LET ME TELL YOU

A SECRET

A Journalist's Career Covering the Rich and Famous

Courtney Hargrove

Bullying; Pregnancy loss and infertility; Body image, eating disorders, weight loss, weight gain; Murder; Missing children.

One Moment Books
Snapshots of remarkable lives

Table of Contents

For my family.

Here are some places I went, some things I did, and some people I met.

—Courtney Hargrove, April 2026

Preface

In 2016, I said I was done writing about celebrities.

And I was. I pivoted to independent journalism and published nineteen books.

Yet here I am again, writing about the stars I said goodbye to in my viral resignation letter ten years ago. A few things happened along the way. First, with the passage of time, my memories of meeting fascinating people and working as a correspondent in dozens of different cities and countries began to fade. I never want to forget those days, so I set out to chronicle that period of my life.

Second, when a young family member said to me in 2025 with wide eyes, *Wait—you met TUPAC?!* I realized that what was once stale is now vintage. My mini memoir from 2016 wasn't the whole story, and I felt a pull to document it all.

I had a notebook for many years, then a mini tape recorder, then a smart phone. Only in the final stretch of this career did I take a few unremarkable selfies on red carpets. I wish I'd captured more of that time on film and on tape, but I thought there would always be more opportunities. I thought it would last forever. I thought I'd always remember.

This book was my chance to write it all down before it's gone, and I wanted to include it all: The fun, the glamour, the ugly, and the extraordinary.

I'm also here to share some fun history a lot of people weren't around to witness.

There's a whole new generation discovering old news now. Social media is flooded with vintage gossip presented as shocking new revelations as the young ones post about history that I and my cohorts watched unfold in real time. This book is for those who forgot some of what happened back then or never knew the origin stories of today's stars or the mega-scandals of Gen-X Hollywood.

It's for people who didn't know Ryan Reynolds was engaged to Alanis Morissette, who wrote an entire album about their love story and then, later, another one about their breakup. Or that Ryan then went off and married Scarlett Johansson. You might know him as Blake Lively's husband now.

It's for those who don't know that Gwyneth Paltrow and Brad Pitt were once engaged, and styled themselves alike and dressed the same, and were so lovey dovey that he gushed from the stage when accepting his Golden Globe, *I love you, my angel. You are the love of my life.*

Who haven't heard that Julia Roberts and fiancé Kiefer Sutherland, some of the hottest stars on the planet in 1991, called off their wedding at the last minute (for a long time she was blamed for "leaving him at the altar"). *It was going to be the fantasy wedding of the decade,* the big *People* magazine story began. Julia ran off to Ireland with Kiefer's close friend Jason Patric, and was later married country star Lyle Lovett for about five minutes.

It's for people who weren't around when Demi Moore was *the* biggest star in the world, at which point her agents pushed hard to get her paid anywhere near as well as equivalent male movie stars, which led pissed-off studio execs to leak their nickname for her: "Gimme Moore." The sexism shone through without a filter: Instead of the tough negotiator Sly Stallone was, Demi was a greedy bitch.

I left the business in 2016 with an open resignation letter that went viral, and I'll tell you in the final chapter what happened next.

You might have questions when you're done reading. Find me on my Substack *Everything is a Mystery*, where I'll address more vintage news and answer some of the queries that come my way.

xoCourtney

P.S.: For those wondering why I wrote this book under my pen name, it's because Courtney has many more readers and followers at the online book retailers and sells a ton more books than Sara Hammel does.

The Sexiest Political Scion Alive

John F. Kennedy Jr., the de facto handsome prince of a royalty-barren America, is so close I could touch him. I usually see him on the pages of magazines, shirtless and suspended in one-dimensional gloss, except when he's campaigning for various Democrats, in which case he'll be pictured fully clothed in the *Boston Globe* or New York *Times*.

John is in the flesh today. His button-down shirt is white. His tie is maroon. I'm at this Irish restaurant in a Boston suburb to interview the man *People* magazine anointed Sexiest Man Alive six years ago, in 1988. He is as conventionally, objectively good looking as he appears in photos. He is not as tall as I expected. His thick chestnut hair is poufy and perfectly coiffed despite the heat and the mess of people who are getting too close. They all want a piece of him.

Including me.

I'm a newspaper intern in the summer of 1994, and I need to prove I deserve a real job. I need dental insurance. I intend to get the exclusive quotes that editors sent me here for.

John's jaw is clenched, his eyes distant as he exits the restaurant.

It hasn't been a good year for him. He's spent the past months supporting his mother, an icon called Jackie who only ever needed one name. She endured chemotherapy and radiation to treat non-Hodgkin lymphoma, only for the cancer to spread to her brain and liver. In May of 1994,

America lost a legendary historical figure, the elegant first lady of Camelot. John lost his mom.

Adding to John's troubles is chatter that his relationship with longtime love Daryl Hannah, an actor who shot to fame in the 1980s after starring in *Splash* with Tom Hanks in 1984, is over. Which means he's possibly unattached.

He's in this Boston suburb stumping for his uncle, Ted Kennedy, the incumbent Democrat who's been challenged by upstart Republican businessman Mitt Romney. Teddy needs to keep his seat in the Senate, but he's shown weakness in recent months. The scion of a political dynasty, a liberal lion, had now become the lion in winter, some say. Age, health problems and scrutiny on his personal life are taking their toll.

Enter the hot young heir to the Kennedy legend. He understood the assignment. He's injecting glamour into a flatlining legacy and reminding Massachusetts that Camelot is still here, and still theirs, and they must vote to keep it so.

I'm outside as John leaves the restaurant. I push through the throng, draw closer to him.

His entourage and the crowd move with him like an exoskeleton. He's not panicking, nor or is he grinning and waving. He appears mildly annoyed.

It's not an option to let him slip by me. My determination is reflective of my refusal to let a story get away, ever.

I bust through the crowd, but am pushed sideways, and he ebbs further away. I push back and call his name. As they block the crowd from closing in on him, turns and faces me. *Just one question?* I am loud but polite.

Okay, he says. I always remember the eyes. I have the full attention of our country's version of royalty shining on me. It is hot there.

"If you could say anything to Massachusetts voters today, what would it be?" I say, probably too loudly.

Perhaps not the most penetrating or original question of all time. He gives me the once over.

"Vote for my uncle," he says flatly, and keeps moving.

Ouch. I hope this is not the pinnacle of my journalism career.

I've never heard John's voice before. I'm not alone in this; you'd have to know when and where he'll be on television to tune in and listen to him speak. If you don't catch him at that moment, you miss it.

I am surprised at the sound, the inflection. I'm surprised by the lack of gravitas. I grew up on the sharp, forceful, distinctly emphasized words of his father, President John F. Kennedy: *Ask not what your country can do for you, but what you can do for your country.*

I listen to Junior talk to other people, and note his delivery is more reminiscent of a surfer dude than a president, which is fine, because he isn't running for anything, and it's the nineties, not the sixties. He is a piece of history, and expectations are high; perhaps unfairly so.

So it goes with those we put on a pedestal. They can't possibly meet our expectations, nor match the stories we form in our heads about who they are and what they owe us, nor is it on them to try.

That summer, unbeknownst to many JFK Jr. watchers, he'd already met the woman he would marry. Carolyn Bessette was a publicist at Calvin Klein who wasn't sure about dating

John, wasn't sure about *him*, and there was reportedly some messy crossover with Carolyn and Daryl before John made a clean, final break from the actor.

I didn't know then that I'd one day move to Manhattan, where John and Carolyn would live a life hounded by paparazzi and press and fans through the streets of TriBeCa, where the green door of 20 North Moore Street would become a beacon, a curse, and a memory.

Senator Ted Kennedy once said that his nephew John Kennedy Jr. believed "politics should be an integral part of popular culture and that popular culture should be an integral part of politics."

I met Teddy one year before my JFK Jr. encounter, when I was covering Capitol Hill as an intern for a wire service. The liberal lion was affable. He seemed tired. He was in his early sixties, and he walked old, the hitch in his gait the permanent result of breaking three vertebrae in a small-plane crash in 1964. I was close enough to see the gin blossoms on his face.

He'd met a gazillion people in his life, and I was number one-gazillion-and-one. He was nice to a cub reporter like you'd be nice to the valet handing you your keys, one you've never seen before and never will again.

Politicians are meant to be public servants, not celebrities, but in fact they are both, and the journalist covering them is at that crossroads whether they acknowledge it or not. I didn't set out to write about celebrities as a career. When you cover Capitol Hill, you will meet nobodies, and you will meet Kennedys. It's the same job. Some of them are just harder to get to and have less time to talk to you.

Yet the fascination with celebrity is always there, hanging in the air like a promise when someone famous walks into a room. In my experience, the same people who denigrate any talk of celebrity are the first to brag about the 2005-era B-lister who smiled at them at Trader Joe's. Trust me on that.

Even famous people are not immune to the allure of others like them; even celebrities get starstruck.

In 1988, JFK Jr. had a brief relationship with one of the biggest stars on the planet.

"You could see it in his eyes that first time they met," said dancer Erika Belle, one of Madonna's closest friends at the time. "John was totally in awe."

The world's most eligible bachelor at the time, JFK Jr., went wobbly in front of the blonde megastar, because who wouldn't have? Everyone's eyes were on Madonna. Madonna's eyes were only on John.

That dalliance didn't last long, and by all accounts John continued sampling the smorgasbord of beautiful women who crossed his path or threw themselves at him.

His friend Billy Noonan once said that John, a Manhattan Assistant District Attorney at the time, was "sleeping with every hot chick…'Check out the cover of *People* (or *Vogue* or *Vanity Fair*),' John would say. 'I banged her last night. Just thought you might like to know.'"

As with every high-profile person you'll ever meet, what they show the public and who they are as a human being are two different things. John was a prankster. He talked crudely about women sometimes. He also, said his uncle Teddy,

...joined Wall Street executives on the Robin Hood Foundation to help the city's impoverished children. And he did it all so quietly, without ever calling attention to himself.

People are never just one thing, though fans often want celebrities to be heroes or villains.

Let me tell you a secret: They're usually neither.

The difference between a regular person and a celebrity is that many more people want to be in the presence of the celebrity for whatever reason. Famous people have to be selective about who they let near them in order to survive. That's what separates us from them. They are no more special than you are. In a lot of cases, they are less special than you.

On July 16, 1999, I was cruising for toothpaste in a Duane Reade on the Upper West Side when I heard John's plane had disappeared off the coast of Martha's Vineyard. There were no cellphones, no hand-held internet. If breaking news happened while you were doing errands, it was the radio, the television, or nothing.

It was a while before we heard anything, before we knew for sure if he was just missing or if the plane he was piloting had crashed. It was days before they recovered the wreckage and the bodies of John, Carolyn, and her sister Lauren Bessette. Eventually, it was determined John had grown disoriented while flying through thick fog, and the plane plummeted into the Atlantic Ocean. One year later, in July 2000, investigators determined the cause of the crash was due to pilot error.

John's uncle Teddy did not dwell on his nephew's mistakes, but mourned him with heartfelt words, saying he had thought maybe John would've escaped the so-called Kennedy Curse.

We dared to think, in that other Irish phrase, that this John Kennedy would live to comb gray hair, with his beloved Carolyn by his side. But, like his father, he had every gift but length of years.

California Love

Everyone who's anyone is seen at the Roxbury. The iconic nightclub on the Sunset Strip is the ultimate celebrity hotspot in the nineties, which I know because magazines regularly run photos of famous people blinking at the camera flashes as they exit.

I am a reluctant clubber. I am terrible at it. I never found the fun in standing around holding a fifteen-dollar vodka cranberry unable to hear what anyone's saying over *Nce nce nce.* But if I'm going to L.A. for the first time, I intend to try to get past that storied velvet rope. If I'm going to sip an overpriced cocktail at a nightclub packed with sweaty drunks, I might as well do it with Leo or Jen or Brad or Johnny.

If you're a hot and/or super-cool girl living in Southern California, hanging with the stars on the Sunset Strip is a standard Friday night. You might have Leo's home phone number. Maybe you've skinny dipped in Kiefer Sutherland's infinity pool or sipped vodka tonics with the Red Hot Chili Peppers at the Viper Room.

For me, this visit to L.A. will be like going on safari, but the reserve is a series of dark rooms, and the big game is human. I am a tourist. I've always wanted to move to Los Angeles, so this is also a reconnaissance mission. I've even set up meetings with newspaper editors for the few days I'll be in town.

I head to L.A. in October 1995 with my friend Elle in tow, taking the redeye from Boston's Logan Airport. We make friends with the flight attendants, who give us a bottle of champagne from first class, and the pilots, who take pictures with us in the flight deck.

On our first night, with no way of knowing if we'll be let in, Elle and I teeter up to the Roxbury's velvet rope.

We're almost at the front of the line when a bouncer beckons us over.

"We're in," I nudge Elle with my elbow.

"Private event. It's Magic Johnson's birthday party," the bouncer tells us.

"Shit," I whisper. "We'll just go to the Viper Room." I figure we can check out the music club and pay tribute to Generation X icon River Phoenix, who died at the venue almost two years ago to the day.

"You coming in or not?" The bouncer beckons us beyond the ropes.

Apparently Magic Johnson, whose actual birthday is in August, would be delighted to host us at this evening's celebration.

Elle and I meet famous people even before we get past the entrance. Ricky Bell and Ronnie DeVoe—from New Edition and Bel Biv DeVoe—are hanging outside, and we get to chatting about growing up back in Boston, and they tell me how hard-won their success was. I lived a couple miles from them in Dorchester in the 1970s, a time of unrest, rioting and protesting on the streets of Roxbury and Dorchester, when racial tensions were high after a 1974 federal court mandated busing between predominately Black and white schools in an effort to dismantle systemic racial segregation.

I'm at the Roxbury night club talking about the rough streets of 1970s Roxbury, Massachusetts with people who know. That is more exciting to me than what lies inside. Still, not wanting to overstay our welcome, Elle and I bid them goodbye.

We split up when we make it to the party. She dances away to get some drinks while I check out the scene. As I make my way through the crowd, I recognize one man right away, a guy about my age who's weaving through the sea of people, his particular head shape and signature bandanna making him instantly recognizable.

We are facing each other, ready to either pass or stop. We both stop.

"Hi," I say to Tupac Shakur, stage name 2Pac.

The bandanna is blue today, and tied in the front, the two ends bobbing as he speaks.

"Hi," he says back. "How you doin'?"

"Great," I say. We make meaningless chatter, and then he shifts in the crowd to get closer to me so we can hear each other. *Where are you from? What's your name?*

And then, when things are about to get real, someone barges into our meet cute. A gorgeous, glamorous woman pushes toward us and shakes her head at me. She tells me off as she brushes by.

"What are you *doing?*" She holds the glare and adds an eye roll. "Why are you talking to *him?* He just got out of jail for *rape.*" She is disgusted by both of us. I am baffled.

I take a moment to absorb what she's said. I'm blinking and watching her go. Tupac is focused on her now.

He is not upset or angry. Tupac appears mesmerized by the beautiful woman and her obvious—and presumably alluring—disgust for him, and he ditches me in a hot second.

I yell after her, "I didn't know! I'm with *you*. I'm a feminist!"

As Tupac turns to follow her, I snap a prehistoric selfie, which involves holding up a disposable camera, waiting precious seconds for the hissing flash to kick in, crossing your fingers, and pressing the plastic button.

I had no idea that days earlier, Tupac had been released from Clinton Correctional facility in Dannemora, New York, after serving part of an eighteen-month to four-and-a-half-year sentence for a sexual abuse conviction in a New York rape case.

I didn't know that Tupac was out of prison not because his sentence had been served, but because he'd been bailed pending an appeal of his conviction. I didn't know that two of the alleged assailants in the gang rape at a New York hotel had their charges dropped in the case. I didn't know Tupac was married when I met him, or that the union would be annulled within months.

I didn't know his music, either, even though my life at the time was all about finding songs that could keep me going during a prolonged and exhausting endeavor I'd taken on (my experience as a U.S. Army test subject is chronicled in the book *The Strong Ones: How a Band of Civilian Women Made Their Mark on the Army*, by Sara Hammel).

It turned out that Tupac, a diehard New Yorker, was in L.A. because he'd jetted straight here after walking out of prison, at which point he signed on with Suge Knight's Death Row Records. Those days were special, his fans say now; that night at the Roxbury we were smack in the middle of history in the making. Tupac's sound engineer at the time, Dave Aron, recalled later,

"The day he got out of jail, he didn't go to the clubs. He didn't go try to meet women. He went straight to the studio like he was on a mission, and he recorded 'Ambitionz Az A Ridah' and 'I Ain't Mad At Cha.' Tupac came in and he was fresh out of jail. I seen them give him his Death Row Medallion that same night. And then he came right in. He was ready to go. He was very hyped, very focused, a lot of energy-mad energy."

Though Tupac did in fact go to clubs and did in fact meet women at some point after getting sprung, it didn't matter. Hip-hop magazine *XXL* called *All Eyez on Me*, the product of that post-prison creative frenzy and the last album he'd release in his lifetime, *A bona fide hip-hop classic that is considered to be the game's first true double LP released to the masses, and a project that is largely responsible for the shift toward widespread mainstream popularity that the genre was experiencing at the time.*

I had no idea I was smack in the middle of the East Coast-West Coast rap rivalry as I stood in front of Tupac in flats from Filene's Basement and a twenty-eight-dollar cotton black dress from Express. A famous *Vibe* magazine cover from 1996 explained the feud this way:

What's clear is that a series of incidents—Tupac Shakur catching bullets at a New York studio in November '94, a close friend of Death Row CEO Suge Knight being killed at an Atlanta party in September '95, the Notorious B.I.G. and Tupac facing off after the Soul Train Music Awards in L.A. this past March—have led to much finger-pointing and confusion.

If you asked me what he was like that night, how he seemed in the four minutes I knew him, I'd say he was open.

Friendly. Alone. Searching. No visible entourage. Not nervous, not scared, not high, not drunk. Interested. Was this the new 'Pac I was meeting?

Months before, he'd opened up to the journalist Kevin Powell in a jailhouse interview for an iconic *Vibe* magazine cover, and he had made promises: *The addict in Tupac is dead. The excuse maker in Tupac is dead. The vengeful Tupac is dead. The Tupac that would stand by and let dishonorable things happen is dead.*

None of us knew he would be actually dead inside eleven months, though he was sent portents, had a premonition based not on superstition but on the reality of his situation. Tupac told Powell that he'd summoned the journalist because, *This is my last interview. If I get killed, I want people to get every drop. I want them to have the real story.*

Tupac Shakur was killed in a shooting in Las Vegas on September 7, 1996. Six months later, Biggie Smalls was killed in a drive-by shooting in L.A.; many in law enforcement and in the rap world believed it was revenge for Tupac's shooting. Both murders went unsolved for decades, and while no one has ever been charged with killing Smalls, a man was arrested and charged for orchestrating Tupac's shooting. Duane "Keffe D" Davis is awaiting trial in Las Vegas at this writing.

It wasn't until 2018 when the victim in the rape case Tupac was involved in spoke out. Celebrity firebrand TMZ reported it this way:

The victim in the harrowing rape case, Ayanna Jackson—the woman Tupac Shakur sexually assaulted—spoke publicly for the first time since the trial about the incident that sent the rapper to prison.

Tupac was convicted not of rape but of forcibly touching her buttocks. The case itself stemmed from an alleged gang rape by his associates in a hotel room. At sentencing in February 1995, the victim told the courtroom how the assault harmed her physically, emotionally, and psychologically.

He took advantage of his stardom to abuse me and betray my trust, she said, adding that the attack turned her into a villain while Tupac was glorified by his peers and fans.

Ayanna said in her first on-camera interview about the case—an exceptionally brave move considering Tupac's still-active fanbase and vehement defenders—how she can never recover, and there is "no justice" after what happened to her.

She recalled, I'm looking at him dead in his eye, and I'm like 'what's going on?' And he's saying to me he's like 'relax baby, these are my boys. I like you so much I decided to share you with them.'"

I am oblivious to all this the night I first visit the Roxbury. After meeting Tupac, I run into Elle and tell her about it, which impresses her somewhat, and we dance and sip watered-down drinks. After wishing happy birthday to a slightly bored-looking Magic Johnson, we're forced to run away from some randy members of the Toronto Blue Jays baseball team that Elle had been speaking to, racing to our car before they can follow us.

She leaves L.A. the next day.

My meets-and-greets with editors in California lead to nothing. If I want to move out west, it's starting to look like I'll have to go without a job.

The One at the Hockey Rink

I nail the first celebrity scoop of my career when Matthew Perry comes to town in the winter of 1996.

The adorable *Friends* star, who plays Chandler Bing on the popular sitcom, is in a suburban rink practicing for the NHL All-Star Game's celebrity exhibition in Boston at the Fleet Center this weekend.

The practice rink is covered in famous men. Like ants on a frozen puddle, they're sliding around everywhere. *Beverly Hills 90210* star Jason Priestley. The original MacGyver, Richard Dean Anderson. The grouchiest, broodiest man alive, Michael Ironside, who I learn today plays himself in everything. Cameron Bancroft, also a member of the *90210* cast and a future star of Hallmark and Lifetime movies.

I'm a full-time reporter at the newspaper now, and I'm standing at the edge of an ice rink, pen and notebook in hand, watching the guys whiz around the ice. I wave to Matthew as he takes a break. He catches my eye, nods, and glides toward me with hockey stick gripped in both hands. He's bulked out with protective pads and wears that Chandler grin, part smirk, part I'll-let-you-in-on-a-little-secret.

I flinch as he barrels towards me and gets too close, but at the last second he *whooshes* to a dramatic ice-stop. He's good; he grew up playing hockey in Ottawa.

"Hey," he says.

"Hey," I say.

My first celebrity interview—which happens to be with one of the biggest TV stars of the moment—is off to a sizzling start.

I hit him with the important questions: I ask him about his love of hockey (duh! He's Canadian, *eh*). About the people who are helped by all the money their celebrity team raises. He's sweet and funny, amenable and charming.

I've heard he might not be technically single.

I make a quick decision. He's been smiling all interview long, he's listened to my questions with tilted head and focused eyes, and he seems to like me. I go for my bombshell question. It's always a risk to stray too far into a subject's personal life, but I need a story and, frankly, I want to know the truth about the recent gossip.

"Are you in fact," I say, "dating Julia Roberts?"

He smiles wider, sheepishly, and tells me that yes, the rumors are true: one of the darlings of the most popular show on the planet is officially embroiled in a romantic entanglement with one of the most famous movie stars on said planet, the *Pretty Woman* herself.

I've confirmed this mega-couple that so far is only chatter and rumor. I got it straight out of Matthew Perry's mouth.

With that, I've broken a major global news story. Because there have been rumors in the magazines, references in *People*, maybe even photos of them together, but neither of them has said a word. But Matt said the words to me.

The story runs as a blurb on the inside pages of the *Middlesex News*, a daily paper that reaches thousands of people in our corner of Massachusetts.

Before long, Matthew and Julia are seen together at the big hockey game, so my scoop is no longer exclusive.

Welcome to life as a reporter before the internet.

29

It's Been 84 Years…

It's time to go, so I pack my things.

I have a bit of savings, an aging white Nissan 300ZX with removable roof panels, and a dream. I quit my job, one I love that's in a location I *don't* love, and take it all out West in the summer of 1996.

It's Arizona for now. I have a friend's apartment to crash in and a job interview at a big newspaper.

Not long after I arrive in the Grand Canyon State and shrivel under its arid 109-degree heat, I'm craving the beach. I drag my friend Caroline, who's visiting me in Tempe, on a road trip to L.A., and back to the Roxbury.

House music shakes the nightclub. I carry my drink through the crowd, breaking the waves for Caroline trailing behind me. I see a familiar face within minutes. He's got floppy, sun-streaked light brown hair, a baby face, and a bunch of guys around him.

It's Leonardo DiCaprio.

He addresses me when my friend and I draw near to him and his boys: *Hello, hi, hey.* I reply with something equally scintillating like, *Hey. Yeah, great. How's it going?*

Leo in the wild presents with the same innate confidence and boyish good looks he has in movies and on TV, which I've seen on *Growing Pains* and in *The Quick and the Dead.* The actor also known for *What's Eating Gilbert Grape* is like any other partygoer, standing around looking slightly bored as if he's certain there's something better happening somewhere else, if he could just find it.

Leo, Caroline and I exchange more pleasantries along the lines of *I love this song, don't you?* He gives me and my friend the once-over as we all stand at the edges of what might be the VIP room. I don't see his rumored on-off girlfriend, a beautiful blond actor called Kristen Zang, anywhere in the vicinity. These are perhaps the last days of Leo being in a romantic relationship with a woman who's older than he is, albeit by five months.

Slim and lanky, Leo is clearly the alpha dog among the male friends he's clubbing with. From afar, they are a generic blob. When I first saw them, I thought they were a bunch of everyday dudes, Hollywood's version of frat boys scamming for chicks.

They are, in a way. My friend and I are being vetted.

A young guy I suspect is actor Jay Ferguson steps between us and Leo (I can't be sure it's Jay, but I do know it's not 1990s posse members Lukas Haas, David Blaine, or Tobey Maguire). Another pal quickly joins "Jay" in vetting the two of us. They pepper my friend and me with questions: *What are you doing here? Where are you from? Do you know who that is over there; do you understand who you're talking to?*

We know, and we're *meh* about it. Leo is not that big of a deal, and he's practically a kid. I'm on the lookout for grownups like *Legends of the Fall*-era Brad Pitt.

The chatter continues nonetheless, and we stand around sipping drinks and checking out the scene. Leo's role seems to be sheltering in place, glancing over tops of heads to look for someone better, and leaning down to yell things in a friend's ear over the music, a curtain of streaked hair falling fetchingly over his eyes as he does.

This encounter is unfolding with the bland sense it has all been done this exact way a million times before in this exact place. There are no other young women hanging around them. It's just Caroline and me, two unfamous, casually dressed New Englanders on a sightseeing tour of L.A. clubs.

Before long, there is some shuffling among the group, and then: "Leo wants to leave," the original entourage member tells us. "Yeah, this isn't working. We'll probably try somewhere else."

It is said with a question mark at the end. Is it an invitation or a blow-off? The ambiguity is mutual. My friend and I aren't overly impressed with these boys, either, so we take the parting shot for what it is and prepare to move on. I shoot a glance to the big guy, the alpha Leo, and he's still looking for something I'm not sure he'll ever find.

Eventually the guys leave the club, and that's that. Leo's posse was doing its job, surrounding him and protecting him from people he might or might not be interested in, speaking for him and carrying his money. I didn't ask Leo anything personal or talk about movies. It was about the music, the drinks, the weather. Not our names.

Other, more exciting memoirists, true Hollywood insiders, would write about the night ending with a wild party where things get out of hand and coke is snorted and there's jumping naked into a famous person's pool. But part of me always suspected that if you immersed yourself fully in it, the superficiality would chew you up and spit you out somewhere in the Hollywood Hills, where you'd awaken to find that Uber doesn't exist because it's 1996 and you're stuck because there are no cellphones, either.

I'm almost certain Caroline and I didn't talk to Leo or his posse first, or bother them, because he was just another boy in the crowd.

Weeks after we hung with Leo, he traveled down to Baja, Mexico to shoot the blockbuster movie about the iconic ship that was never supposed to sink.

One year after we met the accessible, approachable club kid, *Titanic* made him Hollywood royalty.

Soon after that, journalist Nancy Jo Sales introduced the world to the Pussy Posse.

This crude term refers to Leo's fraternity of Hollywood carousers, and it entered the lexicon with a juicy 1998 *New York* magazine profile by Sales, who wrote,

They are the fun-lovin' guys you always see Leo around with. Even before there was Leomania, Leo always traveled with his pack of devotees, known in Hollywood circles as "The Pussy Posse."

My friend and I didn't know we were being vetted by the posse. We hung with Leo's legendary pack at a time when it was still in development, when it was Pussy Posse 1.0. We met pre-*Titanic* Leo, a guy who had to sneak into Victoria's Secret shows because he wasn't on the list.

Titanic, the first-ever film to gross $1 billion globally, changed all that. By 1998, when Sales's magazine piece ran, the Posse's cohesion was complete, its gameplan fully developed.

Venturing out at night with him feels like climbing onto the set of The Jerry Springer Show, Sales wrote, and added a quote from New York gossip columnist Liz Smith: *He seldom sleeps, so intense is his partying.*

The picture painted in that evergreen magazine article is a far cry from my half hour with the guys. For a group that we were later told would start fights on the streets of New York City, throw grapes at paparazzi from hotel windows, prank call top journalists, and (allegedly) semi-stalk beautiful famous actors like Elizabeth Berkley, these men are, in the summer of 1996, dull as fuck.

It's been thirty years since I met Leo at the Roxbury. (My stomach lurches writing that. Where did *thirty years* go?). He's still clubbing, still dating women the same age I was when I met him back then. Still a confirmed bachelor, still seen traveling the world and showing up at glamorous events with his boys.

While his always-twenty-something girlfriends come and go on a metaphorical conveyor belt, Leo keeps his true, lifelong friends around him. For example, you'll find Lukas Haas, who made a name for himself as a young actor in *Witness* and *The Ryan White Story*, in the background of paparazzi photos of Leo from his travels around the world. They share a house, according to an interview Lukas's grandmother Cornelia Haas gave a German publication, though she adds that they have separate quarters.

When you're so famous that no one wants to say *no* to you, having close friends and family around you to tell you the truth must be extremely valuable.

Then again, maybe I'm being naïve. Nancy Jo Sales suggested in her article that maybe even Leo's "real friends" weren't putting him in check when he needed it.

In 1998, an actor friend of the Posse told Sales, *Some of them have completely lost their careers…All they do now is hang out with Leo. If Leo wants to go to Paris, it's let's go to Paris. Las Vegas? No problem…The people closest to him have Leomania worse than anyone.*

At this writing, Leo is dating Italian model Vittoria Ceretti, who was not yet alive when I met him at the

Roxbury; she was born a few days before the *New York* magazine story ran in June of 1998.

Though Leonardo and I are close in age, one imagines that if I bumped into him now, he'd offer a crooked arm and say, *Let me help you to your walker, dear.*

After all, I'm probably around the same age as his girlfriend's grandmother.

Leo and Everything After

The same night I encounter Leo's posse, a few hours later in fact, I bump into Counting Crows frontman Adam Duritz. I am properly starstruck. *August and Everything After* is the soundtrack of my life in the mid-90s. I've been listening to "Mr. Jones" on repeat since 1993.

When I meet Adam in a tight hallway downstairs at the Roxbury, his dreads sprouting so wild and so big they seem in danger of touching the walls, I flash him the peace sign. He stops, gives a melancholic smile in return, and flashes back. He's a nightclub fixture in L.A., a Viper Room regular, a rockstar who recently split from Jennifer Aniston, that huge star from NBC's Must-See TV staple *Friends*.

When I met him in that hallway, I didn't know that Adam, also a composer for the Crows, had been diagnosed with dissociative disorder and felt "untethered" from reality. It appears nobody knew, not even him. Describing the year his grandmother died and his girlfriend broke up with him, Adam wrote in a 2008 essay for *Men's Health*,

This was not depression. This was not workaholism. I have a fairly severe mental illness that makes it hard to do my job—in fact, makes me totally ill-suited for my job. I have a form of dissociative disorder that makes the world seem like it's not real, as if things aren't taking place. It's hard to explain, but you feel untethered. And because nothing seems real, it's hard to connect with the world or the people in it because they're not there. You're not there.

I met him at a *Golden Globes* afterparty a year or so after that essay was published, and he was happy to stop for a chat. I asked him how his music-making was going, if there were new songs or albums in the pipeline, and he said he was optimistic and working in L.A. as we spoke.

Then I ruined it. As a reporter for *People* magazine, I was expected to ask about his romantic life, so I did. Here I was with a brilliant lyricist who put his stamp on the nineties while churning out music that fans would say captured the human condition, and I was bothering him about women.

Adam shook his head like he was disappointed in me. "No, no," he said. "I'm not talking about that."

I thanked him, and we parted ways.

I ran into him once more a few years later, in New York this time, but I will leave it there.

Hypocrite and the City

Sarah Jessica Parker's hair is in my mouth. Her curls, gathered up in a prickly blonde bush sticking out from the back of her head, swat me in the face as she wriggles past me through an overpacked party. Crispy and big and intrusive, the nest stays in my eyes for a beat as SJP laughs with a high-pitched giggle when another civilian congratulates her on her new show. They're all saying it'll be a huge hit.

I'm not so sure. I didn't like it much at the screening earlier this evening, a warm night in June of 1998.

I spit out the hair. My cosmo splashes down my chest, and I become a victim of drinkicide. Luckly, the cocktails are free, so I can order another.

SJP is moving on and accepting congratulations left and right and will never know (I presume) what her hair salad hath wrought.

I smell like booze now, but I plow on. There are servers carrying trays of passed apps to chase, and there are people to watch.

It's weird I ended up in New York City, a place I never wanted to live because it's expensive, crowded, and terrifying. But it's where fate dropped me.

I ended my Arizona experiment after a month and drove back east. I landed a temporary job covering Capitol Hill in Washington, D.C. The salary was an unlivable fifteen-thousand dollars a year, so I took a project-length gig at a newsmagazine. In the breakroom one day, I told the guy who sat across from my cubicle that I thought he must be quite important because of all the people who gravitated to his office to seek his counsel. He cocked his head, looked me dead in the eye, and said, *I've noticed you're a hard worker. Always on the phone and typing furiously.* Days later, he beckoned me into his office, told me he was the Chief of Correspondents in charge of every bureau from Berlin to Moscow to L.A., and asked to see my work. I gave him my award-winning articles about the seven months I spent as a test subject in a U.S. Army women's strength study. The next day, he offered me a full-time job as a news assistant-slash-reporter in the New York office.

Working for a major national newsmagazine—number three in circulation after *Time* and *Newsweek*—means I get to report on women's issues and culture and exciting breaking news. My mission is to add a new perspective to big issues of the day for our ten million readers.

It also means I get invited to random events, which is how I ended up at the Home Box Office (HBO) premiere of its new half-hour dramedy, *Sex and the City*, which is happening at Lot 61, a brand-new warehouse/club/restaurant with exposed ventilation, uncomfortable zebra print couches and walls adorned with art by Damien Hirst.

Between cocktails I share a mirror with Cynthia Nixon in the bathroom, and as I blot my left boob with a wet paper towel that leaves a trail of white gunk, I try to place this quirky actress with the flaming crown. I'd seen her face before, usually as a sidekick or a guest star, like in an episode of *Murder, She Wrote*. She's excited; giggly; confident; happy. It's almost as if she's about to break through in a major zillion-dollar TV and feature franchise that will live in perpetuity in syndication and, in the future, something called streaming.

I see SJP a few more times that evening. She works the room like a pinball and then sits where people can pay homage to her, one after the other. Everyone wants a piece of her, and she beams as she obliges.

SJP is not an A-lister. Her movies thus far are such notable romps as *Life Without Dick* and *Dudley Do-Right*.

Tonight is her night. Her husband is with her, hanging back, because it is not his night.

To me, Matthew Broderick will always be Ferris Bueller. Sarah and Matthew have recently celebrated their one-year wedding anniversary. Matthew's popcorn blockbuster *Godzilla* just premiered.

Sarah's new show is already getting mixed reviews. From me, it's getting a thumbs down. Before the party, there was a screening of the first few episodes at a nearby cinema. I was one of the first people on the planet to see *Sex and the City*. I didn't like the show. At all.

My review, spouted to friends later with an irritated shake of my head, was this: *Vapid, superficial, unoriginal, too high concept.* Episode one, "Modelizers," was too cutesy, as if the idea—the shocking *revelation*—that men love to date models was beaten into submission to justify the clever "Modelizers" title (get it? *Get it?*). *This fluff will float away on a breath of wind after one season*, I said.

People didn't quite know what to make of it. Most of us got the title wrong. The day after the premiere, I got a fax (yes, a FAX) from HBO's publicity department clearing up some confusion. No one knew what the hell *Sex AND the City* was. Anyone who hadn't read Candace Bushnell's New

York city newspaper column, and there were a lot of us who didn't, instinctively called it *Sex IN the City*.

HBO's post-premiere press release went to worldwide media saying something like, *Please note: The show is called Sex AND the City, not Sex IN the City.*

Then-important trade publication *The Hollywood Reporter* didn't like the show either, but for different reasons.

"…what may be a reasonable, even sexy premise comes out flat, bitter and flaccid," wrote the THR critic, adding that he felt Darren Star wrote an "awkward script, which is choppy and burdened with impossible dialogue. But worst is that the smarty mood leaps beyond cynical, and his characters are too disagreeable to make funny."

In later years, one of my sisters would remind me that I watched the show all the time. I don't remember being a superfan, but I guess I ended up being sucked into the women's shenanigans as much as anyone.

Being young and single in New York City probably had something to do with my jumping on the bandwagon. The women were always going to the Coffee Shop, and my friends and I were too, ordering Caesar salads and cosmopolitans at the counter. I haven't watched an episode in years, but when the Coffee Shop closed a few years ago, I felt a stab of nostalgia.

Zig-a-zig-*oof*

By late winter in the year 2000, I am as far as one can get from reporting on celebrities. Something called the Internet bubble has been making a lot of people very rich, but I have little interest in joining the gold rush.

I go the other way. Old school establishment.

At work at the magazine one day, I pick up a misdirected call from a recruiter who's looking for a top financial writer who understands the markets—better yet, cares about them—to work at a global investment firm. That's not me, but somehow I end up with a job in the firm's marketing department. The "comp," as they call it in finance, is nearly three times my magazine salary.

One of the newsmagazine's new senior writers, a former war correspondent who added some much-needed buzz to our office, tells me, *If you take this job, you can't come back. You won't come back to journalism.*

It's a seductive argument.

I leave anyway.

The halls smell like money. Some assistants wear five-carat diamond rings. I write about bond yields, P/E ratios and some stuff about stock markets; the learning curve is steep.

I take a vacation first chance I get, and head down to the south of Spain.

Among the docked yachts of Puerto Banus, outside Sinatra Bar, I meet some British guys on a golfing holiday. I get engaged to one of them three months later, and my firm transfers me to the London office so I can move in with him. Due to a paperwork error, I'm accidentally promoted to Vice President, and I'm given an office with French doors and a balcony overlooking Green Park, not far from Buckingham Palace.

I try really, really hard to care about our clients' money and whether they're making enough of it. But the job doesn't work out so well in the end, so I quit in 2002, leaving me unemployed in a foreign country. What's next, where do I go, what do I do? Was the war correspondent's prediction correct? Is there no way back for me?

After a paid summer off thanks to the firm's goodbye present to me (I told you they were filthy rich), I catch a break. A journalist friend back in New York snags me a dinner meeting with the London bureau chief of an iconic American magazine.

The chief takes me for nachos and frozen margaritas at Texas Embassy, London's answer to Tex-Mex. Homesick American expats flock to the grandly decorated restaurant for gloopy frozen drinks and bland burritos in a futile attempt to find some flavor.

The chief and I get along well, though halfway through our apps I ask a question that seems to get his hackles up, and I think I might've blown it.

Then, as we part ways at Trafalgar Square, he says those three dreaded words: *I'll be in touch.*

I hear a final, unsaid, implied word: *If.*

If you impressed me. If you can do anything for the magazine that I don't already have covered. If I can think of a reason to choose your resume over the hundreds I get every month.

To my great shock, he calls a few days later and offers me a freelance assignment. I have never written for a publication with such reach before. Time Inc. is a titan in journalism, and *People* is one of its most popular magazines with some thirty-million readers.

On a cool September day, I hop on the tube to central London to go watch a Spice Girl unveil her wax figure at Madame Tussauds.

That's what I thought the assignment was, anyway.

Shortly before I leave my Wimbledon flat, I'm told there's something else the editors in New York want me to do.

It's not going to be easy, and I can't afford to mess this up.

Ginger Spice, one of the women who made "Wannabe" stick in my head since the late nineties, arrives at the museum. I join the pack of British reporters who observe her marveling at her dead-eyed likeness for the first time, and I think, *I can't believe I'm getting paid for this.*

The wax Geri is dressed in a slinky black dress with slit up to here. The flesh-and-blood Geri wears black pants and black tank top that reveals hints of midriff. She teeters on spiky heels. She has bid goodbye to the ginger; today she is a platinum blonde with a glint of strawberry. I am shocked at how small she is. Compact.

I make notes about everything from the height of her heels to the width of her smile.

Now comes the hard part.

I've been asked to throw in a question about Geri's recent weight loss. The change in her appearance after leaving the Spice Girls was extreme for the diminutive performer, whose height is listed as five feet, one inch. Thankfully, the magazine I'm working for is all about the soft approach, and I was assured it was fine if I couldn't get the question to her, they'd totally understand, but could I try?

In my experience, there is no try, only do.

I get to Geri as she nears the exit, surrounded by her people.

I feel uneasy asking the question. It seems embarrassing and invasive, though not entirely inappropriate considering Geri has an autobiography coming out within weeks, and while promoting it, she'd revealed she'd written candidly about her struggles with body image and eating disorders.

I follow her and her entourage, and I find myself alone with them as she heads to the back door.

Geri walks right by me, swift and jittery, choosing not to answer or acknowledge any questions. She knew the question before I even asked it, and she wanted no part of it.

I write about her dress and her heels and her hair, and her tiny figure, and how it looked a lot like her new wax likeness, and send my file to the chief, apologizing profusely for not getting Geri to answer. He wrote back, *I understand. Thanks for trying.*

I would say this moment in history was peak horror for women and body image, but I'm not sure much has changed. GLP-1s, in fact, have made "emaciated" the new "skinny" in Hollywood, and we don't quite know how to talk about it yet.

We're still criticized for the weight of our bodies—too fat or too thin, wrong shape, wrong size. The Spice Girls were deep in it in 2002 when I watched Ginger Spice meet her waxen doppelgänger, and at least two of the bandmates wrote autobiographies addressing their eating disorders.

Geri's book, *Just for the Record*, was in the news the week I met her because of her candid revelations. These passages were, in part, an answer to unspoken questions about why her body looked the way it did on a given day. The media spent years saying she was too big and calling her "Podge Spice" among other things; now they said she'd gone too far the other way. Geri wrote of attending her first eating disorder support group:

When I came home…I wrote in my diary: "My name is Geri and I am a recovering compulsive overeater, bulimic anorexic." Confessing my problem seemed to reduce my compulsion to binge and take away some of its power. This was just the beginning of the road to recovery.

Fellow Spice Girl Victoria Adams (she became Victoria Beckham in July 1999) was judged just as harshly and was subjected to equally ugly nicknames on front pages. Actual, real, grown-up editors of major newspapers called the twenty-something Victoria, aka Posh Spice, "Skeletal Spice" when she lost weight after the birth of her first child, a son she and David called Brooklyn.

What's worse, her shrinking and subsequent public body shaming came months after she was forced to weigh herself on live television. Victoria was told to get on a scale and show the host, Chris Evans, whether she'd lost enough baby weight to satisfy him. As if he were judge and jury. As if she belonged to him because she was a woman. He did it because he could; it was, after all, open season on women's bodies.

Through Victoria's obvious distress and protestations of *No, no, no,* Evans gleefully brought the scale out from behind his desk and set it where the cameras could zoom in. She dutifully got on, because many—or most—of us would have under that kind of pressure.

That's not bad a'toll, is it? Evans said when the scale revealed her weight.

On that same show on another day, Evans did the same thing to Geri Halliwell while she was battling eating disorders none of us knew about at the time. She, too, was flustered, and objected, trying to wriggle out of the humiliation. *Oh, no…no…I don't believe in weighing yourself,* said Ginger as she prepared to step on the scale.

There are some moments and behaviors we tell ourselves were "of a time," which is a way of saying we filter hideousness wrought in the past through a lens of what was once normalized. What Chris Evans and his producers did was cruel and it was bullying, and there was *never* a time for that. Watching these clips reminds me of how much we're *all* hurt by this behavior. Fuck you, Chris Evans, and fuck everyone around you who supported and allowed this.

Both Geri and Victoria shrunk themselves down, but it was never going to be enough, because you must not only be thin. You must be precisely as thin as they want you to be—no more, no less.

Here's an idea: Don't comment on women's looks at all. On *anyone's* appearance. Alas, this is not a consideration in the year 2002. Celebrities expect body and diet questions and have answers at the ready; journalists comply; and readers lap it up. Whether we like to admit it or not, we were all in on it.

Catherine Eater Jones and the Million-Dollar Gaffe

Gasps ripple through the courtroom like we're in an episode of *Matlock*. I think I might've laughed. I can't believe what I've heard, and I'm fascinated by the casual way Catherine Zeta-Jones said it.

The actor is testifying in her and Michael Douglas's civil case against *Hello!* magazine. Long story short, the couple struck a deal with glossy celebrity magazine *OK!* to supply authorized photos from their 2000 wedding at The Plaza in New York City. But *Hello!,* a direct competitor, had an inside man snapping pictures of the cake and the couple and the romance, and that magazine ran unauthorized images the couple did not appreciate.

In making her case, a heavily pregnant Catherine actually just said in front of Britain's top journalists and a packed gallery, and I quote, that one million British pounds "is a lot of money maybe to a lot of people in this room, but it is not that much for us."

It is not that much for us.

My mouth is agape. Why yes, Catherine. I'm in this room, and a million pounds, which equals around $1.6 million in 2003 dollars, is a lot to me.

Catherine was responding to a suggestion from the defense that she and Michael are suing *Hello!* because they're upset about the million British pounds *OK!* promised them on condition of exclusivity.

To that, Catherine responded, in essence, that the piddly amount of cash means nothing to them, so could *not* be their motivation.

There are more noteworthy moments in the trial at the Royal Courts of Justice, a grand symbol of Victorian architecture on the Strand in London that was officially opened by Queen Victoria in 1882.

To me, the six-acre courthouse is like a museum with its cathedral-like entrance, the intricate stone carvings, the palace-like feel compared to American courts. Fans of *Bridget Jones's Diary* will remember the heroine outside this stunning building, and, later, at a nearby fictional convenience store where her cameraman rushes in to tell her they've missed the people they were supposed to catch on their way out of the courthouse (like me now with Catherine Zeta-Jones and Michael Douglas).

Bridget, we've fucked up utterly.

I haven't fucked anything up, though. Not yet. I'm back doing what I was trained to do. Covering courts or crime or human interest or breaking news is why I became a journalist. This week it just happens to be a couple of celebrities in the dock.

I'm feet away from Catherine and Michael as they testify one after the other in the High Court. It is a zoo.

BBC News reports on the chaos this way: I counted eight television and radio trucks outside the High Court in London and probably more than 200 reporters, camera crews and photographers awaiting the glamorous couple's arrival. More reporters (admission by ticket only) waited inside Court 35, a cavernous and rather chilly place with terrible acoustics.

Watching the testimony in that room is like having a front-row seat to a high-class reality show where the last great movie stars are forced to speak frankly and step outside of their controlled images. They have to, if they want to sway a judge to see things their way.

On that note, the New York Post covers Catherine's let-them-eat-cake moment with its signature snark:

Catherine Zeta-Jones, pregnant and drenched in diamonds, yesterday griped in court that "stolen" photos of her nuptials made her dream day look like a big, fat, geek wedding…"It [$1.6 million] is a lot of money maybe to a lot of people in this room, but it is not that much for us," said Zeta-Jones, with diamonds on her ears, neck and hands.

The quotable moments are sprinkled generously throughout the official proceedings. At one point the defense shows Catherine a copy of Hello! with the unauthorized wedding photos. She sniffs that they made everything look as if the event was "doused in bad disco lighting." She calls the stolen shots "cheap and tacky."

One of her objections is the publication of moments of intimacy captured by the uninvited photographer.

"There are certain moments of emotion, certain moments of embrace" shown in the Hello! photos, Catherine says.

When the defense produces authorized photos published in OK! that include the bride and groom embracing, an obviously annoyed Catherine shoots back, "There is embracing, and there is embracing."

Laughter rings out in the staid courtroom.

The privacy issue aside, I get the sense her distress is largely about one particular image that was taken and blown up without the bride's permission. This unauthorized Hello! photo ended up as a front-page splash in Britain's The Sun tabloid newspaper with the obnoxious headline CATHERINE EATER JONES.

The image showed Michael feeding his bride a piece of wedding cake.

The defense asks if this is offensive to Catherine.

She replies, "Yes. I did not want my husband shoving a spoon down my throat to be photographed...It looks like all I did was eat. It is offensive and it is obviously a stolen photograph."

The defense follows up by asking Catherine, a woman who's been food-shamed on the cover of a tabloid newspaper in the only wedding dress she hopes to ever wear, why she didn't just laugh it off and move on. He basically said, Don't you have a sense of humor?

Catherine keeps her head when I would've struggled not to go off on a tangent about gaslighting and minimizing. "At this point," she replies coolly, "I had no sense of humor."

She tells the court it was not all about control, but about "being able to let my hair down, do whatever I want, have the security of privacy in my own wedding and not have the stress and angst that happened after the wedding."

Michael on the stand is very chill, until he's not, and he gets testy talking about invasion of privacy. Celebrities have walked this tightrope since the dawn of time, since the hottest neanderthal in the hut was worshiped by his pack.

So the Douglases sell their wedding pictures to a magazine under the condition the couple controls which images are seen by the public. If another publication runs photos the couple *didn't* approve, that's not an invasion of privacy—because if they'd wanted privacy, they wouldn't have revealed *anything* about their wedding…right?

Wrong.

The defense suggests the couple's interest is in money and control rather than privacy.

Michael's answer is succinct. "Control is what gives you privacy."

As Meghan, the Duchess of Sussex once explained, just because you show a coworker a picture of your kids on your phone doesn't mean that coworker gets access to your entire camera roll.

As readers of my work since 2016 will know, I am no fan of manipulative and controlling celebrities who want it both ways. But fans can't have it both ways, either. We don't get the whole camera roll. We get what they give us.

Best to understand these people aren't our friends from the jump, so you're never disappointed.

The other moments of that trial I'll never forget, the little details outside the legal sparring, includes Michael talking about taking their helicopter to Wales (or wherever).

He pronounces it *hell-ee*-copter, and I think, *You're American. Say it right.* I get it, though. I'm married to a British person too. He also says helicopter wrong.

The other memorable thing about this trial is sitting a few feet away from Catherine for hours on end. She's clad in all black, and to me, she's stunning. Her attorney has an open tin of mints on the table. Every now and then she reaches for them, and I think about whether he brought them for her or if he just had them and she finds them distracting, or what.

When there's a break in the proceedings, I write my file, call my editor, then bump into the couple's lawyer. I decide to introduce myself and ask a non-legal question.

Turns out he's a friendly, approachable chap. The magazine likes details. I'll give them details. I want to know about the mints.

What's with Catherine and the mints? Is she a fan of Altoids?

The mints? They're just there. She likes them. Want one?

I'm OK, thank you.

He smiles. I smile back.

I know better than to approach either Michael or Catherine.

No matter. This won't be the last I will see of the couple in my budding celebrity reporting career.

They won in the end, technically, and most headlines about the verdict named them as the victors. The judge threw out several of the claims, but still, *Hello!* had to pay *OK!* damages, plus court costs, plus about $21,000 to Michael and Catherine for pain and suffering.

Which, as we know, is not a lot of money to them.

A Scandal in Scotland

*C*an you get to Glasgow right away?

The chief's on the phone. There's a scandal brewing up in Scotland, where a fellow called Danny is making headlines around the globe.

This will be my first international trip as a reporter for *People*. I've been working from London since Ginger Spice. Most of my assignments are not celebrity related; they are stories about crime and interesting topics and breaking news. *People*'s ethos from inception was to cover ordinary people doing extraordinary things, and that's my favorite part of it.

In the spring of 2003, celebrity news is taking a back seat to the horrors of the real world. In March, a coalition including the United States, Great Britain, Poland and Australia invades Iraq, an unpopular move that sets the world on edge. *People* and its sister publications at Time Inc., including flagship newsmagazine *Time*, allot massive resources to covering it, and the London bureaus are directing it all. I'm new, so I remain back at the ranch making calls to contractors, military families, officials, and anyone with a story to share about the war.

Senior reporters are embedded with American troops on aircraft carriers or on the ground reporting in cities and villages.

One of the journalists on the ground in Iraq is a seasoned war correspondent who's been stringing for various Time Inc. titles. One day he is given an assignment from a newer magazine in the company's stable.

He wears his protective gear, risking life and limb, to gather reporting for this publication.

When those of us holding the fort back in London learn of this, we laugh until we cry at the absurdity of a grizzled war reporter walking up to insurgents and saying, *Hi! I'm with Teen People. Mind if I ask you a few questions?*

I land in Glasgow and get a taxi to Danny's house. A one-on-one interview with *People* magazine is part of the media tour to convince the court of public opinion to see things his way.

Danny's alleged crime? He's been accused of getting a facelift to win an international championship, and competitors are out for blood. They say he cheated by getting cosmetic tweaks that were prohibited by the rules. They want his title pulled. They want Danny and his handlers, at the very least, to be investigated.

Danny, as you might have guessed, is a dog. The Pekingese, whose full name is Ch. Yakee A Dangerous Liaison, just took the coveted Best in Show title at Crufts, the prestigious dog show held in Britain since 1891.

After his triumphant win, even before the euphoria could wear off, an anonymous informant contacted the Kennel Club to say that Danny had gone under the knife for a cosmetic procedure that's banned under conformation show rules.

I'm about to meet Danny.

I'm welcomed into the house by his co-parents, Bert and Philip. The men need me to understand their pup has been falsely accused, and they tell me so in thick Scottish brogues.

Jealous people want to take him down! It's all lies.

Take me to Danny, I say.

They introduce me to the defendant. From far away he looks like an out-of-control feather duster with eyes, but up close he's a wiggly boo with a scrunched-up face. I want to believe in his innocence. I really do.

I can see why he beat 22,000 rivals to take the title. But I'm here to observe and report in the name of justice— whether for the thousands of dogs who competed fairly against one who'd cheated the system, *or* for the poor maligned Danny.

I'm no veterinarian, so I can't tell if there has been malfeasance.

But if there was….*why?*

What puzzles many about this story is the question of why a Pekinese would need a facelift. Turns out it's for the same reason humans do: To tighten up sagging muscles and remove unwanted wrinkles. But nips and tucks are banned under Crufts rules.

He's innocent! Danny's co-parents assure me. *Does this look like a dog who's had cosmetic surgery to you?!*

Absolutely not. I nod along, taking notes.

Of course…we must take into consideration that there *was* a surgery. But it was done to investigate persistent tonsillitis, his parents say.

Sounds plausible to me.

I am here in the midst of a war, asking a dog about any work he had done to win a dog show, and the magazine's readers are lapping it up.

Amid chaos and agony there needs to be joy. There is a place for fluff. Unimportant things. Entertainment. And that year, I'm here to provide some of it.

Weeks later, Danny is cleared of all wrongdoing. The Kennel Club ruled that Danny can wear his Best in Show crown with pride. Bert Easdon, Danny's co-parent, tells a Scottish newspaper, "There was never any doubt about it."

Like many overnight celebrities, Danny's fifteen minutes was up. Can you imagine if they'd had TikTok back then? Still, they couldn't cancel that plucky Pekingese, who has his own Wikipedia page, and later had a son who went on to find great success of his own.

I become a part of the London bureau. I'm working on-site most weeks now as the fighting in Iraq shows no sign of abating, and the magazine needs help covering non-war stories.

On my first day in the office, I expected to be cowed by a sleek, modern space humming with glamorous editors wearing five-inch Jimmy Choos rushing out for lunch with Prince William. But Time Inc.'s London operation is housed in an old, converted mansion off the Strand, its central open-plan desks drowning in newspapers, the smell of newsprint reminding me of my first full-time reporting job. The building is a short walk from Waterloo station over the bridge, and every day I stroll to work above the Thames with Big Ben and Parliament in the background.

I am given a nickname, and I don't know how it began, but I am called HRH in every context. I am assigned stories as HRH. I sign off emails as HRH.

In this bureau, stringers—freelance correspondents, basically—are generally respected and treated well because they need us. We are stationed around Europe and beyond, from Germany to Sweden to Russia, and we know our local territory. We're expected to drop everything and jump on breaking stories whenever they call us, and, like the staff I'm working with in London, we're all able to cover everything from crime to combat to movie premieres to Gwyneth Paltrow's latest detox diet. It does not occur to me there is any other way to do journalism.

An Irishman and a Gentleman

I'm in a taxi crawling through Dublin on my way to a VIP reception for a major charity event in the summer of 2003. Exactly one year has passed since I quit my job making price-to-earnings ratios of Chilean mining stocks sound interesting, and as the River Liffey rolls by outside my window, I think, *This is better.*

I'm early, so it's still quiet inside the huge VIP area when I arrive. There'll be a concert at this indoor stadium later, and I'm in the massive glassed-in area high above the stage making note of the spread: Julienne of Irish beef with Irish whiskey sauce, acres of seafood, and salads for days.

But that's not important right now.

There's Colin Farrell.

Colin arrives like a whirlwind, big brown eyes wide with the urgency of everything he must do this evening. He's holding a clear fizzy drink in one hand and a cigarette in the other.

He's wearing a white button-down shirt and jeans. He's here with a small entourage, hawk-eyed young women who stay by his side. Closest of all is his sister, Claudine, who has worked with him for years.

Colin finishes up an in-house TV interview for the organization he's here to support, and then they tell him, *You're running late. You're due on stage.* His handlers usher him away.

The magazine didn't fly me here for the seafood tower. I *must* get the interview. I have no choice but to give chase. *Sorry, we have to go*, Colin's people say to me.

I am more afraid of the chief than I am of strangers in an entourage, so I defy them.

Uh…Colin? Just a couple questions?

They're on the move.

Sure, he replies.

With that, I embark on my first-ever speedwalking interview. His people let me into the circle.

I have time to ask him two questions about his dedication to the cause, of his desire to help vulnerable people thrive. His answers are humble and heartfelt.

So far, so easy. Now, though, I have to ask one of the out-of-nowhere questions the editors expect reporters to ask celebrities we meet at events. These queries cover several pages and range from dull to cringe to downright insulting. I've come to call this the Apropos of Nothing List.

Chasing a man to an elevator bank as he's about to go onstage with U2 and asking him something mildly ridiculous is not the high point of my life, and it makes me wince, which I can do freely because Colin is looking ahead.

Do you ever use an alias when you check into a hotel?

Colin's quick on the draw. *Yes*, he replies. *Tom Foolery.*

Does it work? I shout after him he steps into the elevator.

I get very few calls, he says, and the doors close, and Colin is gone.

Later that night, I watch U2 perform for the third time in my life—first was *Joshua Tree* in 1987 at Sullivan Stadium and then Zoo TV tour for *Achtung Baby* in 1992 (the fourth would be at the Sphere in Las Vegas in 2024)—and then I meet a few more stars, including Dylan McDermott, who is another lovely gentleman, and Quincy Jones, who agrees to meet over a glass of wine.

I'm at the party for nearly ten hours but never manage to sample any Irish food. Twenty-three years later, I read the file I sent in and it appears I felt quite sorry for myself. I describe the endless buffet in great detail: all salmon, all the time, including salmon terrine, smoked salmon, poached salmon, salmon with dill dressing, spiced smoked salmon…

I included a personal note no one needed or wanted: *Certain people were working and had no time to try it.*

If it doesn't seem like a big deal that Colin Farrell was nice to me in a three-minute interview, it sadly is. The bar is low for basic human decency with the rich and famous. In a world where celebrities are worshipped to the point of being out-of-touch and unwilling to tolerate discomfort for one second longer than they have to—which means sometimes degrading and insulting the people around them and usually getting away with it—the Colin Farrells are rarer than they should be.

So, whenever I run into him, I know I'm going to have a good day.

Like in 2009 when I'm covering the afterparties of the Golden Globes, at which Colin took home the award for his role in the black comedy-slash-crime thriller *In Bruges.*

All the winners participate in press conferences after they claim their trophies. They're swarmed by shouting reporters and photographers, and everyone gets the same quotes.

My job is to get *exclusive* interviews with the stars when the official pressers are over. I need A-listers. Doctor number two from medical TV show *House* won't do. Your best chance is to catch them in the wild, when the champagne's popping and they're out of the tight control of reps and guardians. Nabbing a one-on-one with a winner is what I came for.

My feet hurt as I make my way to the NBC/Universal party at the Beverly Hilton. Dule Hill is behind me on the way in, and politely, oh so politely, says, *Cough, excuse me, thank you.* He passes me and I move further to the right so I don't hold up any other celebrities. They have vending machines for comfortable flats here. I consider buying some, but I'm working; I have to look the part best I can, and disposable ballet shoes aren't trending.

I make my way through the party and then, suddenly, a familiar A-lister appears in front of me. He's alone. Moving fast. About to pass me.

These parties are shoulder-to-shoulder. There are often roped-off sections, but generally, everyone mixes, because ostensibly, the guest lists are already elite enough.

"Hey, Colin," I say. He stops. "Congratulations."

"Thank you," he says to the five-thoustandth person falling all over herself to praise him tonight.

People are noticing him because he's still. He's on his back foot, ready to take off.

I introduce myself as a reporter and ask, "What are you going to do with your award? Where are you going to put it?"

That question is on the red-carpet-cringe-question list, and once again, Colin has a choice. He can ignore it and keep walking. He can roll his eyes. He can tell me to *fuck off* like a certain other low-level "celebrity" once did. Or he can be nice.

He half-smiles and chooses kindness. He deadpans, "Straight to the pawn shop tomorrow."

He waits. *Is that good enough?*

More than good enough. I thank him, and he waves, smiles, and keeps moving.

Celebrities sometimes despise you for these random questions, but most of them are gracious because if they don't want to answer, it's not hard to wriggle out of it with a modicum of civility.

There is, of course, a Coalition of Assholes. Always has been, always will be. Some "celebrities" will use their power to humiliate reporters (or restaurant servers or any support staff) who have been expressly invited to interview them in order to give their projects—and them—free publicity.

I'm not talking about obnoxious interruptions of a famous person's dinner, accosting them for selfies when they're walking in the city, or following them when they're taking their children to school.

I'm talking about how one behaves during professional, mutually agreed-upon meetings in the workplace. And when you have the power, it's even more important to treat people around you with dignity.

As Roger Federer once told me in front of a roaring fire in Switzerland, *It's nice to be important, but it's more important to be nice.*

Fat Actually & the Tits Cake

mma Thompson got married yesterday. Find out everything, an editor tells me when I arrive at *People*'s offices one morning in July 2003.

I'm borrowing the office of a reporter who's in Iraq. I pick up the day's papers and cruise the Internet looking for information about Emma's wedding.

Find out everything.

I know what that means. *People* editors like details, the smaller the better. They don't want to hear about a vanilla wedding cake. They want to know *How many tiers? What flavor is the frosting, what color, what's the theme?* Not a white dress, but, *What shade—ivory, cream, bone?* Not a wedding, but, *What religion or denomination? How long did it last? What other celebs were there?*

I nibble on a thumbnail as I scan every report out that morning and discover the British media has only the basics of who, what, when and where. Emma Thompson and actor Greg Wise married during a rainstorm in Scotland. She wore a white dress and Greg wore a kilt. Their three-year-old daughter Gaia was a flower girl.

That a wedding was taking place at all was kept secret until the last second, even from family and friends. Newlywed pals Kate Winslet and Sam Mendes were invited but cancelled at the last minute. Villagers were treated to champagne as the couple arrived at the Coylet Inn on the shores of Loch Eck, in Argyll, Scotland, for the reception. Sophie Thompson, the bride's sister, told onlookers, *There wasn't a dry eye in the house.*

This is something, but I need more.

Emma and Greg, who first met on the set of *Sense and Sensibility*, are presumably on their honeymoon. If their PR teams aren't talking, there's only one thing to do.

I call the Coylet Inn, knowing that much of the time—if not most of the time—owners of businesses working closely with the stars won't reveal private information to a reporter they don't know. They're much more interested in keeping the celebrity happy and coming back.

But the chap I get on the phone is a chatterbox. I decide he's probably been given permission from the couple to talk to certain news outlets. Perhaps Emma wanted to bring the inn publicity and told management to let it rip, to talk about it all. Whatever his reasons, the proprietor tells me everything on the record. What Emma and Greg's guests ate, what they danced to, what was said.

The cake seemed to be the star of the show (apart from the adorable couple). The proprietor described it as a cake with two peaks, designed like the rolling hills of the Scottish Highlands, pointy and green and iced with a smooth fondant.

When it's time for the next issue of the magazine to go to press, an editor in New York tells me, *No one else has these details. Well done.*

Thank you, Emma and the Coylet Inn.

A few months later, Emma Thompson calls me at home.

This is even more exciting than when Arsenal footballer Freddie Ljungberg called me to talk about being Calvin Klein's new underwear model, at which point I locked myself in my home office and my British football fan husband gave me the side eye.

Emma and I are supposed to be talking about her role in a soon-to-be-released project called *Love Actually*. I haven't seen the movie. This state of affairs is unusual and not ideal, because it means you can't ask targeted questions. I can only go vague: *What was it like filming with X? How 'bout that cast, eh? Christmas, yay!*

We talk about her role in the movie, in which she plays the mother of two young children whose husband has an emotional affair with his young assistant. Great; an *in* to talk about family, a topic the magazine editors love.

I ask Emma how little Gaia is doing. I pronounce her name *Gay-A*.

"It's pronounced Guy-A," Emma corrects me.

Read that in Emma Thompson's voice.

Oof.

She proceeds to tell me something nice about her daughter, which gives me an entrée into talk of her wedding. Surely she hasn't connected the dots that I was the one who called the inn and got all the details, though I probably had a byline on that story.

I ask her, "Talk to me about your cake. I heard it was unique. What was the inspiration for it?"

Emma replies, "Oh, you mean the tits cake?"

I can't help it; I laugh and gasp at the same time. "Uh…"

"It was meant to be mountains in the Scottish Highlands," she says, and explains that something went wrong and the cake ended up looking like a pair of green breasts, and that they all thought it was hilarious and the cake was delicious. Emma Thompson, I've learned, is no bridezilla.

That same week, Richard Curtis, *Love Actually*'s writer and director, calls me at home, and again I must stick to general questions. This moment for me is much more about what I *can't* ask him than what I *do* ask him.

I haven't seen the movie yet, so I can't inquire as to why his Christmas movie is packed with certain icky themes that don't quite fit with a feel-good holiday flick.

The interview is generic. I only know one movie he directed, *Four Weddings and a Funeral,* and I never understood the hype. It was fine…but so, so flawed. The Carrie character, played by the salty Andie MacDowell—look up British talk show host Richard Madeley's quotes about UK presenters' experiences with her, including his claim that *Andie…wouldn't even make eye contact and was incredibly snotty*— was so bizarrely drawn that she distracted from everything else happening onscreen. Don't get me started on that infamous line: *Is it raining? I hadn't noticed.*

Anyway, I want to say, *What does love actually even mean?* But instead I blurt, "Congratulations!"

Richard and I talk about the killer cast. Emma and Liam Neeson are the steady, kindly, yet beleaguered parental figures. The rest of the world will finally meet British TV stars Ant and Dec! Bill Nighy is peak Bill Nighy. Notoriously grouchy Hugh Grant has some embarrassing scenes.

The movie is well received in the UK but gets mixed reviews in my home country. As always in life, one person's schmaltzy, saccharine cheese is another's heartwarming, inspiring, cozy, Christmas staple.

There are those of us who recognize both can exist in the same place. I like me a schmaltzy Christmas movie now and then, and I can tolerate flaws in order to experience the sweet moments. When I finally saw the movie in a cinema, I liked it…for the most part. *Love Actually* didn't age well in many ways. The ensuing generations possess a clear-eyed view of some strangely toxic threads running through the 2003 film. (I am *not* trying to rob you of your joy if this movie is a favorite holiday tradition! You like what you like. In fact, stop reading now if you don't want to read about the negative bits that so many of us can't unsee).

A few examples: Martine McCutcheon's character is relentlessly hammered with jabs about her "size," is called "plumpy" by her own father, and is told she has a sizeable arse and thighs the size of tree trunks; Richard Curtis's script forces Emma Thompson's character to say her clothes are so huge they'd fit the opera singer Pavarotti, a line that manages to insult both Emma and Pavarotti at the same time; Bill Nighy's character frames his loyal colleague in the film as just a fat guy, calling him "chubs" and his "fat manager" to name two instances; and the house cleaner who falls for boss Colin Firth's character after zero legitimate conversations or shared physical affection fat-shames her own sister before the sister even comes on screen, and the "fat" sister is later called Miss Dunkin Donuts 2003 by her father in front of a pack of people.

Here's one you might not know. Remember the stalker scene where Andrew Lincoln's character turns up to creep on his best friend's young wife played by nineteen-year-old Keira Knightley, flashing cue cards professing his love for her? The final card was edited out of the movie—but it remains in the script, and the scene itself was included in an official trailer the studio uploaded to YouTube around 2011. Originally, the final cards were meant to read,
MERRY CHRISTMAS.

FATSO.
To Keira Knightly.
What the *actual*, Richard?

Here's the truth, actually: if I'd seen the movie before interviewing the writer/director in the year 2003, I wouldn't have questioned him about his persistent fat shaming, just as every other entertainment journalist at the time didn't.

I *liked* the movie the first few times I saw it. The endless jabs wouldn't have hit as hard to a woman living in a timeline where Jessica Simpson is called fat in every form of media; where Bridget Jones weighs around 134 pounds and is deemed deserving of an entire movie built around her being the butt of relentless fat jokes and barbs, a movie also written by Richard Curtis; and where model Kate Moss famously validated a spectrum of eating disorders with her pronouncement that *Nothing tastes as good as skinny feels*.

Richard's supposed mea culpa in 2023, marking the movie's twentieth anniversary, was watered down to almost pointlessness, but whatever. He's long in the tooth; I doubt he's spending his life worrying about what he wrote twenty-three years ago. During an appearance at the *Times* and *Sunday Times* Cheltenham Literature Festival, Curtis gave an interview about this to activist and writer Scarlett Curtis.

Scarlett Curtis is Richard Curtis's daughter. Richard explained to the public that Scarlett had told him he can't use "fat" as a word anymore, and added, "I think I was behind, you know, behind the curve, and those jokes aren't any longer funny, so I don't feel I was malicious at the time, but I think I was unobservant and not as, you know, as clever as I should have been."

Um, to say the least…

Side note about Kate Moss: One night in London around 2005, I bump into Kate and Rhys Ifans, who are hailing a cab outside a nightclub opening I was just covering as an invited reporter. I ask for a quick chat about the event; there were no cameras in their faces, no pressing hordes bothering them. Just a girl, standing in front of a model and an actor, asking nicely how their night went.

They mock me like schoolyard bullies.

Hahhahahahahaaaa, they laugh in unison. They're laughing at me, not with me. I know the difference.

Rhys cackles and says, "I don't do *interviews,*" as if I've asked him to spank me in public. "I'm not talking to *you.*"

Who knows why they chose rudeness when they could've said no or simply walked away. Maybe Kate could smell the food on me. There were some yummy appetizers inside the party and I did, indeed, take the chance that some things taste better than skinny feels.

The Young Royals

Dancing with princesses is a new activity for me. The young royals are a lot like regular people, as far as I can tell; we're all bathed under the same juddering splotches of colored lights running across our faces like bugs from the glittering disco ball on a crowded, makeshift floor at the Cartier International Polo Day afterparty in Windsor. We're all glistening at some level. A hot, un-airconditioned evening in Windsor is the great equalizer.

Beatrice and Eugenie Mountbatten-Windsor bop rhythmically on the raised wooden floor, working their shoulders and engaging in some energetic foot-shuffling. The two sisters have matching freckled noses and auburn hair. I see their parents Prince Andrew and Sarah "Fergie" Ferguson in them. I see signs of sweat on all three of us—on our cheeks, our foreheads, in tendrils of hair. Shiny, beet-red faces abound in the exclusive VIP marquee.

Bea and Eugenie are just kids in the summer of 2004, but this fact doesn't compute with me. I view them as princesses first and teenagers second, probably because they're inside the Chinawhite afterparty where booze is flowing like water.

No matter that they're not legally allowed to drink. Their granny, Queen Elizabeth II, lives just up the road in Windsor Castle. Something tells me the cops won't be coming to bust anyone.

It's nearing the end of a long day spent reporting on royals, mostly Prince Harry, who was playing in the Cartier polo match as I watched him, his face aflame in the heat, matching his red shirt.

I'm still dancing with the princesses.

Six hours earlier…

I arrive in Windsor early in the day to interview any celebrities that might interest our magazine. They're few and far between. That is, those who will speak to us. Because a bunch of royals, including the polo-playing Prince Harry, are here, but they're not interested in talking to the media.

I enjoy lunch in the VIP marquee with the upper crust, and my tablemates include a smug sixty-five-year-old aristocrat and his cool-as-crystal thirty-five-year-old wife.

I head out to watch the polo match after lunch. I'm supposed to take notes on Harry. How he plays, who he talks to, who might be paying particular attention to him. Who he pays extra attention to. I see no signs of a serious girlfriend, but that doesn't mean one isn't lurking in the shadows.

The prince is so young, baby faced, not yet twenty. He lost his mum only seven years ago and blames people like me for it. He mounts his white horse and plays polo like a monster. I'm not a polo fan, but I'm gripped. It's not every day you get up close to the British ruling class.

I watch from the VIP section, and there I run into a friend who watches with me for a while, then gets me into the afterparty.

Word on the street is Harry parties just as hard as he plays polo. That is his reputation, anyway. He is the spare to his brother Prince William's heir. Harry is the son the

British media isn't pressured to handle with kindness or grace, the one thrown to the proverbial wolves while the heir, his older brother William, is generally protected.

The match is over, and Prince Harry has a cigarette in one hand and a cigarette in the other (he really does) as he hangs with posh chums at the packed Chinawhite afterparty, face red from exertion and the heat of a crowded marquee on a July night. He's surrounded by Red Bull and half-drunk glasses of champagne.

Harry is wearing a baseball cap and robin's-egg-blue shirt with spilled drinks and sweat stains down the front, and he's generally being a nineteen-year-old man. When I go to use the port-a-potty, I lose him, which is how I end up flailing along with Harry's flame-haired cousins in a last-ditch effort to find him again before I head back to London. Why am I doing this? Let's say Harry is caught making out with someone. Or even a casual smooch. If I see it, it's a story. If I don't, I'm a bad reporter. I'm not doing my job.

I won't be speaking to the princesses or otherwise interacting apart from proximity on the dancefloor. It's a huge no-no for reporters to address royalty unless the meeting has been previously arranged. Even more frowned upon—understandably!—when they're minors, as Bea and Eugenie are. I was already on the floor with someone else when they danced near me; I wouldn't approach, but I'm not going to run away if they come my way, either.

Evening is turning to night, and the air smells of dirt and cut grass and men's sweat and horses. As one of my favorite summer songs come on, I get overly excited. My high wedges are great on grass but wrong for slick dance floors.

My heel slips on the wet spot and I go down hard, slamming my hip and elbow on the wood. In that moment, when I'm certain I'm one vigorous drunken dancer away from getting trampled, the princesses hover above me.

Their quick exchange of eye contact conveys concern. Beatrice mouths, *Are you OK?* I hold up my hand like I'm fine, then I roll to my side and scramble to get to my feet with a modicum of grace, but it's slippery, and it takes me a few tries. There is no grace.

I'm fine! I shout, giving the ladies a thumbs-up, but of course I'm not; I ache and I'm horrified. It's time to go. I give the princesses a wave and they give me pity smiles in response.

I tie up my final loose end, finding someone in the know to tell me that Harry has left the property to possibly attend an after-after party at a mate's country mansion.

Harry has finished up his gap year after Eton and will enter Royal Military Academy Sandhurst next year. He's also recently conceived, filmed, and helped package a documentary titled *The Forgotten Kingdom: Prince Harry in Lesotho.* The young royal shot it with his own handheld camera during his time in the country, capturing some of the work he did with Mants'ase Children's Home in Mohale's Hoek, which was set up for children orphaned by or living with AIDS.

A spokesman for Harry said he "wanted to go to Lesotho to learn more about the problems faced in a country affected by AIDS and to do what he could to help. He was really affected by his experience there and the people he met. He hopes that his visit and now the film will help to raise awareness and money to help tackle the problems faced by the people of Lesotho."

Unfortunately for the young prince, the media is more interested in the fact he goes to parties with friends and smokes and drinks sometimes. Even the BBC can't let it slide when covering Harry's very serious documentary, snarking, *The young prince's dedication to Lesotho's problems may help counter his party-loving, nightclub-dwelling image.*

He's a kid, BBC. Isn't that…what teenagers are supposed to do? He'll be out of that phase soon enough; he's readying to join the British Army and serve his country.

As for Princesses Beatrice and Eugenie, two years after they helped me up off the dance floor, Bea celebrated her eighteenth birthday alongside future convicted rapist Harvey Weinstein, pedophile-rapist-sex trafficker Jeffrey Epstein, and convicted sex trafficker Ghislaine Maxwell. This collection of pond scum was celebrating at a party packed with teenaged girls, thrown by members of the British royal family.

Fast forward to 2026. Andrew's family is in shambles. With the release of a portion of the Epstein Files—millions of pages of evidence gathered in a years-long investigation of his and Ghislaine's sex trafficking operation—some disturbingly horrific content is coming out about people in high places, with much more still hidden and redacted at this writing. Andrew, ex-wife Sarah Ferguson, and their daughters Beatrice and Eugenie are already mentioned multiple times in the files, but the extent of the family's involvement with Epstein and his operation is still developing. What else will be revealed is unknown at this stage. Maybe nothing. And perhaps what we already know is enough.

Andrew has been in hot water for years because of his closeness to Epstein. Meanwhile, his mother, Queen Elizbeth II, his brother Prince Charles, and others in the royal family kept him in the fold and placed him front-and-center at public events.

This ongoing scandal calls into question the behavior of the entire royal family. Not only was Andrew credibly accused of sexual assault by Virginia Giuffre in the Queen's lifetime, he settled with the victim in a civil lawsuit. While he didn't expressly admit guilt, for the deal to go forward, Andrew was forced to commend Giuffre, who accused him of raping her when she was a teenager, for her courage in coming forward. The reported figure Andrew agreed to pay her was $16 million, with a good chunk of that believed to have come directly from his mother the Queen.

With the spectre of allegedly raping a trafficked teenaged girl in Andrew's background, not only was he kept in the royal fold and allowed to stay in the thirty-room Royal Lodge in Windsor, he kept his princely title and maintained his closeness with the longest-reigning queen in the history of the United Kingdom.

Sure, his title has *now* been stripped, and he had to leave the Royal Lodge…and was immediately given another royal mansion to live in for free on a different family compound.

And still, the royal family kept their public statements vague—we are so, so "deeply concerned"—and no one ejected Andrew or firmly denounced him. *Even though* emails and photographs in the Epstein Files show deep ties to Epstein and Maxwell. One of them, from someone called "A," was sent to Maxwell. The British media noted that "A" was corresponding from Balmoral, the royal family property in Scotland where Queen Elizabeth II died in 2022.

I am up here at Balmoral Summer Camp for the Royal Family…How's LA? Have you found me some new inappropriate friends?

The writer signed it, *see ya, A xxx.*

Further, files made public in October 2025 show Andrew apparently emailed Epstein in February 2011 and told him to *keep in close touch* and expressed a wish to *play some more soon.*

But Epstein's tentacles reach further than just Andrew. Turns out others in his family were cozy with Epstein, too. The released files, news reports say, include emails indicating Epstein paid for ex-wife Sarah Ferguson and daughters Beatrice and Eugenie to fly to Miami, where the four of them got together for lunch.

In a sickening revelation that's hard to excuse or reconcile, this delightful lunch date under the Florida sun was held *after* Epstein had served thirteen months of an eighteen-month sentence for a sex crime involving a minor. According to the files, Beatrice and Eugenie, who were then twenty and nineteen, joined their mother for lunch with Epstein on July 27, 2009.

Later, Sarah wrote in an email to the sex trafficker, *I have never been more touched by a friends (sic) kindness than your compliment to me infront (sic) of my girls. Thank you Jeffrey for being the brother I have always wished for.*

In a January 2010 email, "Sarah" wrote to the seedy dweeb Epstein, *You are a legend. I really don't have the words to describe, my love, gratitude for your generosity and kindness. Xx I am at your service. Just marry me.*

That's not the worst of it.

In a shocking exchange two months later in March 2010, "Sarah" makes a vulgar reference to her nineteen-year-old daughter's sex life when Epstein, already convicted of a sex offense involving a minor, inquires when he might see Sarah again.

Not sure yet, Sarah wrote. *Just waiting for Eugenie to come back from a shagging weekend!!*

What happens to the princesses and their place in the royal fold remains to be seen. Their cousin Prince William, who is primed to be king sooner than anyone expected due to his father's cancer diagnosis, once briefed through royal commentators that Bea and Eugenie would remain in the fold because Andrew's sins are not their fault; but then, more recently, someone in his camp briefed the *Daily Mail* that William and Kate aren't close to the women and "wouldn't miss them" if they were gone.

Ouch.

Even so, one can be pretty certain Bea and Eugenie's place in the British royal family has not been sealed yet. Not by a longshot.

Wife to Bono: Make Your Own Sandwich

I'm sitting across from the gate in Dublin airport, waiting for the call. It is December 2004 and a grey, wet cold blankets the city. It is nothing like the New England razor-blade winter I grew up with.

Do I wait, or do I run?

In the next ten minutes I'll either be boarding an Aer Lingus flight back to London or racing out to hail a taxi to meet U2 for an interview.

A text comes through.

Hang tight. Still waiting.

Waiting for management, for reps, for permission, for the green light. Celebrities are nothing if not suspenseful.

The 2003-2005 era is a messy one for me and rock stars. They are alternately flirty, mean as hell, annoyed, funny, sanctimonious, reticent, and open. There is only one woman among them. I ask her less about her music and more about her diet. We're told it's what the readers want, so we give it to them.

In December of 2004, U2's new album *How to Dismantle an Atomic Bomb* sits at #1 on music charts around the world, including the Billboard 200 in the U.S. Its first single, "Vertigo," is everywhere that autumn and winter.

Colin Farrell sends it up on *Saturday Night Live*, mimicking Bono's gravelly, sultry Irish voice and wearing a facsimile of his ubiquitous shades as he belts out the song's opening cry:

Uno…dos…tres…catorce!

In the skit, someone asks "Bono," *You do realize you're saying one, two, three, fourteen?*

Sure.

We never find out why Bono skips the numbers four through thirteen. He is as much of an enigma as his lyrics are.

With this worldwide interest in U2, I've been dispatched to Dublin to see what I can dig up about the band in their hometown. I stay at The Clarence, a hotel partly owned by members of U2 on the banks of the blue-grey River Liffey. The halls are low-lit and my room is cozy. If you don't speak the language, I can tell you that "cozy" is European for "small."

I barely notice it's Christmastime in Dublin as I race past the fairy lights and pine trees and Temple Bar wrapped in ribbons. I have to hit the ground running after being airdropped into a city where I know nobody, with the vaguely impossible goal of finding out where U2 hangs out and what they do when they're there.

My job becomes infinitely more doable when the magazine connects me with a lovely Irish correspondent who's too busy to take on this assignment. In one phone call she gives me her time, sets ego free like a helium balloon, and steers me in the right direction with her insider tips. It's not always like this. Reporters can be, understandably, precious about our sources and secrets. But there are ways to be kind and generous to colleagues without surrendering your hard-earned proprietary information, and this one nails it.

The correspondent points me in the right direction and gives me the names and numbers of some people who are happy to talk to friendly media outlets about the celebrities they know, and it's all I need. I can take it from here. Each person you talk to leads you to the next, every place you visit points you toward your next location. Following breadcrumbs and collecting them, coalescing them until they are a story, is the job.

I make some phone calls, talk to some people, come into possession of the email address of a good friend of the band. I write to him. I visit a pub. I grab a taxi to a nightclub. Dublin tonight is narrow streets, Christmas lights, people spilling out of pubs. Now that I'm a thirty-something married person, I'm even less interested in clubbing than I was as a single twenty-something on the Sunset Strip. But a-clubbing I go, to a cool venue where I have an *in* with a source.

Bono, at forty-four years old, still comes in sometimes to drink and socialize under the strobe lights, the source tells me. Edge comes too. Larry is more of a homebody, but he'll come out to support friends when the situation warrants it. All of them will. Everyone loves U2, and its legendary frontman in particular, because Bono is an extrovert.

Said one person who hangs out with him regularly, *Most locals who aren't in his circle know to leave him alone when they see him out and about, but strangers who bother him, those who are indiscreet, will usually be forgiven by Bono. Worst you'll get is a lack of enthusiasm or a polite reminder he's out as a private citizen, or sometimes, he'll quietly leave.*

One person I meet has known Bono since Live Aid in 1984. He tells me something about the rocker that sticks with me. I've always wondered how megastars who hold marriages and relationships together do it. It's hard enough when you're not famous.

Mr. and Mrs. Bono, real names Paul and Ali Hewson, I'm told, *Have something amazing. They really get each other. She once said to me that when he comes home from tour, he has been like God. When he comes home she might say, "make your own dinner."*

Ali would say to me, "We don't talk for a week." He comes down [from rock star heights] for a full week.

My new friend laughs. You can picture it, can't you; Bono's wife of however many years putting him in his place after weeks of playing to sold-out stadiums, months spent attracting crowds that clog streets and yell your name.

Not in so many words, this source says Ali is unimpressed with Paul thinking he's a big deal, because everyone treats him like a rock god when he's away from home and he gets used to it. When she needs him to pick up his socks off the floor, help with their two kids under six, and not bother her when she's trying to launch the fairtrade fashion label EDUN, maybe it gets tense.

That was the way it is around 2004, anyway, according to some old friends.

When they're together, he says, they are holding hands. *He is always touching her.*

I write in my notebook, *When the band is together out on the Dublin scene, particularly The Edge and Bono, there is no flirting with/hitting on women or picking up groupies. "He's very intense. If you look over, you see them in a huddle; 99 percent of the time, it's about art or something artistic," says the source.*

That's not the only long-term relationship in Bono's life that requires work to stay on track.

They do what they need to for the band, and they don't live in each other's ears, a Dublin source tells me. U2 protects the unit. Sometimes, that means distance from one another. But it always means having each other's back.

I pop into another club and stay until the wee hours, and one of the Corrs, an Irish family band, greets my new friend and brushes past me, though I don't know which one she is.

After clubbing, I grab a taxi back to my hotel and venture into the cozy residents-only bar at The Clarence. I scan for the boys of U2 but it's hard to see in the low-lit bar.

I notice a group of rockstar-type men.

A man in black with black curly hair notices me. He is not smiling. He stops what he's doing to check me out. It is hostile.

This guy watches me as I try to look like I'm not watching them. He stands.

He eyes me with suspicion, something I'm used to and cannot blame him for. I could be anyone. A British tabloid reporter. A celebrity journalist crossing a boundary, invading privacy. A deranged fan. A general weirdo. A threat.

He tells me he's Gavin Friday, and I know the name. His story is intertwined with Bono's, and therefore with U2's.

I tell him who I am, and he's nonplussed.

I am a hotel guest, I assure him. I'm technically off the clock (lie). He says he'll call me later *if* he decides wants to talk to me about his friends in U2, and after that, I don't stay; I'm not going to order a drink and pretend I'm not watching and listening to him and his friends.

Google Gavin Friday and note his dark eyes that are actually blue behind the lashes, his pout, his smolderingly bellicose confidence. This is the gaze under which I proudly remain sure-footed. Listen to his 1995 song "Shag Tobacco." This is the voice under which I do not wither.

But I do beat a fast retreat.

I wake the next morning to taxi my way to the wealthy seaside hamlet of Dalkey thirty miles away. Nestled in the village, on a narrow and winding street, is Bono and The Edge's local pub.

I order a pint to fit in and strike up conversations with locals. Most are friendly, showing only a flicker of suspicion, and it helps that I ask benign questions. I am not the first nosy reporter they've met. I'd pretend to be a regular tourist or even an American expat out for a drink alone in the middle of the day, but we have a rule at this particular magazine. You do not do that. You do not pose or pretend or play a role. You don't elicit or solicit information under false pretenses. Not that reporters haven't done it; I've been with some who have, and it's really bad, and I stayed far away.

One of the white-haired men at the bar is drinking Guinness and he tells me his name, which may or may not be his real one. It's as Irish as Seamus O'Houlihan. Bono comes in quite often, mostly on a Sunday night, Seamus tells me. He tends to come in after dinner at home with friends and family, after the kids have gone to bed. Bono is not here right now. I *just* missed him. I might even be sitting in the stool he warmed up yesterday.

Seamus has been drinking here for twenty years. Bono, he says, is well liked and is generally left alone to stick with his own friends and family unbothered, but is sociable when he wants to be.

"He doesn't like people up in his face. He's a private person. If Bono comes in, we leave him alone. He's entitled to his privacy…We don't interfere with him. That's not done here. He's a nice fellow. Edge comes in too," my new mate Seamus tells me.

Note: They call him *Edge*. Second note to self: stop being uncool. Stop calling him *The* Edge. In my day, the day of the Gen X teen girl, we called him The Edge. Also, Larry Mullen was the hunk. I find out the least about him because Larry stays at home a lot, the locals tell me. Not as sociable as Bono who, by the way, makes his personality about *not* being precious, not being anyone but just another guy hanging around Ireland.

"If he wanted it to be otherwise, he would make it that way," Seamus says wisely. "He wants to be one of the lads. He is proud of the fact his city allows him to do that. If you offer to call him a cab at the end of the night, he'll shout 'no! I'll walk.' I can imagine he goes back to LA and talks about this—'Look what I can do in my city. I get no grief.'"

The next morning, I'm still waiting in the airport for Gavin Friday to call, or their friend Guggi to respond to my email, or for U2's team to give the go-ahead for me to interview the band.

Travelers rush by as I write my file on my laptop and wait for the call.

Finally, my phone rings.

Come home, the boss says. *It's not going to happen.*

Not that day, anyway. My celebrity reporting career is spiraling out of my control now, and maybe, I think, I'll meet Bono somewhere else, some other time.

Later that year, some of my family meet my husband and me in London, and we fly over for a weekend in Dublin. We visit Bono's hometown pub for a Sunday roast. As we are seated, I swear my mischievous much-younger brother to silence for the second time since he'd landed in London: *Do NOT ask about Bono, do not look for him, do not act like we're there for anything but a pleasant pub lunch in Ireland.*

I get a suspicious glance in return that says something like, *Fine. But don't tell me what to do.*

The server comes.

Hey, my brother says to the guy, lowering his voice and glancing around. *I have a question.*

I send him my strongest *Don't you dare* vibes. My brother ignores them.

The young Irishman nods, waits.

Is it true that…

My death stare intensifies. *Don't you dare, don't you dare!*

…is it true that Phil Collins drinks here? My brother asks.

The server knits his brow, squints.

I don't know about any Phil Collins, he says, making us think it's possible he doesn't know who Phil Collins is, *but Bono drinks here all the time.*

You can imagine how the rest of the day went. We cried laughing, which is the point of any good Sunday pub lunch, and all was well.

I return to The Clarence nineteen years later, in 2023, booking a standard room for the convenient location more than the memories. Out of nowhere, the front desk upgrades my husband and me to the penthouse suite.

The suite is bigger than many Dublin apartments and has a roof-top terrace. Back in 2004, I was told this precise set of rooms, wooden and cream and spare and calming, was where U2 used to retreat to hang out with close friends when they didn't want any strangers or fans, even well-meaning ones, to ogle or bother them.

This is where they'd write music. Shoot the shit. Drink. Be.

I venture out on the balcony in the cool autumn night and feel ensconced in echoes of the past. Nearly twenty years have passed since I was young and running around this city looking for traces of one of my favorite bands. The ghost of a young Larry, of Edge, of Bono and their trusted circle is here where I'm standing, throwing open the balcony doors, watching the River Liffey roll by while drinking pints of Guinness and creating music and memories.

Nineteen years pass just like that.

Uno, dos, tres, catorce…and it's gone.

Stung

I lock myself in an office in the London bureau and go over my questions again. I've waited by the phone for men to call before, but never a rock star, and never to talk about such personal things. All the questions have a spicy angle. Every single one.

Celebrities and reporters have a built-in frictional relationship. They need us more than they'd like to admit, and we clearly need them, and within that dynamic lies varying degrees of willingness to go along. Sting, like many famous men, has agreed to be featured in *People* magazine's latest special issue in the Sexiest Man Alive franchise. The former Police frontman is not the cover boy, not the superlative sexi*est* man, but he's in good company alongside the regular sexy runners-up inside the issue. I can only hope he'll have a sense of humor about my questions.

I never thought about Sting much over the years, though I liked plenty of Police songs in the eighties and then, later, the lead singer's solo efforts. Teens everywhere swooned for him. I was more of a Simon Le Bon girl. I was pretty sure, as I listened to Rio on vinyl as a child and memorized the lyrics to every song, that I would marry him. (This assumption turned out to be incorrect).

Maybe I'll be more of a Sting woman now. After all, Simon never called me personally, which is a strike against him.

I stare at the phone until it rings, right on time. The panel reads *private number*. Dammit. I go to answer and instantly panic; what do I call him? *Shit, shit, shit.* I can't call a grown man Sting. I just can't. Mr. Sting? That's even stupider.

I go with, "Hello! Hi!"

"Hello," comes a husky, languid voice. "This is Sting."

The pleasantries are fairly standard, and I manage to choke out my side of things. He's relaxed. His voice is thick and low; he doesn't sound like he's *trying* to be flirtatious. He just is. He's calling from his home in Wiltshire, an eight-hundred-acre estate with a pool, a lake, a wine cellar, a music studio, an ornate fireplace. I picture him sipping tea in front of the fire. The stretches of barley on the property inspired him to write the hit song "Fields of Gold."

I ask him a bunch of the hot-man questions on my list, and every reply is delivered with that same timbre. I have a no swooning, no fawning policy. We're reporters, not fans. Today I will be tested.

"Back in the days when you were single, what were some of the pickup lines you used?"

He takes a moment, then tells me he used to have a great opening line about needing change for a ten-pound note. It's clear he has a sense of humor, so I take a risk: "That's not the most seductive line I've ever heard. I mean, did it really…?"

"It works," he assures me. "It's all in the way you approach it."

Asked what his biggest pet peeve might be, he teases me.

"Does it have to be a sexy pet peeve?"

I chuckle, as anyone would, and say it can be anything he wants it to be. He chooses non-sexiness.

"I hate things that fall out of magazines," he tells me unsexily. "I pick up magazines and all this crap falls out of it. And [internet] spam."

I check the clock. *Uh oh;* we have three minutes left. When you set a time with a celebrity's team, you stick to it, or you might get complaints later.

"How are you doing on time?" I ask.

"I'm doing OK," Sting replies. "I think talking is an aphrodisiac, don't you?"

My brain seizes up.

I manage to comprehend that the query was rhetorical and reluctantly let it go, because every response that comes to mind is inappropriate and would get me into trouble. I glance at my sheet. Here I am, trying to stay professional, and every single question is about sex, love, or romance.

"What attracts you to a woman? What do you look for?"

He thinks for a moment then replies, "I'm attracted to people who speak well. Camilla Parker Bowles is one—I sat next to her at an event once and she's absolutely lovely."

There's more, but you get the gist.

By the time I meet the Police frontman, I've already interviewed one Sexiest Man Alive—JFK Jr. He took the crown three years after the franchise launched in 1985 with Mel Gibson on the cover. Over the years, some problematic men have smoldered sexily from the newsstand.

Some men tried diplomatically to wriggle out of the honor. I remember in London one year a reporter told me they were asked to pitch Cillian Murphy as one of our inside-the-magazine sexiest men. This was pre-meme, pre-extra-famous Cillian Murphy. No one could believe he kept turning us down; stars rarely if ever did. (Makes sense now, though, doesn't it?).

Matt Damon flat-out rebuffed the crown in 2007. Which was odd, because that very summer, he'd joked on the TODAY show about how something was missing in his life because he'd never been offered the title.

"I've got to hire a campaign manager," Matt told TODAY co-host Meredith Vieira. "[George] Clooney's been trying to campaign for me the last few years. It's a whisper campaign."

And guess what? *Bam*, magazine editors called his reps to announce he was officially their sexiest man alive, for that specific twelve-month period anyway.

The reply from Matt's camp was clear, much in the way Victoria Beckham's PR person's was clear to me back in 2004: ...*this would be a no.*

Word on the street is that Matt was the first star to refuse to partake in a sexiest man cover interview. He wrote a letter instead, blaming his strong sense of humility for skipping the iconic interview and insisting he didn't deserve such an honor because he's "an aging suburban dad." He suggested the magazine tap New England Patriots quarterback Tom Brady instead.

I can understand why Matt Damon might view himself as too cool for any of that. He's been cool since birth. He was a celebrity before he landed a single film role, before even *Mystic Pizza.*

I met him in passing on a school bus during a high school field trip to Canobie Lake Park, and to this day I don't know why I was allowed to go, because I didn't even go to that school. I did spend my early years after Dorchester living in North Cambridge, though, and my best friend from Jackson Street invited me along on this Cambridge Rindge and Latin School field trip. No one in authority seemed to notice or care. (It being the eighties, a time of feral disconnection when parents and teachers were equally unbothered about where their children were, could explain it).

Anyway, Cambridge Rindge and Latin had a thriving theater program that, in my generation alone, spat out Matt, Ben Affleck, Matthew Maher, Casey Affleck, Traci Bingham, and others. Matt was a cute as a button, sharp, socially savvy, and could slay a room with wit and profound coolness. I didn't know him or even his name at first, but I knew he was the boss of the bus. He ruled not with an iron fist, but with benevolent sarcasm and clever humor. He was part raconteur, par purveyor of comebacks and hilarious observations. He stood up a lot, so you'd notice him.

Though I knew him as the popular kid from Cambridge Rindge and Latin, he would one day be *People* magazine's Sexiest Man Alive cover boy, whether he wanted to be or not.

Not all rock stars are nice. Around the time I enjoy a rollicking interview with Sting, I find myself racing to keep up with Jon Bon Jovi and his entourage at an event in Europe.

He's agreed to a brief walking interview. Everyone's in earshot. His entourage. Security. It feels like we're going fifteen miles an hour. The exit door, mocking me in all its angry bright neon, is yards ahead, and I have four questions editors want me to ask.

I can't go back with *one* piddling answer, let alone zero. I'm livin' on a prayer as I fire off a question about the event. Jon returns a rote, one-sentence answer; I ask a follow-up, and same thing.

I have mere seconds. Still moving, I grit my teeth and throw him one of the random questions from the Apropos of Nothing List. It's an easy one, if not slightly inane. I try to jazz it up with a perky voice.

"If you had to wear the same T-shirt every day, what would it say?"

This time, Jon swivels far enough that his eyes meet mine. He has a feline quality. "It would say, 'I Love [Insert City Here],'" he says.

He's talking to someone else now. I have seconds before he reaches the exit.

Reporting 101: Always get specifics. Details make the story. "Fascinating!" I shout. "What is it about [that city] that you love so much?"

He slows, turns. "And WHAT does this have to do with what we're talking about? Right. *Nothing*," he snarls. "That's enough!"

That's enough is said in the way you might tell an assailant to stop throwing rocks at you. The door flies open and he is gone.

I'm a bit shaky as he leaves.

Not a fan of the yelling.

There's no doubt it was an out-of-left-field question, one that might've seemed pointless, but editors have their reasons for asking it. This how it works. This is the deal. When celebrities agree to be interviewed, they know that if they only talk about their project, no one will read the article or watch the video. It's why Chris Hemsworth and Halle Berry will promote their thriller *Crime 101* in the year 2026 by smashing fortune cookies and talking about random topics, for example. If you don't package the marketing right, the project fails. Jon knows this.

Normally in the course my reportorial duty, I am prepared for who's going to be combative: a CEO asked why his stock is down, a police chief confronted about rising crime in his city, the child molester who's asked why he's violating his probation living next to an elementary school—they'll be prickly, and I'm always ready for it. The rest of the time, I go in expecting people in the grown-up work world to be professional and polite. Yes, even celebrities.

The Band in the Bathroom

In January 2005, it's back to Glasgow, this time not for a pampered pooch but for a buzzy new band.

I've never heard of them. Apparently The Killers are all the rage, fronted by twenty-three-year-old Las Vegas native Brandon Flowers. I'm told the first single off their album Hot Fuss, "Mr. Brightside," is "a global anthem."

For those who weren't alive or fully conscious during this timeline, my notes from that night will tell you something about the cultural landscape: The Killers, I wrote, …*recently completed a special tour with the hottest acts of last year: Franz Ferdinand, Keane and Snow Patrol.*

I buy the CD on expenses and bring it to the interview. I have not had time to listen to it, nor do I possess a portable CD player with which to play it.

I'm scheduled to interview The Killers *before* I see their show, which is unfortunate, because it cuts me off at the knees with questions and a feeling for who they are when they're on stage.

That's not the worst news.

By the time band members are available that evening, the only private place for an interview is a white-tiled bathroom adjacent to the drably claustrophobic dressing room apportioned to The Killers for their shows at Glasgow's Carling Academy. In the UK, they call this room the toilet. I am not calling a whole-ass room "the toilet." I am not interviewing anyone in a toilet.

The bathroom is the only place we can hear ourselves.
The opening act has already begun playing.
We make do.
Brandon follows me in.
It doesn't smell too bad. I think we can do this.

The bandmembers enter the bathroom with me one by one.

There are comments made as this happens. Shy, nervous chuckles, nothing too offensive from The Killers. I can't blame them. It's a weird scene.

I learn that the band doesn't party much. They do not admit to or present as being wild, or users of recreational drugs, or of finding out where models hang out and going there 'til all hours. They can't—it's already too exhausting being a rock star, they tell me.

Plus, shrugs bass player Mark Stoermer, "We've all got girlfriends."

For him, being interviewed by a magazine journalist in a bathroom is a more normal experience than his previous job.

"I had to go to boxing matches and pick up urine for testing," he recalls of his job as a medical courier delivering everything from blood to body parts. "Sometimes they [the boxers] couldn't 'go,' and I'd have to wait for three hours just for someone to be able to [pee]. I'd have to wait around for hours. I did a lot of them. I carried Lenox Lewis's urine."

He tells me how The Killers see themselves. "We had a similar concept of what we wanted a band to be. We wanted to raise the bar. It obviously worked. We definitely all agree on the Cure, U2, the Beatles, the Cars [as influences]."

I stop myself from mentioning that I *almost* interviewed U2 a few weeks ago, because no one cares what you almost did. The guys probably have Bono on speed dial, anyway.

Later, I ask David how four young men gallivanting around Las Vegas with weird jobs became The Killers.

"I consider the band starting when Brandon and I met. He was looking for a guitar player, and I was looking for a lead singer. I had the music and he had the lyrics."

Brandon sits on a wooden bench in the echo-y room with ramrod posture, waiting for the first question.

He's earnest, doesn't smile or laugh much, and appears to take this job of talking to a reporter very seriously. This is refreshing, because I am the same.

I learn Brandon is LDS (Church of Jesus Christ of Latter-day Saints). This surprises me, because you don't meet many Mormon rock stars. That aforementioned earnestness, the seriousness, the determination to be *nice*, always *nice*, when out in public is familiar to me. I was born in Utah and much of my extended family remains spread out there. My cousin is one of the most famous Mormon athletes in history. He was very nice to people out in public, at least early in his career, during the times I was with him; I didn't see him much after her got married, because he had a hundred kids and lived in Utah.

I ask Brandon about his fear of flying. I don't mention my own plane crash (no one died, including me). Note to budding journalists and interviewers: Avoid talking about yourself unless you decide it's vital to get a subject to open up. It's not about you, and they don't have time for it. They might say they care that your garage band got seven-thousand streams on Spotify, but I promise you, they don't.

As the stories go, The Killers were on a plane that went into freefall on the way to the UK in December of 2003 after hitting an air pocket, leading Brandon to genuinely believe he was going to die; on a flight in Australia, a real killer, in this case not a bandmember but a mass murderer wearing a straitjacket and Hannibal Lecter-style mask, was also on board; and, on that same flight, the jet's tires blew out on take-off, requiring the pilot to make an emergency landing.

"It's all true," Brandon tells me. "We fly so much that stuff's bound to happen. I don't get better every time; I get worse every time I fly. I'm looking into boats. I'm serious. I think on the second album it's going to be boats. I'm having someone look into it. I think it's a five-day trip to London, and then you just take ferries to Europe and stay on the ground the whole time. And then we just come back to America and stay on the bus there too."

He wants to live, that much is clear, and feels boats will keep him in his earthly form, but for what?

I ask him what his ultimate life goal is. What he hopes The Killers will one day be.

"Just to last," he says, then takes a breather and corrects course. "Not just to last, but leave our mark in the right way. There are a lot of bands that fall away. A lot of bands have potential, but they just don't do it. I want to have a couple of songs that are classic songs, like 'Roxanne' on the radio or 'I Want to Hold Your Hand,' and you just know these songs, you don't know why, but everyone just sort of knows. I want to, of course, make enough money to keep doing it."

"There's something special about that," Brandon tells me later. "We want to stay together. They [U2] have grown old with the music. They're not trying to sound like they're twenty-five. They're writing songs talented forty-five-year-old guys should write. They changed the world. They're the closest thing to The Beatles."

When our time is up, we shake hands and thank each other for our time.

It is bad form to ask for a photo, an autograph, merch, or any other favor. Journalists are not fans. We're professionals.

Brandon won't have it. I don't ask, or even hint. He offers before we leave the bathroom.

Please. I want to. I'm happy to.

I hand him my unopened CD, and he signs it.

He looks me dead in the eye.

Listen. You want tickets to a show anytime, ANYTIME, you call us.

He says to call their manager, whose cellphone number I keep.

I walk away thinking maybe The Killers will endure. That Ronnie, the drummer, will stay on this strange ride as a traveling rock star.

"It's like being on the hood of a car for a year straight with no goggles, bugs in your teeth, and never slowing down," he says. "You know you're passing things, but you don't see any of it. A wise man once said, 'you have to burn to shine,' and that's what we're doing," Ronnie says. "We're hopefully not burning *out*."

That night, I hear their music for the first time.

I am blown away, as I was meant to be. I had no idea.

As the house shakes, I ask a young Scottish lass next to me, *What is this song?*

Mester Bray-eet Say-eed.

What?

Mester Bray-eet Say-eed!

WHAT?

Mister Brightside!

Whenever that song plays, I hear it in my head as if I'm in Glasgow listening to Brandon sing it to me.

Mulleting it Over

I slide down the months from January to June. I start at Brandon at age twenty-three talking about Bono at forty-five, and land on Bono at age forty-five talking about Bono at sixty-five. This happens because, in the summer of 2005, I finally get to interview U2. Fifty percent of U2, if you want to get technical.

A few months after Brandon Flowers talked to me about U2's longevity, the Irish rockers are being honored for that very thing on a warm London day.

I pick at my plate at a luncheon at a perfectly fine hotel. My job is to dig up something exclusive from the legendary U2 frontman. The band isn't here, though. I scan the low-lit event room. Dido talks to The Who's Roger Daltrey and the boyband McFly (Google them) makes the rounds. Through salad and rolls and a little white wine, I do not stop looking for Bono's mullet, Edge's beanie, or Larry's blond coiffe.

In the meantime, I chat with Midge Ure and Dido. Midge, a former member of British new-wave band Ultravox, organized Live Aid with Boomtown Rats frontman Bob Geldof. Midge is melancholic and sentimental when I ask him his favorite moment about Live Aid twenty years before, a legendary dual-stadium, dual-country concert with iconic performances by Queen, U2, David Bowie, Paul McCartney, Elton John, Madonna, and Duran Duran.

Midge's favorite moment was going home.

"It's true," he explained when I seem disappointed with his answer. "London is a very cold place if you live here. You don't know your neighbors. It can be very insular. As I drove home in 1985, I saw strangers opening their doors to strangers. Doors were open. TVs, the music, was blaring out windows and doors. Strangers were handing drinks to complete strangers. This spirit was there."

He got me. I am misty-eyed thinking of the old days, when I was a teenager listening to "Do They Know It's Christmas," and watching all the tired rock stars filing into the studio that day in the song's video. And then the unbeatable Live Aid itself, a universe ago.

I meet Dido while table-hopping, and she's happy to chat. It's 2005, so the magazine wants me to talk to people about their bodies and about their opinions about other people's bodies. And by "people," I mean women. I won't perpetuate the toxicity by sharing what either of us talked about or put either of us on blast for what we said about the pressure to be thin, because it was of a time, and we did and said what was expected of us.

This platinum-selling artist, given name Florian Cloud de Bounevialle O'Malley Armstrong, whose smash hit "Thank You" was famously sampled by Eminem for "Stan," also gives me insight into her song-writing process.

She is in the midst of writing her next album. "I do most of my writing on airplanes," she says. "There's something emotional about them. I don't know if it's the lack of oxygen or what."

She's really fun to talk to. I move on, keep looking.
Still no U2.

I head outside before the awards show, hurry after desperate British tabloid reporters, poke around hallways in the hotel.

Their car pulls up to the venue in time for the awards ceremony, and I catch them before they go on stage. Bono and Edge do all the talking. They'll be playing a show in London that night, and instead of talking about the music, Bono muses about the weather.

Ever positive, ever confident, he quotes himself, his own song.

"It's a beautiful day," he says. "It's beautiful in central London in summer."

I can't see what kind of emotion his eyes are conveying, masked as they are by rose-tinted glasses; he's worn them for eons due to light sensitivity from glaucoma.

When asked how they feel about receiving the lifetime achievement award that day O2 Silver Clef Lifetime Achieve Award from the music therapy charity Nordoff-Robbins, Edge, in particular, is miffed. Defensive, even.

"More like half a lifetime," Mr. Edge, I mean *Edge*, who is nearly forty-four, says. "We're mere pups."

"We've still got a lot of unfinished business," adds Bono, who has recently turned forty-five.

The band is not nearly done making their musical mark. They feel young. They are young.

When asked how he remembers Live Aid twenty years before when he was the youngest of pups, Bono replies, "With great embarrassment. This is the man who brought you the mullet. No man should look like he's had his hair ironed."

Ha, everyone laughs. But it's interesting, because he has what I call a mullet *right now,* as we speak. I suppose he is measuring his style choices in degrees of mulletness.

But seriously, Bono says, "I feel sharper, smarter, rougher, tougher than twenty years ago."

Everyone files back inside, and I think to myself, *Now I can say I've interviewed Bono.*

Later, their table covered in empty water bottles, white wine in a silver ice bucket (and is that a red-topped vodka bottle?) the band watches the awards ceremony. When U2 files to the front of the room as the band accepts their award, Bono says something that is timeless.

"I don't think it's the pop stars or the musicians that the politicians are afraid of," he says, referencing the coming protests in Scotland at the G-8 summit, where activists will demand debt relief for developing nations, increased aid to Africa, and stronger action on climate change. "It's the audience. *They are young people and they can change things.*"

At this writing, Brandon Flowers is forty-five years old, the same age Bono was when twenty-three-year-old Brandon said he aspired to have U2's longevity.

I feel like the same person, and I would wager Brandon does, too. Age tends to manifest itself as a sudden shock. Along the ride, you're not old despite what the numbers say, and then one day, you are.

If I was in the bathroom with the boys again, exactly twenty-one years to the day they wished for longevity in that bathroom, I would say,

Hey, Brandon, Ronnie, Dave, Mark.
You did it.

Mission Possible

Part of being a successful celebrity reporter is a willingness to sneak into events you're not invited to. That is an unspoken requirement of the job. The more impossible the mission seems, the more likely your publication and editors are to disavow you if you get caught.

Crashing an event can be a fireable offense. I've only had to do it twice. Working for *People* magazine means you are almost always invited.

Except for this particular weekend.

I fly from London to Lisbon for the Laureus World Sports Awards in June of 2005, tagging along with CNN's London-based sports crew, me with my notebook and a couple of Bics, they laden with heavy cameras and other fancy equipment.

Upon settling into our hotel in Estoril, a seaside town not far from Portugal's capital city,

we meet up with a Lisbon-based CNN International anchor for dinner. He takes us to a narrow street in Lisbon and stops at a heavy door at the bottom of some stairs, with no number or name on it. He knocks, and the door swings open.

The nameless restaurant is intimate, low lit, and happens to have Owen Wilson inside it. The Butterscotch Stallion himself—the origin of this nickname is searchable, but if you can't find it, contact me and I'll tell you—who dated Sheryl Crow and would later have several famous girlfriends including Kate Hudson, is dining with his bushy-bearded brother Andrew.

This hidden restaurant has nothing so common as a menu. The serving starts, and one after another, something like twelve courses are set before us.

As we eat, there is port brought to us, there is wine, and there is vodka at the end, the whole bottle given to us to share as needed, and then we give the bottle back late at night long after the dessert plates are taken away.

We are there long after Owen Wilson has departed the restaurant. I suspect I'll see him again. He's in town all weekend like us.

The next morning, I pick up my press credentials for various events surrounding the awards weekend. A chatty British tabloid reporter approaches. She tells me her name is Mallory.

"Are you going to the *Vogue* party tonight?" Mallory asks me.

"I don't think I'm on the list." I didn't know there *was* a party.

"Meet me outside the hotel at eight," she says.

I'm right on time, and so is my new friend.

Outside our hotel is a glorified shuttle bus with glamourous people draped in Prada and Versace and Vera Wang waiting to board it. I feel comfortable enough in a basic LBD that can blend with polite society if you don't get too close. I'm never going to care enough about fashion to spend much money on designers and handbags.

I remind Mallory, "I don't have a ticket. You sure I'm OK to be your plus one?"

"Don't worry about it," she whispers. "I'm not on the list either."

I want to abort the mission, but I'm already at the door to the shuttle. I give Mallory the side-eye. She keeps walking, like she belongs; she's nearly glued to the back of a woman who is flashing a shiny invitation.

As the invite-wielding party guest is waved on by the driver checking people at the door, Mallory glides past him and is waved onto the shuttle as a presumed plus-one. I, in turn, stay glued to Mallory's back, trying to look like a plus-two, giving a quick smile to the driver, keeping one hand in my purse as if I'm about to pull out one of those coveted invites.

If I'm caught, I might be able to talk myself out of it. If not, the organizers of the awards might be told about my attempted party crashing, and they could complain to my bureau chief.

Shockingly, I'm let onto the bus. I plop down next to my new friend in the back.

Fifteen minutes later, the bus stops on a steep hill outside a modern hotel set into the hillside and ringed by palm trees. It is twilight, and the breeze smells of evening and the sea, and it blows the hair of all the beautiful people walking towards the hotel. Outside, there are long tables with frowny women taking names and crossing things off lists, and security guards. It's a well-oiled machine. It's not chaotic enough to slip inside unnoticed.

I made it this far. But I think my champagne dreams will end here.

Mallory shows no fear. She tries to slip by.

Alas, she is stopped by a name-taker seated at the table.

It's over, I think. I back away slowly. But my new friend goes with it.

"My editor is in there," Mallory says woefully. "Jane Remington? She works for *Vogue*?" The name-taker checks her list, shakes her head.

"No Jane Remington? *What*? Can I go look for her? She told me to meet her here."

This woman can *act*. Mallory's voice grows whinier, more desperate. She almost makes me feel sorry for her.

She is gazing towards the party with squinty, longing eyes, and as the name-checker turns to talk to a colleague about this person who's not on the list, my friend starts moving toward the door. It's now or never for me. I ignore the table lady, nod toward Mallory as if to say to whoever's watching that *I'm with her*, and I walk straight-armed, breath held.

"Wait," desk lady says sharply. "Name, please."

I think fast but not particularly intelligently, and blurt out the party line. "I'm with her," I point to the rapidly disappearing Mallory. "Our *editor's* in there!"

I shuffle past her as fast as I can without breaking into an all-out run.

The name-check lady opts not to sound the alarm.

And that is one of the most important secrets to getting by in life: Act like you belong, and you can get in (almost) anywhere.

The hotel is perched atop a cliff with expansive picture windows overlooking the Atlantic Ocean. Cascais, a coastal resort town west of Lisbon, has a Mediterranean vibe with palm trees swaying in the cooling breeze. The party is in full swing.

Mallory and I split up to do our jobs. I grab a glass of prosecco, take inventory.

There are tables piled high with a rainbow of fruit and shaved Serrano ham and salads and fresh, warm bread, and there are bars in every corner. I scan for the celeb catch of the day and spot Morgan Freeman and, in another corner, Jackie Chan. I don't speak to either one because I don't want to blow my cover just yet. They're both surrounded, and if I break into their conversations I'll be noticed, and someone important might wonder why a non-sports reporter is milling about.

After a quick chat with Joely Richardson, the current *Nip/Tuck* star who possesses both a swan-like grace and a willingness to answer a few questions on the record, I run into someone standing alone who I'm certain is safe to approach. He's not going to make it into the pages of our magazine at this point unless something newsworthy suddenly happens, but he's got multiple Olympic gold medals and I'm always excited to talk to people of extraordinary talent.

I approach sprinter Michael Johnson with a smile and offer him an immediate way out, as I do with everyone I talk to at these kinds of events.

"How are you, Michael? Do you have a quick moment to chat with *People* magazine?"

He seems to indicate consent, so I ask one of the magazine's introductory, softball questions meant to elicit fun responses and maybe lead to something with more meat.

I put on my usual *I know this is a silly question but work with me here* smile and ask what grosses him out the most about daily life, you know, like at restaurants or people's gross habits or bugs or...

Keep in mind track and field legend Michael Johnson is not exactly sought-after tabloid fodder at this point and could have simply declined to speak with me. Or even walked away silently without even a polite nod or smile.

But he does neither of those things.

Instead, he sneers, "Your magazine."

He does not offer a warm smile or a tilt of the head to say, *Hey, just joking with you!* He is not playing. The reply is served up without charm or humor.

In real life, I would tell him to go fuck himself. But I must keep the "celebrity" happy so no one complains to my editor, which is the journalism version of asking to see the manager. I put on a sad pout and pretend Michael has hurt my feelings, so he grudgingly changes his answer to "hair in my food" and walks away.

That's the thing with celebrities: The lower they are on the fame scale, the more obnoxious, dismissive and even cruel they can be. The closer they are to A-list, the more professional they tend to be. *(There are exceptions. Keep reading)*.

After my unpleasant encounter with Michael Johnson, I spot last night's distant dining companion Owen Wilson, his wavy blond mane bobbing like a beacon and his drawly, unique voice carrying over the hum of the crowd.

I move closer to him and see he's mingling with a bevy of lithe, tanned beauties. I introduce myself, ask if Owen will answer a few questions for a *People* magazine reporter. He is happy to oblige. He is chilled out, smiley. Kind of a slower-talking version of his character in *Wedding Crashers* (and *The Internship*, and *Hall Pass*, and *Marley & Me*...)

"How's it going?" he asks me.

"Great! Nice party, right?"

He heartily agrees that yes, it is a great party. The bevy of beauties stays where it is.

"So…how did you enjoy the restaurant last night? I ate there as well."

I choose my words carefully. When talking to a celebrity, one must use vocabulary that won't signal *stalker*. "I was watching" or "I was there" or "I saw" can, understandably, get hackles up.

Owen's eyes widen and he grabs my arm at the elbow, gripping *hard*. He pulls me in and I see that famous face close up. He proclaims that he has *never* been to such a restaurant in his whole life.

"Thank GOD for that place," he says, his eyes staying wide as he holds me. "We were just in Rome, where the food is amazing. The food here was even better! I called a girl in L.A. and told her she has to try this."

I ask him what brings him to this little town tucked away on the southern coast of Portugal. Is he a major sports fan, or has he worked with the organizers before? He releases my arm and thinks for a moment. "Well… I just heard Lisbon was a great city."

That's about all I have for him right now. I will forever like Owen Wilson. I don't know the guy, but such is the job wherein you cling to any semblance of kindness or professionalism. The bevy of beauties, happy to have their celebrity back, closes in as I depart.

That's what it's like to be a celebrity: People and companies fly you places and treat you like a king just because you're you, and beauty follows.

But does that make you happy?

Shouldn't it?

Life doesn't work that way. Mental health doesn't work that way.

Two years after our chat, in the wake of (but not necessarily connected to) a breakup with actor Kate Hudson, Owen attempted suicide at his home in Santa Monica. His brother, Luke Wilson, found him and got him straight to the hospital.

Andrew Wilson, the brother who dined near me with Owen in Lisbon that night, took care of him in the aftermath. Andrew "stayed in his house with him" following the attempt, according to an *Esquire* interview with Owen in 2021. Andrew stayed by his brother's side, the reporter wrote, "rising with him each morning and writing up little schedules for each day so that life seemed at first manageable and then, at some point, a long time later, actually good."

In that article, Owen reflected on his struggles with the way life gives and then takes away.

"Sometimes life seems to be played by Tom Hardy in *The Revenant*, some nightmarish guy trying to kill you, where even if you get the upper hand…He's still going to be there at the end whispering, 'This ain't gonna bring your boy back' or your dad back or any good times from your past back. Or whatever. And when life's being played by that guy, you just gotta hang on and wait for it to pass."

As of 2021, Owen said he was hanging in.

"I've been in sort of a lucky place of feeling pretty appreciative of things…I know everything's kind of up and down, but when you get on one of these waves, you've gotta ride it as long as you can…Feeling pretty grateful," he told the magazine.

The Scandal of the Century (so far)

The biggest global celebrity scandal of 2004-2005 is arguably the fallout from bombshell infidelity allegations against soccer star David Beckham dropped by Rebecca Loos via tabloid giant *News of the World*.

The gossip explosion reverberates globally. Explicit, cringeworthy texts reportedly exchanged between David and Rebecca, who was the Beckham family's former assistant in Madrid, rain down like shrapnel.

The stakes are high because this is no ordinary couple. The claims that David had a torrid extramarital affair with the twenty-six-year-old Loos—who stuck by wife Victoria's side as she looked at homes, who fetched Big Macs for the Beckham kids as she helped settle them all into the Spanish capital after David signed with the football team Real Madrid—shattered the fairytale image of the *It* pair. Posh and Becks, as they were dubbed when they first got together in their native England, is a brand made in heaven.

Everyone is looking for the beleaguered power couple as we speak. They are, in fact, being hunted. The British media in particular are starved for exclusives and are always on their tail to squeeze a quote out of them, get a look at them in real life, nab an exclusive tidbit, a response, catch them in…something.

But David and Victoria Beckham are not easy pickings. The couple's carefully constructed façade is maintained by a hand-picked team of high-powered imagemakers, and their physical being is usually protected by bodyguards. Every precious word Victoria and David utter is filtered and planned, every media interview request vetted within an inch of its life and usually turned down, including one I made that year on behalf of *People.*

The response to me from Victoria's devoted publicist via email was quick and frank:

…this would be a no.

Best wishes.

That's OK. I don't need the Beckhams' guard dog. I found the couple myself and am about to introduce myself to them.

It happens on the final night of the awards weekend. I snag a coveted invite from a connection who hands me a golden ticket to the wrap party. Sadly, Mallory has no such glossy invitation. I agree to help her slip in.

Unlike the Vogue party, this event has serious security, and the guardians of the velvet rope are burly, suited men with earpieces. It's the Oscars of the European sports world, and no unauthorized partiers will be crashing this room full of elite athletic talent.

This will take a miracle, I think.

Mallory is sanguine. *No problem,* she tells me. *Just stall for me.*

I distract the muscly clipboard holder while I search my handbag frantically for my invite, so it appears suspiciously like I don't have one, but wait… *Aha! Here it is.*

I flash the pass, the big guy nods, and I traipse in, waiting inside the doorway to see how Mallory plans to pull this off. Over her head I see the crowd pouring out of the awards ceremony and migrating toward the afterparty, click-clacking in spiked heels and black ties, a well-dressed herd of exotic creatures drawn to where the drinks are.

Mallory doesn't bother pretending she has an invitation. She nods to the clipboard and says coolly, "I'm with John Alessi."

Burly bodyguard man narrows his eyes and checks the all-knowing clipboard. He nods, makes a check on said clipboard, and waves her in.

My husband and another guy from the CNN crew file in a few minutes later. I tell him how Mallory slipped in by catching a peek at the clipboard while the guy was checking me in and picking off some random guy called John Alessi.

You mean Jean Alesi? The racecar driver? This cracks my husband up.

As Mallory told me later, she'd used the first name on the alphabetized guest list. We had no idea Jean Alesi was a world-famous racecar driver and one of the weekend's most celebrated attendees. I just hoped he didn't come looking for Mallory, his fake plus-one.

She and I split up to do our jobs. The first recognizable soul I see is *Jerry Maguire* standout Cuba Gooding Jr., who's making a spectacle of himself by gyrating on the small dancefloor while the party is still sparsely populated. As I draw closer, Cuba races up behind a young woman and tries to grab her ass. He chases her like Benny Hill as she scoots away.

"That booty!" He's moving and dancing to a beat all his own. *Mmm, mmm, mmm,* like she's a pot roast he's about to dig into. Undeterred, he grabs her butt, and she gets away again. I slip between them. I ask Cuba for an interview. I kind of want to see if that stops him.

"I don't do that anymore," he replies, looking over my head for someone better.

(The memory of this experience will horrify me years later when Gooding is accused by dozens of women of misconduct, sexual assault and rape—*he denies any wrongdoing*—and is charged in multiple alleged incidents, pleads guilty to some in exchange for no jail time, and settles at least one civil case to avoid a trial).

I head toward the bar.

And there they are.

Two Tigers

I've happened upon the celebrity world's equivalent of the elusive white Bengal tiger—but not just one. A *pair* of them. *Alone.* No entourage. No agent chattering away and giving the evil eye to anyone who might approach. No scowling bodyguard. I've found them in their natural habitat.

Victoria's publicist would not be pleased to know I am with her precious clients now. Just me. Just them.

If her rep knew I was there, unchained, no barriers, no team, no visible security, she'd tackle me like an NFL linebacker in the final seconds of the game. OK, so maybe only metaphorically, but at the very least she'd have me ejected from the party.

There are no guardrails here.

I seem to be the only person in the place that has any interest in Victoria and David Beckham standing over by the bar not talking. This is meant to be a private party for the stars to let loose, not a time for reporters to bother them. Still, they are hyper-aware that they stand out in every situation.

And boy, does their behavior stand out.

Victoria Beckham is gyrating against the taut body of her husband, dancing on him, running her arms up and down his sides while he stands like a statue. He does not move. He looks bored.

There's no way around it: it's awkward and hard to watch. There is a photo of them you can find online from this night that conveys the sense of need and distance: She is looking up at him adoringly, tilting her head so her chestnut hair flows down her shoulder, focusing everything she has on him while he gazes out at nothing, as if unconnected to what's happening around him, including the touch of his wife.

That is what he's doing right now, too, but without cameras or handlers to see it.

You must understand—this never happens. You can cover Oscar parties and Golden Globe events and New York rooftop parties and obscure European events and never, ever find a big name standing alone for long, if at all.

I toss back the rest of my vodka and pineapple, which is warm now because Europeans do not find ice or cold drinks necessary in the way Americans do, set the slim tumbler on the bar, and go in. As I approach, David—with his strong jaw, dashing black tie and slicked-back hair—does not look at me. If he sees me in peripheral vision, he does not let on. He continues to stare straight over his wife's head.

Victoria sees me and lets go of her husband, puts on a welcoming face. I tower over the diminutive Spice Girl. She's swallowed up by a flowing lime-green flamenco-style dress with a slit up the side and a plunging neckline.

House music is blaring so I have to lean in, and so does she.

I ask if she has a moment to talk to me for *People* magazine.

There is no grouchy pout like the kind we see in most photos of her. She has a deep tan. Her frosted chestnut hair extensions tumble down past her shoulders and tickle her bosom, but ridges of collarbone still manage to poke through. She knows *People*, that we're huge but nonthreatening, that we love the former Spice Girl but Americans aren't obsessed by Brand Beckham yet—their plans to conquer the U.S. are still in the nascent stages—and that there's every chance we'll be safe to talk to.

People? She confirms she heard me right. My American accent helps. She says it in her cute English accent. I hear, *Peepoo?*

Okay, she says. *Okay.*

David's energy is annoyed or angry or both. I can't be sure which. There are strong hints he's not amused I'm there: His jaw is set so hard it's twitching at the joint, and he is focusing on a pulsing strobe light behind his wife's head rather than looking anywhere in my general direction: not to say hello, not to nod, not to make eye contact. Not even to tell me to go away.

I go easy on Victoria because ambushing her here is not something I'm willing do to, especially because the Beckhams are not on our editors' radar in any real way in 2005. I'm not even sure if, or how much, the magazine covered the recent cheating scandal. If this had been Angelina and Brad, I would've asked the question, and then ducked and run.

I ask Victoria one of our generic red-carpet list questions, something about what's in her closet. She thinks about the question and appears to have some fun with it. I jot down every word, though I can't see what I'm writing in this dim venue. David continues his favorite activity of staring off into the distance.

Gwen Stefani's style is a favorite. *Always showing those abs,* Victoria marvels.

What about you? Let's get you showing your abs! You look incredible, I say. That is the way that we start all body conversations in this line of work. *You look great. You look amazing. How do you do it?*

Just three months ago Victoria gave birth to the couple's third son, Cruz, whom the British press shamelessly and cruelly posited might be a "Band-Aid baby" meant to patch up an allegedly ailing marriage. Victoria's pregnancy was announced at the height of the cheating claims.

She tells me she is not comfortable showing her abs, ever. *No, no, no.* She shakes her head at my suggestion she is as worthy as Gwen Stefani in the abs stakes, genuinely horrified. *Are you kidding? I've had three kids.*

She's got a bubbly voice and a tone that makes you want to be her friend. The posing and frowning and hurrying in all those pap photos makes it hard to understand that she's nice. She has a sense of humor. She is self-aware, or at least she knows how to fake self-awareness. I don't know her, so I can't say.

This hasn't recovered, she tells me.

She pats her flat tummy.

David finally looks at me. He does not smile. He is a gorgeous-looking human. I think I prefer him when he doesn't open his mouth.

Decades later, when we talk about Rebecca Loos and David Beckham, we must still say that they *allegedly* had an affair. That Rebecca's telling of their alleged torrid romance are "claims," that the seedy texts she revealed didn't prove a thing.

I cannot find anywhere that David said the dalliance didn't happen, though. His initial statement in 2004 was a carefully crafted non-denial, though media outlets to this day frame it the way David's people wanted it to be framed, without having to do it themselves.

David issued a statement denying the affair, the newspapers write, and then lay out the statement that does no such thing:

"During the past few months I have become accustomed to reading more and more **ludicrous** stories about my private life. What appeared this morning is just one further example. The simple truth is that I am very happily married and have a wonderful wife and two very special kids. There is nothing any third party can do to change this."

Calling a story "ludicrous" is not a denial. The Cambridge Dictionary defines the word this way, including a sentence where the word is used properly:

…stupid or unreasonable and deserving to   be laughed at: Some stories that initially seemed ludicrous <u>turned out to be true.</u>

Nowhere is "ludicrous" defined as untrue.

In David's statement I found no denial. A denial would include such statements as:

Rebecca Loos is lying.

I didn't cheat on my wife.

I did not have an affair.

I never had sex with Rebecca Loos.

In researching this book for the newest updates, I was surprised to see cesspools of vitriol toward Rebecca on social media in the year 2026, prompted in part by *Beckham,* a Netflix docuseries David made about himself.

Instead of being angry about David allegedly cheating on his wife, stubborn fans and misogynists are angry about Rebecca Loos for talking about it.

David was the one who was married. I do not think about Rebecca Loos either way, but she was free and single when she allegedly got together with him.

Victoria herself, to me, behaved later like a woman who believes he cheated. Asked if she "resented" David during the media storm after Rebecca did her big interview, Victoria replied, "If I'm being totally honest, yes I did. It was the most unhappy I have ever been in my entire life."

For his part, David said in that Netflix documentary, "There was [sic] some horrible stories which were difficult to deal with. It was the first time that me and Victoria had been put under that kind of pressure in our marriage."

"Horrible," *not* "false." Which made Rebecca Loos, understandably, irritated at the very least.

"[David] is indirectly suggesting that I'm the one who has made Victoria suffer...he's the one that's caused the suffering," Loos said when the documentary came out and blindsided her (she says David didn't warn her he'd be talking about the hoopla around their alleged affair). "He could have simply said that this was a tough time and I don't want to talk about it."

David has been embroiled in a few scandals in his day. In 2017, we got a behind-the-scenes look at the soccer legend's alleged personal emails when a stack of them were published by the sports-world equivalent of Wikileaks.

The content was ugly. All of it. The crude language, the sentiment, the grammar.

The *Daily Mail's* headline that February was stinging:

*RIP brand Beckham: Hacked emails suggest ex-England captain called gong bosses 'unappreciative c****' after knighthood snub,* *refused to donate $1m to UNICEF declaring 'it's my f***ing money' and railed against tax bill advice.*

The media seized on the emails, which purported to reveal David's anger about all sorts of things. Such as when his PR advisor suggested David put a million dollars into a prize-giving UNICEF dinner in Shanghai.

The multi-hundred-millionaire allegedly replied to the idea of giving to help starving children, *I don't want to put my personal money into this cause...To pour this million into the fund, is like putting my own money in. If there was no fund, the money would be for me. This fucking money is mine.*

According to reports, David's camp confirmed some of the emails published by Football Leaks were fully genuine, and said others had aspects of being "hacked" and "doctored."

The main issue seemed to be David's resentment of never having received a knighthood, something he appears to think he's owed. He allegedly wrote an embittered note about fan favorite Katherine Jenkins, a classical crossover music star who'd snagged an OBE in the same year David *didn't* get a knighthood, according to *The Sun* newspaper.

The paper claims that David made a reference to Jenkins having admitted to taking cocaine in the past, writing in an email, *Katherine Jenkins OBE for what? Singing at the rugby and going to see the troops plus taking coke. Fucking joke.*

He allegedly continued his rant at the honors committee in a most offensive way, *The Sun* reported.

They're a bunch of cunts I expected nothing less... Who decides on the honors? It's a disgrace to be honest and if I was American **I would of got** *something like this 10 years ago... It's pissed me off those old unappreciative cunts.*

David also allegedly wrote, *Unless it's a knighthood fuck off.*

While UNICEF defended him in the firestorm of bad press, putting out a statement that said in part, *As well as generously giving his time, energy and support to help raise awareness and funds for UNICEF's work for children, David has given significant funds personally,* the public was left to wonder what the motivation was behind his giving.

According to the leaked emails, David allegedly demanded UNICEF pay around nine-thousand U.S. dollars for a business-class flight—even though his sponsors splashed out on a private jet, which he used.

Further, the *Daily Mail* wrote, *Football Leaks claimed Beckham admitted in emails that his charity work was part of a conscious effort to win an honour.*

The newspaper went on to say that the PR advisor:

…wrote to Beckham's agent and best friend David Gardner after the OBE snub: "This gives us even more reason to work this year on UNICEF, the armed forces, and other charitable commitments…We need to remain dignified if asked [about the honours], but if you want me to work up something cutting I will work up one, but my advice is it's not productive."

One could argue—as I have done since I've spent too much time around celebrities who love their causes, and others who use charity work to launder their reputations or gain favor—that it doesn't matter why they do it.

Someone once said to me about a British male celebrity, *He's such a phony. He's only visiting that children's hospital for publicity.*

I replied, *Probably. But the sick kids don't care why he's there, and neither does the charity, who's attracting more funds because of the media coverage.*

I think it's depressing that someone with David's privilege would seem to be so entitled and crude, but that's just my opinion. I tend to believe that what you do and say when the cameras are off is a good barometer of who you are. When the world isn't watching. While someone isn't keeping score.

What you see filtered through the PR machine means nothing. It is not real. It is content designed to manipulate you.

And all too often, it works all too well.

In any case, my one-on-one meeting in Portugal would not be the last I'd see of the Beckham family. Nor would the Loos affair be the family's last major scandal.

The Iceman Always Rings Twice

In the summer of 2005, London is rattled by a coordinated terrorist attack on the Tube system. Fifty-six people lose their lives on the morning of July 7, 2005. This dark day will be known as the 7/7 bombings.

I'm ensconced at home in Wimbledon that morning. Reporters already in central London when it happens are dispatched to cover the immediate aftermath.

I am put on cleanup. In the days that follow, I throw on jeans and a T-shirt and head to a council estate (we call it public housing in the U.S.). The British reporters, the men, turn up in suits. This is how they do their reporting, even on a weekend, even in a place no one else will be wearing a suit. I thought it was a peculiar custom when I first started working as a journalist in England.

I am dressed to blend. I find it makes people more comfortable, more willing to talk, more open.

As I'm talking to people on the estate where one of the alleged bombers lived, one of the suited reporters tries to interview me, asks me if I knew the alleged bomber. I laugh and tell him to try someone else.

If I was a different kind of person, I might've gone along with it and given him his interview.

There is a club opening in Mayfair that summer, and two of us head out to cover it.

The place is not a nightclub so much as a palace decorated by some combination of a drunk sheik, Kelly Wearstler, and Liberace.

We head to the bar. There, we run into Robbie Williams, whom Americans know from his days in the boy band Take That and his international solo hit song "Angels." In the UK, many view him as a national treasure (I looked it up). He's in the UK Music Hall of Fame and is one of the most successful music artists in the country's history.

He's leaning with one hip against the bar. I smile at Robbie, then the bartender, and order a cosmo. I notice he's drinking an espresso.

As I'm handed my pink cocktail, I ask him, "Coffee?"

He replies, "I'm sober."

He is serene as he is as he says this, but I also see sadness in those eyes. Or not. Maybe I'm projecting.

Either way, he seems relaxed and he's friendly, even happy to have someone to talk to, and not in the least offended that two magazine reporters have joined him at the bar.

Robbie has an album coming out in October, just a couple months away, but he doesn't talk about it. He talks about this five-a side football pitch—aka soccer field—he built at his Los Angeles home, and a bit about sobriety. We don't ask him anything too personal. We just let him talk.

In the distant future, in 2008 when we still don't have jetpacks, my husband will kick around on Robbie's football pitch with a local team he joined. He graciously lets British expats play soccer at his L.A. home whenever they ask.

The year after I met Robbie sipping coffee at a nightclub, the pop star was tired and messy and a wreck, and coffee was *not* his main social lubricant or source of comfort. Out in L.A., he'd managed to set up a date with a woman he'd met, an American actor called Ayda Field.

Before the date, he invited over the drug dealer he was having sex with. "She'd given me all these pills—morphine, Adderall, Vicodin, a few more things. So I'd slept with the dealer, taken a bunch of pills," Robbie would recall later.

There was a party that night, and he quelled his anxiety with more drugs.

"I took a turn for the worse, because I started to cluck like a chicken," he later recalled of the moment he and Ayda hit the hot tub.

Says Robbie, "There was a moment in the Jacuzzi where Ayda had gone and got changed and she came in wearing this Ursula Andress bikini, and she had a killer body. So I was in the Jacuzzi with a very, very hot girl in Hollywood doing a Hollywood thing. But then I got ill, started to cluck, had to leave, embarrassingly."

A year-and-a-half after I meet an ostensibly sober Robbie in London, he will check himself into rehab in Arizona to treat what his reps called a "dependency" on prescription drugs.

He checked into rehab in 2007 on his thirty-third birthday, a choice he said probably saved his life.

He and Ayda will marry, have four children, and, in January 2026, Robbie Williams will surpass The Beatles to take the all-time record for the most UK No. 1 albums with his sixteenth chart-topper, *Britpop*.

As I head for the exit of the Mayfair party after finding no A-listers to interview after Robbie, I almost bump into one of the most fearsome celebrities you'll ever hear of. He's been described with such off-putting adjectives as "difficult," "childish," and "a prick;" so dickish, in fact, that some directors refuse to work with him.

He once said, "I don't really have too much of a notion about success or popularity. I never cultivated fame, I never cultivated a persona, except possibly the desire to be regarded as an actor."

This is not a guy who wants to be questioned mid-party at one a.m. by a stranger from a celebrity magazine. I'll risk it, though, because I'm face-to-face with Val Kilmer, my favorite actor since the eighties.

He appears to be heading for the exit too, so it's now or never. My chest tightens. *Don't do it, don't do it, don't do it.*

They say to never meet your heroes. Val is *Real Genius. Top Secret. Top Gun.* I mean, the guy's Iceman. So maybe he hates me on sight. Ignores me. Rolls his eyes. It'll be an experience.

I introduce myself.

"Hi, Sara." He says my name, my real name, warmly, stopping dead in his tracks and lightly touching my arm to guide me out of the melee. "What's up?"

This is where I nearly black out.

I don't remember what we talked about. He has floppy hair and he acts happy to talk to me.

He's in town for a while, actually, headlining *The Postman Always Rings Twice* in London's West End. Reviews have been mixed, and not always kind.

Even braver, then, for him to bother stopping for me. His blonde hair is wavy and shaggy, long enough to tuck behind his ears. He's kind and we have a fun chat. I know this because I never forgot it. I just can't remember what the words were.

The next time, I promise myself, I'll collect his words and store everything he says to me so it can never be forgotten.

Let Us Eat Cake

I t's a dreary September day in Falmouth, a port town on the south coast of Cornwall. I'm waiting with a small crowd on a pier overlooking the English Channel, looking out for young adventurer Olly Hicks, who will momentarily be floating to the shore after a grueling 124 days alone at sea.

Upon landing today in the Scilly Isles, Olly will become the first person to row solo across the Atlantic Ocean from the U.S. to Great Britain and the youngest to row any ocean solo.

This day is about him.

But…*uh oh.*

Walking by me in a black windbreaker, jeans, and a dark blue baseball cap is someone I recognize.

It's Prince William.

No one else seems to notice him, as we're all facing the water.

He blends with the casually dressed group of upper-class friends accompanying him. The Prince and Olly bonded a few years ago after meeting through mutual friends from their exclusive high schools (Eton for the Prince, Harrow for Hicks).

This is a momentous occasion for a reporter, especially one for a magazine that's featured Princess Diana and her sons on its cover more times than anyone else in history.

William is strolling around casually and comfortably because there is only a smattering of local media—most of whom still don't realize he's here—and me. This is an unannounced visit. He's here to support a friend, not steal the spotlight.

He stops at a point along the railing near me, and I sidle closer to him. Prince William is an imposing man, not a college kid anymore. His height is reported as anywhere from six-two to six-three. I'm five-nine, and in low-heeled shoes he towers over me.

This is part of what gives him a presence. That, and the hawk-eyed security team giving me the once-over as they decide whether I'm likely to shank the Prince in the spleen with my Bic.

As I hear William shout at the top of his lungs, blow an air horn and utter British-man type encouragement at his friend rowing toward us, I note authentic passion and excitement that I rarely, if ever, see now (this is my opinion).

I watch him, clad in jeans and a baseball cap, being a young man. Not an heir, not a prince, not a trapped future king. Just a guy.

Olly's taking a while to row in, so William and his chums go for a coffee break at the café next door. I've been told to keep an eagle-eye out for Kate Middleton, William's new-ish girlfriend who many people have never heard of, though keen royal watchers will know her because just a year earlier, *The Sun* tabloid caught the young couple on the slopes of Klosters, Switzerland, and ran a photo with the headline, *Finally…Wills Gets a Girl*.

William sits outside at a table with friends, including a striking brunette, but it turns out she's not Kate Middleton.

Olly cruises toward the dock. He lights sparklers as he nears the shore, and Prince William and his friends keep the air horns going. They sing to the tune of the FIFA (soccer) World Cup anthem Three Lions, and instead of the iconic line *Football's coming home*, they sing *Olly's coming home*.

Richard Branson sprays Olly with champagne because Virgin Atlantic sponsored the row. After Hicks greets his family and gives some TV interviews, William and his friends run down to the pontoon and carry their triumphant friend on their shoulders, though William isn't involved in actually holding him up. Olly greets the Prince with a pat on the head.

The small reception is held inside the National Maritime Museum with champagne, red and white balloons, and a vanilla sheet cake.

William has a glass of champagne in hand by noon. He and his friends are talking about how they're hungover, and they plan to keep things going because there's a party at a chum's estate after this.

The Prince is animated, often talking loudly, laughing heartily and gesticulating. During the cake cutting, the young men are shouting again, and Olly is swaying a bit, and William shouts, "It's the champagne!"

Which I assume is irony because it might also be the 124 days he spent alone at sea; standing on solid ground must be a strange sensation. As people settle down and have cake and champagne, I try to be unobtrusive in my staring. It's hard when you're so close to a future king in such a real, casual situation. I notice, perhaps inevitably, a sort of court-jester-at-William's throne vibe. His friends talk and joke and chat, and William indicates his approval by loud chuckles and enthusiastic nods.

It's fascinating, memorable, to be so close, in such an intimate space, eating cake with Prince William. Or nearby Prince William. Either one works.

The Windsor Knots

The streets of Windsor are packed with people and Union Jack everything, like the most unhinged block party you'll ever go to. It is a joyous occasion for some and an exhausting marathon for others, i.e. members of the media. Journalists have come from every town and every nation, and they've rented out many of the apartments and residences around the Guildhall so their cameras can get the money shots.

My feet hurt. It's a slog. Today's events do not interest me particularly, partly because I grew up when Diana was alive and heard the quote that went 'round the world in real time: *There were three of us in this marriage, so it was a bit crowded.*

With the icky affair between Charles and Camilla while they were both married, the Tampon Tapes (Google it, they're vomitous), the ugliness, the betrayal, and the tragic way Diana died and left two sons without a mother, I can't grip onto these two as any kind of romantic love story.

I'm not alone. NBC News reported this week that opinion polls show most Britons don't want Camilla to be queen, and that many blame her for breaking up the marriage of Charles and Diana.

I have a general sense of apathy, which is what you want for a journalist covering a story. The British newspapers, whose treatment of the bride and groom in recent weeks has been described as "merciless," agree. The *Daily Star* greeted the news of their engagement a couple months earlier with the headline, "Boring Old Gits to Wed." The byline was *Hugh Cares, royal correspondent.*

The first line: *Prince Charles is to marry Camilla Parker Bowles after 34 years of dithering—but last night the nation sighed: who gives a damn?*

Charles doesn't find any of it amusing. At a photo call not long before the wedding, hot mics picked him up calling reporters those "bloody people" and referring to a BBC correspondent as "that awful man."

And yet the atmosphere today is jubilant. The crowds, the mood, the celebration, say it all: I am in the minority on this day, in this place. There are royalists decked out in Union Jack garb ringing bells and making a racket. Some of them camped out overnight to get a good view of the Guildhall and, if they're lucky, a peek at Prince William, Prince Harry, or even Charles and Camilla.

Charles's mother, the Queen, won't be here. As the head of the Church of England, Queen Elizabeth II didn't like the optics of attending a civil wedding of two divorced people, though she and Prince Philip will host a reception at Windsor Castle after the Service of Prayer and Dedication at St. George's Chapel.

By the end of the day, Charles and Camilla have done their best to clean the slate. At

the blessing held at St. George's Chapel at Windsor Castle, the freshly minted Duchess of Cornwall and her new husband would repent, reading out a passage that included the line, *We acknowledge and bewail our manifold sins and wickedness.*

It was a weird one, for sure, but their wedding provided a few days' work for me and I was happy to have it.

I didn't know at the time that Charles's sons, Princes William and Harry, had reservations about their father's wedding. Harry wrote in his bestselling memoir *Spare* in 2023 that, *Willy and I agreed that Pa deserved better…Pa deserved a proper companion. That was why, when asked, Willy and I promised Pa that we'd welcome Camilla into the family. The only thing we asked in return was that he not marry her…*

You don't need to remarry, we pleaded. A wedding would cause controversy. It would incite the press. It would make the whole country, the whole world, talk about Mummy, compare Mummy and Camilla, and nobody wanted that. Least of all, Camilla. We support you, we said. We endorse Camilla, we said. Just please don't marry her. Just be together, Pa.

But their father *would* marry her. And Prince Harry believed the nuptials were the result of canny machinations by their mother's love rival. Charles never responded to his sons' pleadings, Harry wrote, suggesting that Camilla *began to play the long game, a campaign aimed at marriage.*

I'm back at the Windsor Guildhall for another ceremony months later, a few days shy of Christmas. This one is more fun. It feels like victory, though my feet hurt all the same, and I really need the bathroom, but they're hard to come by.

David Furnish and Elton John are among seven-hundred couples getting hitched in Britain today under a new law that allows same-sex civil partnerships. While this gives gay couples legal recognition for their relationship under UK law, they still can't get married.

Elton and David arrive at the Guildhall around eleven a.m. They wave and pose and beam for the fans and journalists and photographers who came to witness history.

After the ceremony, witnessed by close friends, family, and their dog, the beaming men emerge. Some say they are showered with rice, others describe it as confetti. Could be both, so to be safe we'll call it ricefetti.

Mallory is here today too, darting around the streets of Windsor looking for her exclusive. She manages to sneak into the Guildhall and get herself a scoop. To my knowledge, no one else gets in that day, or even tries. I officially like her. She tells great stories and she's happy to share information. She seems like a real one.

After the obligatory photocall outside the Guildhall, a pack of uninvited members of the media travel a few miles to hang outside Elton and David's Windsor estate.

That's when things become mildly amusing.

Picture it: The pinnacle of British 2005 celebritydom—Liz Hurley, Victoria Beckham, Ronan Keating, Ringo Starr, Lulu, Claudia Schiffer and Matthew Vaughn—in their Rolls Royces, dressed to the nines, ready to mingle at the event of the year, with no interest in interacting with the dreaded press creeping around.

Problem is, the poor dears are stuck. They can't move for famous people in Jags and Range Rovers clogging up the narrow country lanes leading to Elton's house.

Their windows are rolled up and most of them stare straight ahead like they're avoiding beggars at an intersection. Like we're about to carjack them. The paparazzi snap tons of photos of mildly annoyed stars who sit trapped beneath their lenses.

Lulu, who I'm pretty sure is a Scottish singer, interacts briefly. She points at the traffic jam and pronounces, "This could only happen for Elton."

The most memorable moment of that day, though, happens a few hours into our mass stake-out.

It's boring, the party we're not invited to is dragging on, and we're getting nowhere.

Somewhere between my exhausted thoughts of *Get me out of here* and *I'm so over this*, members of Elton's staff drive through the gates. Security team, I think.

They drive slowly out, through our pack.

They stop.

They unload stacks of small paper cups.

And then they drop off a case (or more) of Perrier-Jouët rose champagne. We are all shocked as we watch this happen. Most celeb couples want to send out cases of tear gas for us.

The whole pack of us serve it up, toast the couple, and drink.

To this day, no celebrity has ever beat, or even matched, that classy move.

The Brangelina Origin Story

Working at a celebrity magazine in the 2004-2006 Brangelina era is a wild, wild, wild time. The world stops when the lives of three megastars collide to form a Bermuda Triangle of gossip, sucking people in and disappearing them, including Jennifer Aniston herself, who said she never wanted to be a part of it. The London bureau is infused with the auras of Brad Pitt, Angelina Jolie, and Jennifer Aniston like a celebrity-scented essential oil.

The amount of money and staff and resources thrown at the dissolution of a marriage and the forming of a new family is staggering. Their stories feed the gossip machine and keep it satiated for years, and Brangelina benefits as much as anyone.

Jennifer Aniston and Brad Pitt were married atop a Malibu cliff on July 29, 2000. They foiled the paparazzi by booking a no-fly zone and covering the reception with a gigantic white marquee.

They recited vows they wrote themselves, famously agreeing that she'd continue making his favorite banana milkshakes and he'd split the difference on the thermostat. They settled into married life, Brad guest-starred on her show *Friends* in 2001, and they renovated a Beverly Hills house together.

The Hollywood marriage of the century lasted until 2005, when the Malibu dream crumbled like cliffs in a landslide.

Rumors Brad is cheating on Jen have been flying since he costarred with Angelina Jolie in the film *Mr. & Mrs. Smith,* which began shooting in 2004.

Everyone involved denies Brad and Angelina are having an affair. Repeatedly.

Even after they're caught holding hands (while not in character) and the photo gets tongues wagging, even though they look like they're more than coworkers, Jen and Brad maintain that their relationship is not affected by a third person floating in their orbit.

Whatever the reasons, the marriage is souring, and Jen and Brad announce they're splitting in January 2005—and the official word is it has nothing to do with Angelina Jolie. I am vaguely aware of all of this, but the story is handled by HQ back in the U.S., so I'm busy with other things.

As rumors and speculation and pictures of the three actors cover every magazine, Jen files for divorce in March, turning up the heat still more.

Little do any of us know Jen's move will set the table for a bombshell photoshoot, one that is not in any way staged, planned, or set up whatsoever.

It is a month later, eons in celebrity relationship terms, when Brad and Angelina are coincidentally caught by a professional photographer on a stretch of beach in Africa. It is simply happenstance that, just weeks after Brad and Jen officially broke up, Brad is suddenly so close with Angelina that they're vacationing together at a luxury resort in Kenya where he looks so comfortable with her son that it's like they're already a family. This new romance comes out of nowhere; it has nothing to do with why his marriage is ending, you understand.

Even more coincidental, of all the beaches in all the world, one lucky photographer happened to catch the hottest, most controversial *rumored* couple on the planet frolicking on Diani Beach, a stretch of white sand in Kenya. Brad was acting like dad of the year to Maddox, Angelina's son.

People's direct rival, *US Weekly*, nabs the photos and blasts out a world exclusive cover that changes everything.

The magazine's cover image very deliberately projects an image of wholesome family time. It very pointedly does not depict two gorgeous movie stars on a steamy getaway in an exotic locale. As *US* put it, *Maddox, 3, frolicked in the sand as Pitt handed him a bucket and a barefoot Jolie held a red shovel during a three-day vacation.*

That said, *US* wants us to know that they've confirmed what everyone already knew, and we can now acknowledge that Brad and Angelina are not just two costars hanging out as pals:

…the Mr. & Mrs. Smith costars allowed themselves to pack on the PDA while they thought no one was looking. "They wrapped their arms around each other [at the pool] and shared a long, passionate kiss," a source told Us.

(Pro tip: if an "onlooker" or "source" is commenting on paparazzi photos, it is almost always the photographer).

The couple that will become Brangelina are still not admitting they're romantically involved. But we have our senses, and they tell us the two of them are an item.

For those of us working in celebrity media, it's also obvious the couple staged the scene. It is a classic maneuver to ease the public gently into our new reality.

The media knows it's a set-up, even if many consumers don't understand how it works or realize that many stars, even the biggest ones, call paparazzi on themselves. Brad and Angelina apparently felt enough time had passed for them to come out as a couple, and that their adoring public would find it plausible that their romantic relationship has nothing to do with his pending divorce.

Whether the Kenya shoot was planned by one or both of them, it is Angelina who gets the blame. The criticism of Angelina is pointed and cutting, and she is painted as a homewrecker who stole the husband of America's sweetheart.

This narrative, however, is challenged almost immediately. The three stars are suddenly cast in new roles by a public starved for details: Angelina as earth mother; Jen as the cold, career-obsessed woman who wouldn't give her husband children; and Brad as the easily led family man desperate to throw off the shackles of Hollywood superficiality.

When I tell you the media implodes the day those exclusive photos drop, I'm not kidding. It's not just celebrity focused media, either. Storied wire service the Associated Press, to name one, is all over it. But of course, it's those of us in the celebrity world who are in a *frenzy*, and it's all hands on deck.

I fear heads will roll because of *US Weekly's* scoop. I'm not privy to the high-level goings on at the magazine in this case, and I don't want to speak out of turn—for all I know, *People* had their own operation in progress but didn't get to Kenya fast enough (though I doubt it)—but when our bitterest competitor nails a world exclusive of this magnitude, some shit is going to go down. I've sat there while an editor lost their temper, shaking and yelling at us when *US* scoops *People*, including over something as meaningless as a couple of exclusive quotes from Lindsay Lohan.

Anyway, seemingly endless resources are thrown at this story. Reporters are sent to Africa to hunt down the couple and vacuum up every crumb of information about where they'd been and what they'd done. I'm put on phone calls, whether it's to Kenya or to any person I've ever met in my life who might have a connection to Brad, Anglina, Jen, or the places Brad and Angelina have been seen.

Some of us are sent on a wild-goose chase thanks to *The Sun* newspaper. The tabloid gets a spicy exclusive that many view as a bit over-the-top, but then again, given what we know about the individuals in question, it's not impossible to believe. This is the gem we're assigned to follow up on:

Brad Pitt and Angelina Jolie made so much noise during a hotel romp that other guests thought they had been attacked by wild animals.

Armed guards dashed to protect the smitten pair in the early hours of Wednesday morning after guests reported "terrifying" noises coming from their £1 200-a-night Kenyan hotel suite—which sounded like "like something being killed."

But hotel staff were stunned when they reached the couple's room and discovered the pair locked in a passionate embrace.

I have no idea if it's true, but I believe there's every chance it is.

The Case of the Missing Sensitivity Chip

The dismantling of a marriage is soon reduced to a ground war pitting two women against each other. It's now Team Aniston vs. Team Jolie, complete with merch and an endless battle about who's to blame for the marriage ending. Paris and Nicky Hilton are memorably photographed stepping out with dueling T-shirts from Kitson, and the store reports that Team Aniston regularly outsells Team Jolie by twenty or twenty-five to one.

Meanwhile, some say Brad is standing by and helping, or at least allowing, Jen to be dragged through the mud. Just a few months into it, in July 2005, Brad rubs an entire ocean's worth of salt into his estranged wife's wounds when he participates in a sixty-page *W* magazine photo spread in which Brad and Angie are posing as a 1960s-style married couple with adorable children in the background. With the headline "Domestic Bliss" splashed across it, this package is, unlike the Kenya shots, *confirmed* to be Brad's doing. He created the concept, made sure he kept the international rights to it, and profited from it.

Meanwhile, none of us can believe what he's just done. It's seen as a tacky and cruel move, and many of us in the media spend far too much time analyzing the motivation behind it. *Could Brad really be that dense? Could he be that mean? Was it a deliberate message to Jen? Was Angelina behind the scenes, goading him into doing it? WHAT IS THE STORY?*

We, of course, are mere observers. We're outsiders with no stake in the lives of three real people with feelings and a right to privacy. These are the people who would be the most hurt and horrified by the ill-timed magazine spread, and they are having their own reactions behind the scenes.

Come autumn 2005, there's another earth-shattering bump in the news cycle: Jen *finally* talks.

She sits for an interview with *Vanity Fair*. She cries with the reporter when she arrives at Jen's new Malibu rental house. Jen reminds readers that she has done nothing and said nothing about her husband's new relationship, and yet her life has become consumed by Brangelina.

"I am not defined by the part they're making me play in the triangle," she tells the reporter. "It's maddening to me."

We find out how *W*'s "Domestic Bliss" package, featuring a man whose current wife is likely in "Domestic Agony," affected Jen.

For starters, her close friends tell the magazine that their circle was "horrified" by the *W* photo spread. "You want to shake the shit out of him and say, 'Your timing sucks!'" says one. "He's made some choices that have been tremendously insensitive."

For her part, Jen will utter one line through this years-long, slow-motion car crash in an attempt to explain Brad's behavior. It is a statement heard 'round the world, and one I've never forgotten:

"There's a sensitivity chip that's missing," she says of her soon-to-be ex-husband.

Indeed.

Jen explains that she's been taking care of herself while a storm not of her making roars around her, trying to suck her in at every turn. She is mourning more than a lost marriage; she had expected to be pregnant in the year her husband is gallivanting around the world with his new family.

"A man divorcing would never be accused of choosing career over children," Jen says. "That really pissed me off. I've never in my life said I didn't want to have children. I did and I do and I will! The women that inspire me are the ones who have careers and children; why would I want to limit myself? I've always wanted to have children, and I would never give up that experience for a career. I want to have it all."

The article points out Angie's abrupt about-face, too, and how her shiny new image helped paint Jen as shallow and dull:

In the blink of an eye, the twice-divorced Jolie—previously known as a tattooed vixen with a taste for bisexuality, heroin, brotherly incest, mental institutions, and wearing her husbands' blood—had morphed into a globe-trotting humanitarian who seemed to be channeling Audrey Hepburn.

I can tell you one thing for sure: After getting reamed by *US Weekly* on the Kenya photos, *People* was not going to get scooped on Brangelina ever again. When Angelina gave birth to their daughter Shiloh in June 2006, the couple sold rights to photos of the newborn to the magazine for an estimated $4 million. In 2008, twins Knox and Vivienne were born in Nice, France, and the magazine forked over a reported $14 million for images of the babies.

Angie and Brad were chased, hounded, and hunted. They also actively fed the machine. The couple benefited greatly from the mystique of Brangelina. As I've said before, we're all in on it. We're all complicit. Make no mistake: Following the personal lives of celebrities is an industry. Everyone gets paid, starting with the stars, and trickling down to the freelancers making phone calls to snoop around in Kenya. The paparazzi makes a ton of cash, as we know; the photos from Kenya, for example, sold for half a million dollars. Brad retaining the rights to the *W* images makes him money. He and Angelina selling the rights to pictures of their children nets them millions. They said the money went to charity, and I'm not saying it didn't, but I'm not sure how we can ever know exactly how every cent of that payout was distributed.

There are two secrets most people don't know about Brad and Angelina. First, while she ended up with the reputation for controlling everything and became the bitch who demanded money for pictures of her children and the brat who pissed everyone off with her demands, sources say Brad was, perhaps, the true puppet master. He did much of the negotiating and *he* made the demands, allegedly.

Second, sources who've worked with him say Brad thinks he's a lot smarter than he is. I've never met the guy, but he doesn't seem like the most stable fellow in the world to me. That is just my opinion.

In any case, the globetrotting hotties' wild, animalistic coupling ended as dramatically as it began. In a lawsuit filed years later, Anglina would describe Brad as "abusive." She recalled in court papers how he was allegedly verbally and physically abusive with her and their children—all minors between the ages of eight and fifteen at the time—on a private plane in 2016:

Pitt's aggressive behavior started even before the family got to the airport, with Pitt having a confrontation with one of the children. After the flight took off, Jolie approached Pitt and asked him what was wrong. Pitt accused her of being too deferential to the children and verbally attacked her.

He pulled her into the bathroom and began yelling at her. Pitt grabbed Jolie by the head and shook her, and then grabbed her shoulders and shook her again before pushing her into the bathroom wall, court papers say.

One of the children defended Angelina, the lawsuit says, and Brad lashed out.

Pitt lunged at his own child and Jolie grabbed him from behind to stop him. To get Jolie off his back, Pitt threw himself backwards into the airplane's seats injuring Jolie's back and elbow. The children rushed in and all bravely tried to protect each other. Before it was over, Pitt choked one of the children and struck another in the face.

The document says he later poured beer on Angie and dumped beer and red wine on the kids. Brad denied many of the family's claims, calling them "lies," though a source close to him explains that Brad admitted things got rough on the plane. The source told *People* that he ...*was "drunk" and "there was an argument between him and Angelina"*—as well as a *"parent-child argument, which was not handled in the right way and escalated more than it should have."*

The source explained that "no one was physically harmed" and denied that Pitt had "hit his child in the face in any way."

Be that as it may, his adult children reportedly have no contact with him now, and daughter Shiloh petitioned the court to change her last name from "Jolie-Pitt" to "Jolie." His two other daughters, Zahara and Vivienne, have apparently dropped "Pitt" professionally, if not legally.

Upon hearing about Shiloh's name change, a source close to Brad told *People* magazine something that he may have immediately regretted: *He's never felt more joy than when she was born. He always wanted a daughter.*

Commenters flooded social media to point out that Zahara joined the family in 2005, Pitt adopted her formally in early 2006, and Shiloh was born later that year. So…he already had a daughter when Shiloh, the daughter he "always wanted," was born.

No matter. Brad still has Hollywood in the palm of his hand. He continues to star in blockbuster films, he is fêted and fawned over, and he makes bank off the production company he and his partners launched years ago, Plan B Entertainment.

Brangelina is just a memory.

What Remains

In the four years I work for *People* out of London, I pitch in on every kind of story. Sometimes it's celebrities, sometimes it's terrorism or crime or dogs accused of plastic surgery. You never know what you're going to get when you wake up in the morning.

Sometimes it involves watching two sides of a star's personality in one evening, like when I meet Orlando Bloom at the European premiere of Ridley Scott's *Kingdom of Heaven* at Whitehall. Orlando doesn't come near my section of the red carpet in the mass chaos of Leicester Square. Television comes first. Fans second. Print, possibly not at all; what I know is I didn't get anywhere near him.

At the afterparty, which is held on multiple floors and is exotic, decadent, and like nothing I'll ever attend before or again, I hunt down the film's publicity department. It's great that there's hummus and kebabs and pomegranate cocktails, but I'm here to work. I tell the reps that Orlando the only A-lister my magazine sent me here to talk to, but I didn't get him. Can they facilitate a chat?

He's doing some select interviews upstairs. But you're not on the list.

Put me on the list, please.

Well…

Can you put me on the list?

They do.

I wait in a private room at a table with a few journalists allowed to talk to the young star. Orlando is fidgety and appears like he doesn't want to be there. He was animated out on Leicester Square. Engaging with fans, posing for photos, smiling on cue. Here, he seems to be shutting down. The fans got Mr. Charming and we get Mr. Bored. He isn't terrible, but…Orlando, buddy, give us something to work with.

Back downstairs, everyone is approachable except Jeremy Irons, who I want to talk to just for fun, but he does an epic job of ignoring me. At first I think he can't hear me, but then I realize he absolutely can and is simply not reacting. I leave him alone. Sadly, Liam Neesons (I call him that because of Key & Peele; he'll never be Liam Neeson to me again), can't make it.

The coolest person I meet that night is Julie Delpy, who is like the best friend you always wanted, one who's done stuff and done it well, and I have to force myself to walk away after we spend some time deep in conversation. Talking with the woman who was a major part of the definitive Gen X romantic drama *Before Sunrise* might be the most fun I've had with any Hollywood type so far in my career.

But I know to never overstay my welcome, so I say goodbye before she has to start giving me hints.

I don't remember many other standout stars from my time in the UK, but that's not unique to that time or place. I've forgotten a ton of them. It is a byproduct of age and interviewing too many people in thirty years.

That said, as I was writing that last sentence, one came back to me. (This is sometimes how it happens). I haven't thought about singer/songwriter James Blunt in years. All I'll say about him is I did two separate sit-down one-on-one interviews to publicize his breakthrough album *Back to*

Bedlam, and it was another one of those not-great experiences. James, who for some reason changed his last name from Blount to Blunt, is apparently known in the year 2026 for his killer comebacks to online trolls, and has been called "social-media savage."

He is above it all when I meet him, even before he's famous. Certainly above me. It's like pulling teeth getting him to answer even the most ingratiating questions. In the files I send to editors, I try to hide how difficult he was. If you can't get a subject to open up, the journalist gets the side-eye. *It's probably your own fault*, they think as they read your boring file.

I guess I didn't hide it so well, because when I started working years later in *People*'s Los Angeles bureau, a colleague dug up my old file and whistled, *Whew. James Blunt REALLY didn't like you.*

Anyway, just because I forget a celebrity doesn't mean they're forgettable. When Robin Williams died, I thought, *What a shame I never got to talk to him.*

But as I went through my old files later, I discovered that I…did. At a movie premiere, apparently.

If you'd asked me a year ago how Kenneth Branagh treated me, I'd say, *I dunno, because I never met him, but man, he did Emma Thompson dirty.* Yet my diaries say I interviewed him in L.A. Same for Bill Nighy. When you ask me who from *Love Actually* I've met or interviewed, I'd have said Emma Thompson and Richard Curtis. But, apparently, also Bill Nighy. I'm sure he was nice. I'm sure they were all nice, or I would've remembered.

One thing that still sticks out for me, though I didn't cover it personally, was the introduction of Apple Martin to the world.

Her parents are Oscar-winning actor Gwyneth Paltrow and Coldplay frontman Chris Martin, who were hunted by the media from the moment they got together. The British media thought they owned the famous couple. They scraped up every bit of childhood intel they could on Chris, the posh British popstar who grew up with a tennis court in his backyard and went to the best schools. A former girlfriend did a literal kiss-and-tell with a tabloid newspaper and told the entire world that Chris was *not* a great kisser. I remember reading that story and thinking, *How invasive, how subjective.* But I also never looked at him the same way again, if you know what I mean.

He and his new wife lived in the Belgravia (and later, Belsize Park) part of London, and with the birth of their first child in 2004, they knew they'd be hounded even more than before.

Chris tried to strike a deal with the paparazzi for a pre-planned view of the little girl they called Apple. At one p.m. on a warm spring day, Chris told the media, the family would give snappers their "one and only chance to photograph them for a very long time." The expectation was that the family would be left alone after this up-close view of the new mom and her six-day-old baby.

The world's media pounced on the offer. A phalanx of photographers showed up as Gwyneth, pushing a covered pram, paraded up and down the sidewalk in front of her London flat flanked by a burly security team.

Asked how she was taking to motherhood, she smiled gamely and told the strangers ogling her and her pram that,

"It's absolutely wonderful and I feel great," adding that baby Apple "is wonderful. I think she looks a bit like both me and Chris." Which, of course, is not an unusual state of affairs when two people procreate together.

They asked her how Chris was doing, and Gwyneth replied, "He's great too," as her husband watched from their flat's balcony above.

Most of us never thought there was a baby in that pram.

I'm not sure anyone was fooled; there were a lot of reporters who suspected Apple was not there for her own paparazzi debut.

I always pictured Chris and Gwyneth reveling privately in their alleged subterfuge, finding a thrill in getting one over on the vermin who made their lives so difficult. Regardless of what the truth is, the media got their quotes, the paps got their shot, and the editors got their front page splashes.

Whether the images were actually of the baby didn't matter in the end.

And that pap walk didn't matter, either; nothing would stop the media from watching them and cataloguing the Paltrow-Martin family's every move.

Side note: The couple was dragged mercilessly for naming their daughter Apple. The Brits were so flustered by this choice that chatter among newsrooms (and maybe in print, I don't remember) was that the couple put out a fake name so the public wouldn't know their daughter's real one, so they could hold onto one last crumb of privacy. Judging by Apple Martin's current career as a model, influencer and singer, I think it's safe to say the name was real all along.

The Expat Wife

Once again, it's time to move on. My husband gets a job offer that's too good to refuse, and though my first reaction is, *Over my dead body are we moving to Switzerland*, I change my mind when the company flies us out to Lucerne for the weekend. The city is a fairytale. It is surrounded by snow-capped Alps and sits on the banks of a stunning lake. The Old Town is in the shadow of impeccably preserved medieval and renaissance architecture and laid with cobblestoned streets. There is cheese and chocolate for sale wherever you look.

Four years to the month when I picked at those bad nachos with the chief (who has since moved on), I leave England for good. Before I do, my colleagues meet at a bar in London for a very sweet sendoff. Twenty years later, I still use the pink passport holder/travel wallet the then-bureau chief gave me as a goodbye gift.

I'm sad to leave, and I'm worried again that my career will stall; I fear I won't get many assignments living in the middle of the Alps.

It turns out my concerns are unfounded. A few weeks after I move to Lucerne, Switzerland, I'm asked to zip down to Italy.

Tom Cruise and Katie Holmes are getting married, and for a few days Rome will be the center of the universe.

5-Star Hotel, 1-Star Behavior

One in the group raises his bottle of beer. "To life, and to new friends."

"What about me?" whines his wife.

"To you, too," Marc Anthony says to Jennifer Lopez.

Everyone at the table cheers with him, including *King of Queens* firecracker Leah Remini, whose tart New York accent is no less thick in person; her husband, Angelo, who I recognize from his recurring guest roles on the show; towering beauty Brooke Shields who, in person, is impossibly gorgeous; and her underdressed, wry, writer husband Chris Henchy who admits with a cool shrug, "I know I married up."

It is one in the morning. I finish my macchiato and prepare to stick to water for a while before ordering an eighteen-euro glass of prosecco. I must rotate my beverages to blend in during this endless shift in the lobby bar of the antique-filled, five-star Hotel Hassler high atop the Spanish Steps in Rome.

We are here for, of course, the wedding of the century. A wedding so epic it will bring together superstars from far and wide and, in turn, attract hordes of press from around the globe to the Eternal City. And I was invited.

Well, not *invited* invited. But I was assigned to hang out for a few days gathering whatever reporting I can get on this historic occasion. And here I am, doing my damndest to pretend I'm not listening to the chatter just inches away from me.

At one-thirty, down comes Tom Cruise and his fiancé Katie Holmes, both in jeans, greeting their friends like it's any old get-together. She orders a cappuccino, he sticks to water with lemon. They sit close, and he puts an arm around her shoulder. She is smiley and gracious and relaxed. He appears uncomfortable with social small talk, is very intense, and doesn't laugh much, save for one outburst that includes a fist pounded on the table and one loud guffaw.

The celebs start swapping stories about their first dates. Marc first wooed Jenny from the Block (*cough*), they explain, at a sold-out show at Madison Square Garden. J. Lo says one of the reasons she ended up going out with him was because of all the "fun" they were continually having. Marc does not appear to be the most jovial fellow.

Anyway, I suspect the topic of meet-cutes is an uncomfortable one for the Cruises, the germination of whose romance has never been convincingly explained in a verifiable timeline, and tonight we hear nothing from them on this issue.

I cannot tell you how normal this group is. Normal in the dull, everyday, uninteresting sense. I reflect on the banality of evil; I believe I am witnessing the banality of celebrity, albeit in a fascinating location. It's like watching any awkward wedding guests who don't want to offend each other and sometimes get caught up in one-upmanship, because that's what it is. They just happen to be rich and famous.

Tom, one of the world's top action stars, listens intently but is never the leading force of the table. Tom does not show himself to be a natural raconteur. He is less charismatic than his onscreen characters but looks exactly the same. There are no surprises in my close-up view of

Tom Cruise. Katie is the same, but more under-made than even the pap shots portray. She doesn't appear to be wearing much makeup if any, and her hair is casually messy in a going-out-to-get-the-mail kind of way. She looks bride-tired.

At one point a staff member—who appears to be heavily involved in the event organizing—approaches, asks her a question, then thanks Katie profusely for her response. Katie is Midwest horrified to be thanked for being catered to.

"No, no—thank *yooo*," she says. "You" is all downhome Ohio lilt: *Yoo.*

Over time, during a few of these lobby sit-ins, Will and Jada Smith will wander by, as will the Beckhams, and David will play with seven-month-old Suri, cradle her head, show off some warmth and some biceps.

Watching this from feet away at our little European café-style table, it occurs to me they must know we're not casual hotel guests. I'm not convinced we've done an Oscar-worthy job of playing Bored Tourists Who Sit a Lot and Drink Many Fluids. But no one bothers us.

During this time, I'm looking out for signs Tomkat is a real couple or, as internet chatter sometimes suggest, are engaged in a contracted, old-Hollywood-style pact. But I'm less than ten feet away from them and Tom and Katie appear close. They are actors, but even actors must struggle to fake chemistry for long. A face has to fall at some point. The body language has to give it away during a millisecond of a guard going down. The camera—or I—will catch them in the moment their mask falls.

But they stay close and relaxed and happy in public. Are they in love? Who knows. I can tell you they rubbed noses (though no kissing) in the Hassler's bar.

Tom Cruise is nice to the staff, friendly to the two fans he bumps into, smiles a lot, and has a memorable conversation in the lobby with an elderly couple who've been married for a hundred years. "I'd love to have what you have someday," he says, and they glow in return.

All of Tom's children are around. Connor Cruise is just a kid. He bops around the Hassler's golden lobby like he lives there. He plays with a soccer ball; he's greeted by Hollywood power players, lawyers, reps, stars like he is on their level. Bella hangs about the staid, marble-ridden hotel too, quiet and shy. Suri, the third child, I see up close only on the night of the wedding, though I watch her colorful, soft playpens and mobiles carted to the elevators on the bellhop's wagon.

It's not all macchiatos and plush hotel bars. On my first day in Rome, I'm assigned as a watchwoman. My job is to use my considerable journalism experience to wait outside for the Tomkat crew to emerge—and write down every detail, hopefully somehow (*how?*) getting an exclusive tidbit.

I settle into the melee and wait, alternately on tiptoes looking over the crowd and staring at two entrances: the front door and the exit to the underground parking lot. I am jostled, stepped on and pushed, cold in the November afternoon shade, feet already hurting. The air smells of autumn and dying leaves.

In the middle of all this waiting, I feel a tap on my shoulder and whip around.

I'm excited to see a friendly face. It's Mallory, clearly stressed but attempting to smile a greeting, though it does not reach her eyes, a sky-blue that pops against a white scarf she's wrapped around her neck to fight the chill. She leans in for a quick double-cheek-kiss.

Mallory tells me she'll be staying up all night following celebrities around Rome, mostly on foot, and getting exclusive stories to please her editors, and she has to go.

She texts me later.

Come to dinner. I got us in.

She snagged a table at Nino, Tom's favorite restaurant and the site of the intimate welcome dinner he hosted the night before. I'm assigned to get some fun details about how it was and, of course, what they ate.

Later, I meet her there, and I try to order truffle pasta. "I'm sorry," the server says. "That was for the special menu only." Ah, Tom Cruise's special menu. Which is not for us.

Mallory and I enjoy a quiet pasta dinner with Tuscan wine while chatting up the waiter casually, ordering three courses on our expense accounts. We make notes about the cozy place with its wood paneling, simple white tablecloths, tables close but not claustrophobically so. We learn that Tom's guests dined on ravioli with white truffles while baby Suri *spent most of the evening in her parents' laps…No truffles for her—only a bottle of milk.*

Finally, the big day is here. We watch the celebs line up to face the crowds waiting outside for them, the paparazzi, as all the megastars head out to the wedding and reception.

As Katie and Tom say their vows at an Italian castle witnessed by best man David Miscavige, I am at the Hassler, waiting for their return.

When the beautiful people start filtering in after one a.m. in a trickle of satin and foofiness and Prada, I am stationed in an unthreatening and smiley manner next to a marble column where I can gently inquire about how the night went. My colleagues are similarly stationed within the long lobby. First up, around two in the morning, Victoria Beckham and her sister Louise stroll in and bestow a polite *It was great* before making a clean getaway upstairs. Minutes later the gruesome foursome parades in: J. Lo, Leah, Marc and Angelo. I ask J. Lo: "How was the wedding?"

Ms. Lo speeds up, and as she passes in front of me she *almost* I-think-she-kind-of-did spit with a fierce *Pss-fff-tsshh* in my direction. I am taken aback. Other responses, mannerly and humane things, would've sufficed. Examples being: I'm sorry, no; not tonight; a silent smile of thanks for asking but no; or absolutely no reaction at all. Just keep walking. Every one of those would've passed without note. This response shows who she is. Not Jenny from the Block. Jenny with mansions and an attitude. In the same way I'll never forget that moment, I'm certain she'd never remember. It is effortless and reflexive.

Behind her, Leah does me the courtesy of swiveling her head my way and saying in an ultra-strong New York accent: *Sorry, honey, can't.*

After acting as a virtual spittoon, I mosey on over to watch a spectacular, rare show that one will not see every day. After Tom—who's carrying little Suri—and his brand-new bride glide in, there is a ten-minute moment captured by the wedding photographers and my own brain. As Katie, dressed in a long strapless silver dress, looks on, Tom lets Suri explore a bronze sculpture of a girl on a swing she's become entranced with. Tom holds the infant and gazes at her with absolute wonder painted on his face as he lifts her, lets her get closer to the sculpture, lets her reach out to touch it. She can't yet talk or walk, so her attachment to the sculpture is conveyed with her smile and her wide eyes. Dad is smiling proudly, eyes sparkling. Whether it is actorly wonder for the audience or real dad-pride, only he would know. There are only a few hotel and/or wedding guests in the little enclave of the lobby, and otherwise it is just their photographer, Tom, Katie, Suri and me. I am so close I could touch them.

When it's over, Tom deposits Suri with David Beckham, who cradles her head and chats with the star. Soon after, Leah and J. Lo and their men slip into a back part of the bar, order pizzas, and scoff them down just like regular people. The Hassler after party goes until five a.m. and the poor hotel staff are beat. As are we all.

Tomkat: The Aftermath

Before I encountered Jennifer Lopez in Rome, I'd never thought much about her. I liked her 2002 movie *Enough*, never took to her music, and thought she and Ben Affleck would not last. But after she almost-virtually spit in my general direction, I developed strong opinions about her.

Only later would I learn I'm not alone. Search for "rude behavior," "bad tipping," "not nice to wait staff," and anything about her recent self-made documentary, and you'll learn a lot about her.

As recently as 2026, Jennifer was slammed for her dismissiveness when a photographer asked her how she'd like to pose for a video on the Golden Globes red carpet. She neither looked at him nor acknowledged him in any way, leaving him seemingly talking to himself. The comment sections were savage.

One publication spelled it out in the most basic terms: *The moment quickly sparked backlash online, with Instagram and TikTok users branding her behavior "rude," not just during the Golden Globes, but throughout her life in general.*

I began to suspect she might be a bit out of touch with everyday people. As the New York *Post*'s Page Six put it, *The Bronx-born beauty is famous for her demands. In 2001 she arrived for a BBC interview with a 90-person entourage and ordered nine dressing rooms for the group.*

Another time, the paper pointed out, *before she filmed a music video benefiting African AIDS victims in 2010, her team submitted a backstage rider that included items such as a 45-foot trailer, white drapes, Diptyque candles, white couches, white lilies, yellow roses with a red trim, white tablecloths, and apple pie (à la mode).*

The worst has to be those infamous gigs where she cashed in by performing for the world's most cruel and corrupt people. The Human Rights Foundation added it up and reported that, as of 2013, Jenny from the Block had enriched herself to the tune of more than $10 million by singing to despots and moguls from eastern Europe and Russia.

After the fur-wearing diva warbled a birthday song for Turkmenistan's authoritarian ruler, Gurbanguly Berdymukhamedov, in 2013, Jen got dragged. Her team, which was shocked, *shocked*, I tell you! said, *Oops, Jen didn't know, we swear!*

Steven Colbert roasted that response, joking, "How could [J. Lo] have known about Turkmenistan's appalling human rights record: Google?"

It was probably not a difficult decision for her to do these appearances, anyway. You can bet the ten million bucks lasted longer than the backlash.

Speaking of Jennifer Lopez, it certainly got reporters chattering back in 2006 when she and Marc showed up at Tom Cruise's wedding, considering they weren't known to be friends. Turns out…they weren't.

According to Leah Remini, who was friends with Jen and Marc, Tom suggested Leah invite the superstar couple—though Tom and Katie only knew them as passing acquaintances. When they arrived at the wedding, Tom's team wouldn't let Leah sit with J. Lo, prompting protests from Leah. Still, I saw them together around the hotel a lot, including for that late-night post-wedding pizza party.

Jennifer was there was for optics, Leah said, because that wedding was enmeshed with the Church of Scientology. "Tom and Katie's wedding was now being regarded as 'official church business.'"

This also explains Brooke Shields being there. (She and Tom had publicly feuded).

"The church, in a very calculating way, could point to this photo or that photo and say Posh and Becks or Jennifer Lopez and Marc Anthony are associating themselves with this wedding, and therefore with Scientology," Leah wrote in a memoir published years later.

During those days I was flouncing around Italy, I was oblivious to the Church of Scientology's influence on the wedding festivities. I never saw a hint of the inquiries Leah Remini says she made about missing Shelly Miscavige, who is church leader (and Cruise's best man) David Miscavige's wife.

Where's Shelly? Anyone know where she is? Remini says she was very surprised not to see David Miscavige's wife at this high-profile event, but when she asked about Shelly, she faced reprisals for daring to ask Cruise, his team, and Scientology officials about the woman's whereabouts.

When everyone returned home from Italy, Leah says she was sent to Scientology's Flag Land Base building (known as "FLAG") in Clearwater, Florida, which "is considered the spiritual headquarters of Scientology." The actress claims she was forced to "undergo a quick 'ethics cycle,'" which as a decades-long Scientologist, "was one of her life's worst nightmares."

Leah sensationally quit the organization in 2013 after thirty-five years as a member and, in 2023, she filed a lawsuit against the Church of Scientology and its leader, David Miscavige, for harassment, defamation and other unlawful conduct after years of alleged blowback for speaking out.

For 17 years, Scientology and David Miscavige have subjected me to what I believe to be psychological torture, defamation, surveillance, harassment, and intimidation, significantly impacting my life and career, she said in a statement.

In the suit, Leah elaborates on those four months she was in Clearwater.

"Upon arrival, Ms. Remini was presented with dozens of internal reports from Scientologists complaining about her behavior at the wedding. It was clear to Ms. Remini that she was being punished for asking where Shelly Miscavige was…Ms. Remini was held at FLAG for four months while she was put through a process that cost her hundreds of thousands of dollars and nearly led her to have a psychotic breakdown," the suit says.

Scientology has vehemently denied all of Leah's claims.

Six years after that cozy, glamorous Italian wedding, Katie Holmes filed for divorce from Tom Cruise. The settlement was finalized in 2012.

Tom hasn't been seen with Suri in public since around 2012. The day after she graduated from LaGuardia High School in 2024, Tom was spotted at a Taylor Swift concert in London.

Meanwhile, I didn't meet Tom Cruise in Italy in 2006, but soon enough, I will.

We'll Temporarily Have Paris

*P*ARIS — *The paparazzi are circling, the guests are jetting in, and the last touches are being applied at the church before "Desperate Housewives" star Eva Longoria marries French basketball ace Tony Parker in Paris on Saturday.*

The actress, who plays the scheming Gabrielle in the hit series and the Belgian-born San Antonio Spurs point guard may wish for an improvement in the unseasonably rainy weather.

But otherwise, things appear to be on track for the Paris celebrity wedding of the year, on the supposedly auspicious date of July 7, 2007 (7/7/07). —The Hollywood Reporter

I fly in from Zurich and check in at my five-star hotel near the Place Vendôme. Jessica Alba is next to me. She's makeup free in a casual pony, and I wouldn't have noticed her if I wasn't looking for celebrities.

I sign the credit card slip and choke on the price. In July 2026, a basic room at this hotel would be 2,200 euros a night. I head to my room to freshen up and get ready to work.

As the wedding weekend kicks off, I dress to blend best I can. When I'm not on crowd duty on the streets of Paris, I'm inside, working on my novel over café au laits or Perrier or the occasional prosecco in the lobby bar. There's no visible media around, because like Catherine Zeta-Jones and Michael Douglas did back in 2000, Eva and Tony have sold the rights to their wedding photos to *OK!* magazine. They got seven figures for the exclusive, according to several media outlets, and they can't afford any spies or spoilers.

I'm not here to bother anyone; my job is to blend in with the crowds and report on the stars milling about in between events during this long wedding extravaganza.

Over several days, I observe a giddy Eva, Tony and their famous friends flitting about the hotel and the streets of Paris. Eva is a lovely, happy host, and one memorable moment is when she and some friends (bridesmaids?) dressed in matching red track suits settle at a table near mine. She gushes about how she *loves* that Tony gives her jewelry, and her bridesmaids squeal.

Football legend Thierry Henry is in the house, his French accent deadly. All I can think when I see Terrence Howard a bunch of times is how he basically said women are dirty, and how I would not pass his test. Why? In a magazine interview, Terrence answered the question, *What one item could you find in a woman's house that would prove that you weren't compatible?* This way:

TH: Toilet paper—and no baby wipes—in her bathroom.

REPORTER: Wait. I don't think I understand.

TH: If they're using dry paper, they aren't washing all of themselves. It's just unclean. So if I go inside a woman's house and see the toilet paper there, I'll explain this. And if she doesn't make the adjustment to baby wipes, I'll know she's not completely clean.

I keep running into a woman looking after a baby in a stroller. We meet by the elevators, by the front door coming back in, in the lobby. At one point we both happen to be waiting for people on a soft bench off the lobby. We get to chatting about Paris. Neither of us asks personal questions. It's polite small talk, stranger to stranger.

That baby again, I smile when I see her another time. *So cute.* The child is one heartbeat way from a newborn.

Later that night, I'm waiting for the elevator, dressed up and ready to report on a glamorous wedding event full of famous people.

The door opens. Everyone's leaving the hotel at the same time, so it's packed.

But there aren't that many people in it—it's the baby carriage taking up a ton of space, and I've already let another full car go by. People beckon me on. *Come on. We'll make room.*

As they shift and I step on, I see my friend, whose name I don't know. I smile, acknowledge her, make another joke.

That baby again! Always in the way. Ha, ha.

A woman I don't know speaks to me. She's tall. I recognize her from various roles in television shows…I'm thinking CSI Miami. Christina Chang, maybe?

Don't you talk bad about that baby, the tall woman says. She's not kidding.

I look at her, then notice the woman next to her.

Sheryl Crow is in the back of the elevator, unsmiling. She is not amused by my gentle joke about this baby's presence. Her expression is like ice, or, as they love to say in British tabloids, her face is like thunder. My friend, it turns out, is the baby's nanny. The baby, it turns out, is Sheryl Crow's son. He was born in April. I'm sure he's a very nice baby, and I want to say so, but I decide keeping my mouth shut is the best way forward.

Eva and Tony have two wedding ceremonies—one civil, one religious—and the celebration dinner on that first night is held at Baccarat, where everything is crystal and probably breakable. No one should let me in there.

Our team has dinner there the following night so we can give readers an up-close description of what the celebrities experienced. The food is creative, like art. The portions are fit for a flea, but there are enough courses. Champagne flows like wine. The bill is embarrassing; we could've fed a family of five for a couple of weeks for what the magazine paid, but at least we can report on what kind of experience Eva and Tony might have had at the Baccarat restaurant.

The second wedding is a Roman Catholic ceremony at Saint-Germain-l'Auxerrois Church, a 12th century cathedral visited by French royalty in distant centuries. Although hundreds, if not thousands, of fans and onlookers gather outside to see some star wattage, the public's view is obstructed by ten-foot-high panels erected in front of the church to protect the couple's exclusive deal with *OK!*

After the second wedding, my colleagues and I dive in for interviews in the crowd. The senior reporter helping direct our coverage says to me, *You go that way. I'll go this way.*

I go that way, and there's the priest who officiated the wedding, and among the throbbing, pressing crowd and celebrity mania on the streets of Paris, he gives me an exclusive quote, which is what literally everyone is after, and this makes the team happy.

It is on the last night when things turn weird for me.

A few of us are reconnoitering at a table in the hotel restaurant. I leave to use the bathroom, and on my way back, in the lobby, I hear some guys calling out like *Hey, what you doing, who are you, blah blah.*

I look to see who they're yelling after. Wait, it's me. The guy in the middle of what looks suspiciously like an entourage is shyly nodding to me, ducking his head smiling when I make eye contact. I lose him under his baseball cap. He seems shy and tame. It's his entourage that goes nuts with the come-ons.

My man says this, my man wants that, ha hah, ooh, ooh, types of things. I am caught off guard.

I'm sorry, I shrug. *I don't know who you are. Sorry…*

I'm thirty-something with a wedding ring. It's just some harmless catcalling.

I return to my table and tell my colleagues that some guy who might be a famous wedding guest—he seemed famous, what with the fawning pals—was talking at me loudly in the lobby. One of them makes a face like she's thinking about my claim, then gets up and leaves.

She comes back. *That's 50 Cent,* she says.

Oh, I say. *Him.*

I decide to see for myself, see if I recognize him. I need a copy of my bill to review ahead of checkout tomorrow, so I head to reception and get an early peek at the multi-page monstrosity, which has line after line of ten-euro Diet Cokes and coffees and a few twenty-euro glasses of prosecco. I end up passing the rowdy entourage again near the hotel's front door where they're waiting for their car.

They start talking to me again as I pass by. I think I recognize the guy after all, though I couldn't name a 50 Cents song.

That's your bill? one of the men with him shouts as he rolls my way. *We can get her room number! Yeah, let's get it. Show me your room.*

Ha, ha, I laugh, but it is a nervous laugh, and I realize I need to get out of there. I get chills—not the good kind. The big man reaches for my paperwork and I pull away. *Whoa—uh, nope*, I say. Things go from flattering to sinister in the flap of a page and the grasp of a meaty hand. I hug my folio to my chest and stalk back to my table.

I don't know it then but I will, unfortunately, see the famous guy again in the course of my work as a journalist.

Three years later, Eva filed for divorce from Tony, citing irreconcilable differences. The pair, it seemed, burned hot and then burned out.

Eva told *People* magazine in 2006 that her first encounter with Tony after a Spurs game was "lust at first sight." Of the French basketball star, who was twenty-four at the time, she said, "He's only been with one other person in his life."

When Eva filed, she Tweeted out a statement: *It is with great sadness that after 7 years together, Tony and I have decided to divorce. We love each other deeply and pray for each other's happiness.*

News outlets around the world reported that the split came after rumors of infidelity by Tony, with sources saying Eva found hundreds of texts on his phone from another woman.

Years later, I don't see her in the news in the U.S. much, but she shares a home with her current husband in Marbella, Spain, the town where I met my husband so long ago. You can find her very white, very big house in the pages of *Hello!* magazine.

When I was down there in the summer of 2025, she was spending the day at the beach with friends, and they ran photos of her all over the local news. She's big down there.

We're living in a different timeline now. Paris was a different universe.

As I browsed through those images, I thought back to 2000 when I frolicked on that same beach with my future husband, and I thought, *Where does the time go?*

The Snow Prince

The weather is diabolical. Grey skies, high winds, bitter, icy conditions, and "significant" avalanche risk that ruins the perfection of skiing in the Swiss Alps.

It's also bad for me, a reporter who's running around Klosters covering the latest ski vacation of Prince William and his on-again-off-again girlfriend Kate Middleton. There are around fifty lifts and eighty runs in the Klosters-Davos area. I've just driven nearly two hours from my apartment overlooking Mt. Pilatus, and I'm hitting the ground running.

Which slope to choose? Where do I start?

I pick the one with a bar at the bottom. This place is the definition of *après ski*. It's a semi-outdoor space that sits at the base of a slope, so that the instant you glide off the lift, you can whip off your skis and have a drink in hand in seconds.

I order a drink and wait, scrutinizing every person who glides off the lift. With everyone bundled up in fancy ski gear, I'm constantly worried I'll miss them. Or, worse, that I already have.

I needn't have worried. I meet another reporter there, and he's English, and he's here for the same reason.

After few minutes of small talk, our work begins.

Look, he says. *They're here.*

Before I see the prince and the girlfriend, I see the photographers. They rise up outside the bar, unfurling like the rock trolls from *Frozen*. It all happens at once: the photographers start snapping; I jump out of my seat, run out of the bar, and find my position away from the fray. I have a close-up view of everything.

The couple alights from the lift. I sip casually from my plastic cup in the snow outside the bar, pretending to barely notice Prince William and Kate Middleton, staying well out of their business.

They swish towards us. William is joking and laughing, then lets his face settle into a look of concentration as he waddles over to lay his skis in the rack between the lift and the bar, just a few feet from me; Kate keeps grinning. William says something to a friend. Kate's still smiling, flashing those dimples. Her white ski gear contrasts with tumbling brunette locks.

What strikes me then is how comfortable she looks in this role, though they've recently come off that famous 2007 breakup and the British media is still calling her "Waity Katie" because the Prince hasn't proposed. As I hang well back with a few ogling tourists, the royal group heads to a waiting van. William ducks in first to get away from the flashing cameras, doesn't help her, doesn't chivalrously let her slip in before him so he can protect her. She follows, and is still smiling.

After a light dinner of white bread dipped in a cauldron of melted cheese, a few of us head to the coolest nightclub—maybe the only nightclub—in Klosters.

Casa Antica is a rustic, low-lit, simple little club typical of small Swiss towns. No velvet anywhere; no ropes, no plush lounge. It's got simple stools, some little round tables, exposed beams, an incongruous disco ball and all sorts of creatively nauseating shooters for late-night binge drinking.

And whaddaya know. The future king *and* his likely future wife are here.

We sit at the bar while the royals, just feet away, guffaw and generally make merry inside the club. William is holding court, sitting in a corner, his distinctive booming voice rising above the din, while Kate flits between two tables. She'll sit across the room and then drift back to check in with him. They don't strike me as particularly lovey dovey.

Safe from the prying lenses of the photographers that follow him everywhere, the one bit of affection the two show is when Kate approaches the table William's sitting at, and he reaches up to grab her arm gently to pull her in slightly to hear what he was saying.

She heads to the bathroom and comes back to sit with him. The place is small, intimate, and not particularly crowded. I do not see him tend to her, not once, not in any way. No one bothers them or even seems to notice them. We stay at the bar.

This royal romance is unfolding before me. Reporters are in town because everyone's on engagement watch, now that the 2007 breakup passed, and the pair came back together as tight as ever. It's fascinating to pick up on the nuances, looks, postures and habits of royals when they don't have the eyes of the world on them. Kate keeps an eye on Wills; she watches that boy like a hawk. He is the quiet leader of their pack of chums; she is glued to his side, and is not going anywhere, except to the next table or the bathroom.

I am struck by Kate's ease among William's upper-crust chums. As nervous and unsure as she sometimes appears in public, in the club, Kate Middleton behaves like a confident woman.

She is not as tall as a lot of people like to say on social media. I'm five-nine and I'd peg her at no taller than five-eight.

About twelve-thirty a.m., Will's crowd orders a round of Jägermeister shots.

And that is all we are going to see. There will not be more rounds of shots, no close-up view of royals dancing on tables.

Because we're caught.

A royal minder emerges out of the ether and approaches the royal reporters next to me. *Either you go, or William goes.* The minder leaves the most important part unspoken: if *they* have to leave, the palace will be unimpressed, and your bosses might even hear about it. We can't have that.

I act natural, stare at the wall. Sip my drink robotically. Alas, I too am screwed. One of the reporters throws me under the bus. She slides off her stool, points to me, and says loudly to the royal minder, "SHE'S A REPORTER, TOO."

How very unsportsmanlike. When the journalist you're with is not a direct competitor, there is no need to screw her over, and we could've shared, like a press pool. But she chose violence on this night.

William's father, Prince Charles, arrives in Klosters near the end of the week. On the slopes, William and Kate take notice of reporters in the vicinity, with both of them loudly joking that one of the male journalists nearby "skis like a girl."

Later, William implores photographers on the mountain to leave him alone, pointing out that they've already taken tons of photos. *Can I just have some peace?*

As everyone knows by now, the prince proposed in 2010, and he and Kate Middleton were married in 2011. The British media had to stop calling her Waity Katie. She became the "rock" and the "glue" holding the royal family together, which the Windsor clan badly needs in the year 2026 as the Epstein Files continue to reveal disturbing connections to some high-ranking members, notably Andrew, brother of King Charles III and favorite son of the late Queen Elizabeth II.

Pictures or it Didn't Happen

Tupac Shakur *and me at the Roxbury, Los Angeles,
October 1995. He is only a week or so out of a New
York prison and has just left our conversation to chase
after the woman who scolded me for speaking to him.
Eleven months after this photo was taken, 2Pac was
killed in a Las Vegas shooting.*

*My plus-one took these photos of me interviewing **Ray Liotta** and **Winona Ryder** in 2012.*

Both of them were very nice and answered all my questions. On the way to the afterparty, Ray asked us how to get there. Sadly, he died in 2022 of natural causes while filming Dangerous Waters.

*Waiting to interview **Nacho Figueras** at a polo match on Governor's Island, New York (2015). He's considered the most famous polo player in the world, is always a good interview, and told me of his friends Princes William and Harry before the brothers' estrangement, "They are great guys. Very well brought up, they're great friends, great brothers, good sons. They have their values very in place."*

Taylor Swift in a screengrab from a video I took of her
in December 2014 at a luncheon in New York City.
Below, the CD The Killers' frontman *Brandon Flowers*
signed for me in 2005.

Ollie, 2/2002-2/2013

On assignment with me, Prince William and Kate Middleton in Klosters, Switzerland, March 2008

A good boy in the dog pen at a Malibu pool party, August 2008.

©Sara Hammel

Ollie getting a much-deserved massage before meeting Mischa Barton

I regret taking so few photos during my travels as a journalist. Only toward the end, around 2013-2016, did I take a few half-hearted selfies to try to hold on to a few memories.

Clockwise from top left: Neve Campbell; Michael Douglas & Catherine Zeta-Jones; Nicholas Hoult & Hugh Jackman, a rare star who made sure to know and say my name (Tom Cruise & Val Kilmer are the other two); Norman Reedus.

One of my last interviews for People *was in 2016 with **Ethan Hawke**—at Cipriani, of course. I can't decide if I look like I'm telling him off or begging for money, but it's all very serious. "Antoine Fuqua gave me a leg up in this life," Hawke says of the director. "Nobody wanted me in* Training Day *except Antoine and Denzel Washington. They championed me and got me that part. It changed my career."*

...my sneaky shot of **Paul Bettany, Mark Ruffalo** and **Jennifer Connolly** seconds later would be so invasive. I felt awful and hid behind a friend until they passed...and hopefully got their sight back.

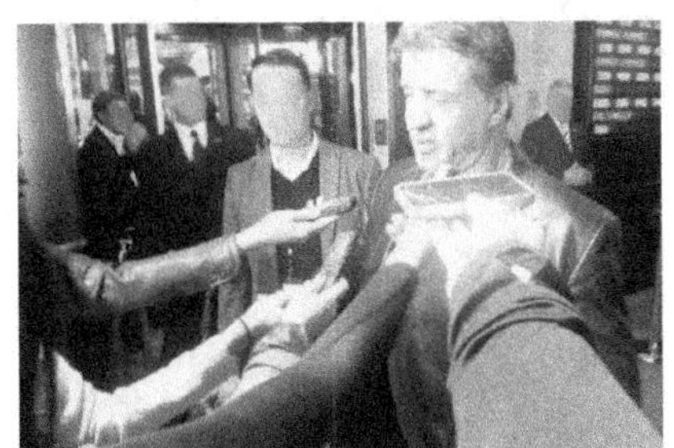

Sylvester Stallone at the Escape Plan *Screening in NYC, 2013*

Feeling nostalgic in the penthouse at The Clarence Hotel in Dublin, 2023, nineteen years after staying here while reporting on U2

There's no Place Like Home

Moving to Switzerland opens up new opportunities with the magazine. As a Swiss correspondent, I'm unofficially put on the Roger Federer beat, interviewing him twice for our Sexiest Man issue; once in Zurich, once in Basel. The tennis champion is a delight, seems to have advanced self-awareness, gives thoughtful, interesting answers, and is all-around sweet and interesting. There's nothing I can do to ruin him for you.

Between 2006 and 2007, I'm dispatched to cover two of the biggest crime stories in the world. Both tragic, both dark, both messy and so badly bungled that they'll keep true-crime podcasts, blogs, documentaries, and comment sections on fire for years to come.

The first story takes place in an ancient, walled city in Umbria, Italy. An American student called Amanda Knox has been accused of murdering her English roommate, twenty-two-year-old Meredith Kercher, in their shared house in Perugia.

The British media descends and the American media, including our magazine, are beside themselves. That the accused killer is a pretty blonde and the slaying was as horrific as it gets takes it over the top.

I land in Rome and set foot in Perugia late at night, getting straight to work, traipsing into a deserted alley with high walls on both sides without a thought. I realize I have no bolt hole to escape to if someone wants to come for me. I stand in front of Le Chic, the nightclub where Amanda worked for boss Patrick Lumumba—who she then accused of being in on Meredith's killing. He's in custody as I knock on a windowless black door, but it has a chain across it letting us all know the owner, and its staff, are not here and no drinks will be served anytime soon.

I hear a noise and look behind me; it is a murky darkness; no one is there.

Amanda, her boyfriend Raffaele Sollecito, and Patrick are all in custody, but these were just arrests, not convictions. They are suspects. There might very well be another mad stabber who's still on the loose.

I am back at it the next day, in the sunlight. Let me tell you, if you think covering true crime is challenging, try doing it in a country where you don't speak the language. It feels quite possible Amanda is guilty of what the Italians are accusing her of. She acts so odd, so confident doing cartwheels and splits and enjoying PDA with her boyfriend in the police station, that no one knows what to make of her. That's how she's painted. I visit the house where it happened, down in a ravine. A lot goes on that week.

Amanda is found not guilty of murdering Meredith after years of legal wrangling and time spent in prison. Her conviction for slander—because she falsely accused innocent Patrick Lumumba—was upheld.

Months after I return from Italy, in May 2007, three-year-old Madeleine McCann disappears from her family's rental apartment at the Ocean Club in Praia da Luz, Portugal. It happens when her parents, Kate and Gerry, are out for dinner with a group of friends at a restaurant in the resort. Madeleine and her younger twin siblings are left back in the apartment, one-hundred yards away from the tapas restaurant. When Kate goes back to check on the children, she finds Madeleine gone.

The world watches, invested, horrified, sad, and ultimately, confused when authorities name the parents as suspects in Madeleine's disappearance.

I'm put on phone calls to the McCann extended family and friends, and then I am sent to Portugal.

I am shocked when I visit the apartment and see how exposed it is, and how it's close to a well-traveled road; I'd pictured the apartment cossetted within the resort, buffered on all sides by other holidaymakers. We are beyond judging the family (aren't we?) but I remember thinking upon seeing the place, *I wouldn't leave my dog there with the door unlocked.* I mean that literally. I love my dog more than I can express in words. That's my personal choice, not an indictment of other people's choices.

I can't see the tapas restaurant where her parents and their friends ate and drank from the apartment, but maybe my eyes aren't good enough, or I'm looking in the wrong direction.

In the year 2026, a lead that German law enforcement had on a possible suspect seems to have not panned out, and we still don't know where Madeleine is. I truly wish for the McCann family to receive answers and the outcome they deserve in the case of their missing daughter.

Living in Switzerland is a life-changing experience. Swiss life is safe, outdoorsy, and full of real, wholesome food, great wine and spectacular scenery.

I'm on the German side, and there are a lot of rules. It takes a while to figure them out, and I usually fall into them, screwing up and learning the hard way. Such as when you discover it's illegal to idle outside someone's apartment block for more than a certain amount of seconds, and doing so will get you admonished by passersby. Don't dump your recycling on a Sunday, or a neighbor will glare at you and watch your every move through binoculars.

The most important word I learn is Entschuldigung. *I'm sorry.*

I use it for everything, especially those times when I don't have a clue what I've done wrong. Fewer people than you'd think speak English in Lucerne, and my German lessons are not as effective as I'd hoped, so I get a lot of finger wags and deep frowns while no one can explain to me my transgression.

Don't get me started on Fasnacht, the yearly carnival that takes over the streets like an invasion from your nightmares. Seriously. Check the footage at your own risk. Much of my psychological thriller novel *The Expat Wife* incorporates how thrown off I was much of the time while living there, even with all the incredible things Switzerland has to offer.

It is not for us long term. My husband quits his job, and I contact the chief about freelance work with the magazine back in the USA, thinking maybe I'll come full circle. He writes back that there is, indeed, work available for the likes of me.

As readers of early chapters of this book will know, I've always wanted to live in L.A. We can't think of anywhere else to move to from here, so we head to the embassy in Bern, get my husband an American visa, and leave the country.

There's an earthquake within about twenty minutes of my arrival in Marina Del Rey, where our starter apartment is located. Coincidentally, I'm on the phone with an agent asking about earthquake insurance. She's from the East Coast, too, which becomes evident when she yells, *I have to go!* And drops the phone.

This Sh-t is Bananas

I've covered every kind of story for *People* for six years in eight countries, but never in my homeland. No one knows me here.

It is a rough entry to the Los Angeles bureau in the summer of 2008. My first assignment is a children's movie premiere on a boiling-hot Saturday in July. The steaming pavement of the Fox Studios lot is laid with a yellow carpet, the décor is bunches of bananas and brown balloons I assume are supposed to be coconuts, and the cast arrives tired from enduring a junket before the premiere.

I am demoralized as the cast travels down the yellow carpet. Not because I'm too good to cover a kids' movie, but because I'm being forced to listen to poufy-haired Andy Samberg talk to me about poop, farting and vomiting.

The former *Saturday Night Live* cast member and I stand face-to-face at this premiere for his incredible and unforgettable movie *Space Chimps*. A hot wind blows grit into my eyes as it roars through like Mother Nature's hairdryer, pummelling palm trees and whipping my hair into my mouth.

After he answers a couple of movie-related questions, our conversation goes like this:

"Can you describe your worst dating disaster?" I ask him, blinking a bit of dust off my eyeball.

"Sure! There was a time when I went on a date with a girl, and we both just barfed all over each other, and then we both farted."

Andy cracks himself up. He reminds me of a bespectacled Greg Brady. I have to stop myself from shooting back with an acerbic dig, because the magazine is all about making nice, and I can't cause ructions on my first assignment on U.S. soil.

I think to myself as Andy talks about farts, *I've won multiple awards for my investigative reporting on women in the military, wrote front-page crime features for the UK's Sunday Times Magazine, exposed sexism in sports. Why am I putting up with this in the workplace?*

These negative thoughts eventually dissolve, because I am glad for the paycheck. I am happy to be a working journalist. My weekend could be spent doing much worse things than being messed with by Andy Samberg at a children's movie premiere, and I'm acutely aware of this.

Back to Samberg.

"Seriously? How about a real example?" I ask wearily.

Faux indignant: "If you're saying I can't have that quote on that page of worst dates…"

"So you're insisting that is true?"

"Oh, yeah. I had a date where we both barfed all over each other and we both farted."

"Did you eat something bad that night?"

"No. It was just a bad date."

Sigh.

"Did you go out with her again?"

"Oh, *yeah.* The first date was nothing compared to the second date when we totally took dumps in our pants. You can put that in the magazine, right?"

I give up and thank him for his time with a well-concealed fleck of sarcasm.

Cheryl Hines is up next. She is chill, smiley, happy to talk about working on another movie with Lindsay Lohan, who everyone is talking about these days, so editors will be happy I got quotes about her. I ask Cheryl, "Working on this film, were you able to get Andy Samberg to give a serious answer to anything?"

She laughs, throws him a glance. "I'm not even sure that's Andy Samberg. You can't believe anything he says."

Wanna know the depressing thing? When people ask me to name the worst celebrities I've ever met, Andy Samberg doesn't make the top five.

That night, I send in my story, the first I've ever turned in to the L.A. bureau. These files go to dozens of staffers around the world, and someone in the London bureau replies to me privately, *Currently in Nice…missing you on the Euro reporting battalion. You could be in the South of France right now covering Angelina and Brad's twins.*

I write back, *Don't be jealous that you're breaking news in Nice while I'm covering the world premiere of SPACE CHIMPS. Cheers!*

Later, in response to another file I've sent, the colleague writes, *Space Chimps rule!*

It's not a bad life, not at all.

But I am questioning my life choices right now, and I suddenly want to go home.

Problem is, I don't know where home is anymore.

My husband and I settle in West Hollywood, where my bathroom window overlooks an alley where WEHO's heroic firefighters regularly get shirtless and polish their ladders, soaping them up, suds flailing everywhere. The park nearby has avocado trees, and we have lemons growing in our back yard.

I start to get some fun assignments here and there. One day they tell me to buy a ticket to a sold-out John Mayer concert. I should talk to them first if it's more than a few hundred dollars. They're spending the big bucks because Mayer is dating Jennifer Aniston, and once again, her relationship is all anyone can talk about.

I head to the outdoor show down in Irvine, and immediately see that Jennifer is here, watching from the wings as John strums his guitar.

When it's over, I race to the exits to see if I can see Jen and her entourage. Unlikely. I spend the time interviewing every security guard and venue staffer I can find, and I soon hit on one who confirms Jen is here tonight, and that the staff was instructed to get the star in and out quickly and quietly. In my file, I quote a concertgoer who's a mega-Mayer fan, who talks about how she was watching John and Jen exchanging glances throughout the show.

Jen followed John around the world that summer, even traveling on his tour bus sometimes. I think to myself after that concert, *Brad, my friend, you are a distant memory.*

The Dog Sitter

I'm invited to a Malibu pool party, and I'm told to bring my dog. I pack Ollie into the convertible Saab and head up the PCH. It's a stunning day in August 2008, and the beach house (mansion) sits high atop a cliff, with the Pacific Ocean rolling on until it becomes a white wall.

I need to get to work right away and get the lay of the land. There's a little pen to put our pups in for short breaks. I'm assured the dog experts on site will be supervising, so I pop Ollie in and head into the party. I sit by the pool with Ian Ziering, who I spent my young adult years watching in *Beverly Hills, 90210,* and he tells me his father died recently, and talks about how he understands that Steve, the character he played in the show, "lives in people's hearts."

The big names in attendance today are Ashlee Simpson and Pete Wentz. She's heavily pregnant and relaxes on a sun lounger on her side while Pete DJs for about an hour. Neither of them talks to the media or appears to engage with anyone other than the party's sponsors, who clearly paid them to come. It's an awkward scene. The two of them are guarded like presidents. I'm sure they're both talented, nice people and deserve privacy, but the drama feels over the top. It's a chill party and all the other well-known guests are hanging around like regular people. To me, Ashlee and Pete seem to be taking themselves a bit too seriously.

I chat with a few other TV actors I meet on the lawn, and then I remember I left my favorite family member in a pen surrounded by strangers, so I race back.

Ollie sees me and wags.

"Would your dog like a massage?" A woman in scrubs asks me.

I accept on his behalf, and I watch as the skilled dog masseuse works Ollie's tired shoulder muscles as he gazes out at the sea.

When she's done, I take Ollie into the party area with me to see if I can grab some food, but quickly realize it's a ridiculous idea to bring a food-obsessed Labrador to a beach-house buffet.

I'm stuck in a crowd between the pool and the cabanas as I make this decision, and apparently I seem lost and confused, because a tall blonde woman rises from her sunbed in a cabana and says, "Let me take him. I love dogs."

"I—I couldn't," I say.

She holds out a hand and takes the leash. I don't feel like I can say no to Mischa Barton, who already appears to adore my little Ollie.

"Go get yourself something to eat," she says. "He's adorable! He'll be fine with me."

But he's not.

Ollie has found her bowl of pasta under her sun lounger and is dragging her down to get to it, jerking her arm, knocking things about, rubbing against people's legs to get that food.

Mischa giggles, then grits her teeth under the strain. "I'm so sorry," I say. "I'm so sorry, ugh." The best trained dog ever is making a scene at a Malibu pool party, and I want to crawl under there with him.

"Go, go! He's fine. I've got him."

As I make a dash to the buffet, I think about some good questions to ask her. She shot to fame starring in the rich-kids-behaving-badly show *The OC*, which became an overnight success and catapulted a teenaged Mischa into the spotlight for her role as Marissa Cooper. I was old and living in Europe during *The OC*'s entire run, so I don't know Mischa's work beyond a ghostly turn as a child in *The Sixth Sense*.

I mostly recognize her from trashy gossip sites, where this then-teenaged girl was regularly shamed and verbally abused from afar by grown men, including a disgusting documented misogynist who we are going to ignore into oblivion (first name starts with P).

I return with a little bowl of pasta salad. Mischa invites me to sit with her and we chat about things that are on my Apropos of Nothing List. It's easy for once, because they're all questions women would talk about anyway. Favorite workout. Favorite tipple. Favorite snack.

She tells me, "I cook a lot, so I like all kinds of stuff. I like vegetarian dishes, salads, the basics. I'm into cheese and crackers. I'm living in Paris part time so I'm really into cheeses. Paris is fantastic, I love it."

Maybe that's why we get along. Expat to expat. Dog lover to dog lover.

I wave goodbye after a while and drag Ollie from his new best friend. She goes back to her friends, a couple of pals and her boyfriend, Taylor Locke of the band Rooney.

She takes a risk befriending me. She was arrested for DUI in L.A. a few months ago and then entered rehab, saying how sorry she was and how disappointed she was in herself. I didn't think to ask her about it, and though she knows we're a friendly magazine, we're journalists, and we're apt to ask anything, anytime.

I just want to hug her. I want to say, *I'm sorry you were treated that way. I'm sorry you grew up in the fucked-up Hollywood machine and it's not fair that sicko misogynist blogger ever had your name in his mouth.*

I don't know if Mischa's a great person or not. As you know, I don't pretend to know any of these people beyond how they behave at events or behind the scenes when I'm around. But she has a way, and she's just really, really sweet.

And yes, if you like my dog, I'll admit to a bias in your favor. (This also works in the reverse, like with my feelings about Yale student Jack Schlossberg, President John F. Kennedy's grandson, who, in the future, will bump into me and the pitbull I rescued from the New Haven animal shelter on our walks around town. Not once did Jack pay proper homage, kneel, scruffle his neck, or ask him who's a good boy. I never liked that guy).

I think on the way home how Ollie's been more places than a lot of humans. He was with me in Klosters for part of the time when I was covering William and Kate. He accompanied me to Montreux, Switzerland when I was reporting on Shania Twain's shocking split from her husband, and now he's in Malibu with Mischa Barton. Not a bad life for a pup.

I put Ollie back in his supervised pen for a very short time as I check the inside of the house. I run into Natasha Henstridge and six-foot-four Scotsman Darius (Campbell) Danesh, whose hit "Colorblind" took the UK by storm when I was living there. Natasha is always so fun and sweet whenever I meet her, and he's easygoing and happy to chat. They are, as an aside, a super hot couple.

The story goes they met at a pedestrian crossing in L.A., which is believable given how gorgeous they both are. I hate to gush, but they *are*. She appeared in his video for "Kinda Love."

End note: They got married in 2011 and divorced a few years later. In 2010, Darius was in a car crash in Spain and broke his neck; in 2021, he was in a smaller accident. After that, his family said he lived with chronic pain. In August of 2022, at age forty-one, Darius was found dead in his Rochester, Minnesota apartment. The manner of death was accidental, caused by inhaling the painkiller chloroethane, which led to respiratory arrest. *He had taken pain medication, marijuana and chloroethane to manage the intensity of the pain prior to his death*, his family said. *The night before Darius passed, he had dinner with close friends, who reported that, 'Darius was in a lot of pain, but he was in good spirits when he was with us.'*

His close friend and fellow Scotsman Gerard Butler put out an emotional tribute to his friend on Instagram, saying in part, *I am devastated by the sudden passing of my dear friend Darius, a true brother in arms.*

Later that night, after I send my file about the party, one of my colleagues back in London shoots me a note. They seem to be feeling more positive about my new position. Wrote one in response to the email blast I sent,

Wow! You get invited to all the best parties!

They are mostly British or Australian, so everything is cheeky and slightly in-jokey and even mildly sarcastic, but all in good fun. Always banter.

Either way, I'm hoping my time covering the likes of *Space Chimps* is in my rearview mirror.

Beckham vs. Beckham

A quiet, hot Saturday in early September, so hot that everyone's at the beach. That is, except me and my fellow guests. I am at an exclusive Pacific Palisades country club for a seven-year-old's birthday party, and it should be all about this little boy.

What I will never forget about that day, though, is the Beckham children.

Three boys, all with dirty blond hair. Brooklyn is nine, Romeo is six, and little Cruz is just three years old. They are brought to the party by a selection of grown-ups.

They behave like a family. Three boys, strapping bodyguards, one or two of them, and at least one woman who appears to be a nanny. The kids don't appear to know anyone here, and as soon as they can, they head to the empty tennis courts.

The Beckhams' staff acts as friends, babysitters, ballboys. They're separate from the party. You cannot coax Brooklyn off that tennis court. *More, more, more.* The bodyguard obliges and lobs balls toward the nine-year-old. The nanny collects them.

Salma Hayek and her on-again-off-again billionaire boyfriend Francois François-Henri Pinault arrive at the outdoor affair with their eleven-month-old daughter, Valentina Paloma, who's wearing an adorable white and red sundress.

They stop on the way into the main party, by the tennis courts, and have a quick visit with young Cruz Beckham.

Valentina is fascinated by the boy as she toddles around under her parents' eagle eyes. Angela Bassett has brought her twins to enjoy the festivities, and Laurence Fishburne is here, too, with Gina Torres and their kids.

The DJ is really mixing it up. One minute we're listening to gunshots and the dark lyrics of M.I.A.'s summer hit "Paper Planes," and the next we're treated to a rousing rendition of "If You're Happy and You Know it Clap Your Hands."

This mix of deep cuts continues. I pick at the food, as does Salma, who noshes on sushi and, later, fruit.

But then the music stops.

The biggest popstars of the moment have just entered the party.

Whatever time period you're living in when you read this, think of the most famous, most worshiped, chased, sought-after popstars of the moment, the ones that make the tweens scream the most. That is the Jonas Brothers in the summer of 2008. Nick, Joe, and Kevin enter the grounds in the late afternoon. The children squeal, the adults gasp. They stand on some steps in the middle of the party, which is held on a sort of patio between two stretches of tennis courts, completely un-buffered by bodyguards or handlers.

There are no barriers. People press so close to them they barely maintain a few feet of free space around them.

Nick Jonas gently asks the birthday boy, *Is it okay if we sing Happy Birthday to you? Would that be ok?*

The little boy agrees, and the brothers perform an a cappella version of the classic song. When they finish to claps, cheers and screams, they spend a few minutes signing autographs, chatting with the kids and posing for photos.

Everyone is snapping photos (except me; why do I live my life this way? Why do I not think ahead?). Brooklyn is standing not far from me, and keeps inching closer to get a better look at the brothers. I catch a melancholic feeling. He's alone, and he seems untethered. Lonely. But maybe I'm projecting.

One young pre-teen girl, several parents say, appears to be "hyperventilating," and she is soon granted a quick audience with the band. When the Jonas Brothers leave, she announces, "Nick is definitely my future husband!" Another kid mumbles ruefully, "When my best friend hears about this, she's gonna kill me."

After the band leaves, all three Beckhams line up for snow cones. I'm not going out of my way to observe them, even if they are the offspring of two celebrities. But it's hard to avoid because there are so many in their group; three kids and their staff take up space.

After dessert, which includes wagons serving cotton candy, churros and popcorn, Brooklyn spends most of the time on the tennis court hitting the ball with a bodyguard while a nanny acts as ball girl. Romeo and Cruz are more interested in wandering around the party with their (presumed) nannies.

Before the party ends, there is a kids' dance-off. Now. This is where, again, you cannot avoid the Beckhams at this party. Little Cruz, just three years old, has already gone viral in his young life. Earlier this year, his mum performed with the Spice Girls in Toronto, and at the end of the show, Cruz came out and wowed the crowd with his breakdancing moves, complete with full head-spins.

This is Cruz's moment. He takes center stage, pulling out a selection of killer breakdance moves, just like he did at the Spice Girls show. He perks up every time the video camera turns his way and has the crowd hooting and cracking up. There are other children in the circle, dancing and entertaining the crowd in a wholesome moment, but Cruz is the star.

Years later, when Brooklyn is a twenty-seven-year-old man, a bitter rift will tear him away from his family of origin—brothers Romeo and Cruz, sister Harper, and his parents David and Victoria—and the memories of that birthday party will roar back to me. The Beckham children on the outskirts, not appearing to know anyone, playing mostly with their adult minders.

It hit me a certain way when Brooklyn posted a statement on Instagram addressing the sad estrangement, which included, in part, For my entire life, my parents have controlled narratives in the press about our family. The performative social media posts, family events and inauthentic relationships have been a fixture of the life I was born into.

As of 2026, Brooklyn is not speaking to his parents. He's cut off his family.

The trouble began when he struck up a romance with Nicola Peltz, whose billionaire father is a major Trump donor and is pals with Elon Musk. When the happy couple got engaged, tensions between Brooklyn and his parents ratcheted up. The firstborn son, it seemed, was inching out of the gravitational pull of Brand Beckham and this was making some people very uncomfortable.

Things blew up around Brooklyn and Nicola's 2022 wedding. Only the two families know exactly what led to the breach, but everyone agrees there are two main issues:

First, Brooklyn and Nicola say Victoria pulled out of designing the bride's dress at the last minute, leaving her dressless, which Victoria denies.

Second, the couple says that at the wedding, Victoria muscled in on the first dance, which was meant to be between the bride and groom. It happened when Marc Anthony called for the most beautiful woman in the room to come up and dance with the groom. That person, Brooklyn says, was supposed to be his new wife. But as if in a creepy psychological thriller, his mother stepped forward instead, prompting a distraught Nicola to burst into tears and run out of the room.

Brooklyn, in that same Instagram post, said of his mother, She danced very inappropriately on me in front of everyone. I've never felt more uncomfortable or humiliated in my entire life. We wanted to renew our vows so we could create new memories of our wedding day that bring us joy and happiness, not anxiety and embarrassment.

The "dancing on" Brooklyn part rang true for me. It whisked me straight back to that night in Portugal seeing her "dancing on" David. It is a peculiar habit unique to her.

The wedding DJ backed up Brooklyn's version of events, saying on a British talk show that The whole situation was really awkward for everyone in the room…Marc Anthony asked 'the most beautifulest woman in the room' to come to the stage, and he says, 'Victoria, come to the stage…[Brooklyn was] devastated."

The Beckham family drama was officially in the public domain thanks to Brooklyn's scathing statement. No one looked particularly good, and so, from their separate corners, each camp spoke to *People* magazine to make their case.

Insiders say the hostility between the Beckhams and their daughter-in-law goes far beyond a dress and ruined dance. "Victoria and Nicola got along in the first few months, but then Victoria started acting like a jealous girlfriend," a Peltz family source says. "She seemed so jealous of Nicola." Not so, counters a Beckham insider: "Nicola is the one who is jealous of Victoria. She wants to be famous."

Ehh…frankly, reading that, I'm none the wiser. You lose me when you start talking about women being "jealous" when we stand up for ourselves, set boundaries, or don't behave exactly how other people think we should. Every single woman I know has had "you're just jealous" thrown at her when she doesn't like something or someone.

The accusation is often projection from people who are themselves struggling with feelings of jealousy. This fallback response also stems from misogynist tropes like the catfight, the hapless man who can't stand up for himself, and the controlling, manipulative shrew. There can be no other explanation other than a woman seeing another woman as a threat, especially if that woman is beautiful, rich, and young. I don't know if Nicola is an awful person or not, but she is not in charge of Brooklyn's choices and actions. He has agency.

And painting Victoria as jealous of her son's wife is ageist and tired.

Is she jealous of Nicola, though? Again, who knows. But to assume it is lazy and unfair.

During the kerfuffle caused by this Instagram bombshell (I recommend reading the whole thing online), I sent up a test balloon on social media. I wrote that my British sports-journalist friends, all of them at high levels, say David Beckham can often behave like a humorless, spoiled brat and a manbaby behind the scenes. I certainly saw his mannerless side, though of course he owed me nothing at that party. I added that I believe Brooklyn, and that some things he says tracks with what we know about the family.

My post was swarmed, and I was lambasted for daring to point out facts about David Beckham. Some of the meanest were obviously bots, and I had to wonder if they were deployed by a crisis PR firm to guide social media chatter about Brand Beckham in their favor, much in the way that the Amber Heard v. Johnny Depp fiasco and the ongoing Blake Lively vs. Justin Baldoni lawsuits allegedly did.

I've gotten furious (always anonymous) replies on social media about how nice David was to them, or how cool he was with their kid, or how he's known for being generous. I'm sure he was. He knows how to turn it on when the cameras are rolling. He knows how to charm when he's at a planned public event. If there are people he needs to impress or show respect to, he will.

I'm talking about who he is behind the scenes. No one is saying David Beckham is the devil. But he's not your buddy, either. Not your mate, and not your friend. He and his family are a brand. They are a money-making machine. If you feel somehow close or loyal to them because of nostalgia or pretty pictures or a parasocial attachment, please know that the adoration and admiration travel in one direction.

Brooklyn seems to want to get off the ride, but his timing and his method doesn't suit his parents' carefully laid plans for world domination. That's not to say I'm Team

Brooklyn; rather, I'm Team They're All as Bad as Each Other And I Have a Life of my Own. If you care enough to take a side and fight a battle for people you don't know, who wouldn't spit on you if you were on fire—and there's a disheartening amount of people who spend their time doing this—you're Team Billionaire however you slice it.

Unfortunately, some people can't help themselves. If a star makes you feel special for even a fleeting moment, you want to hang on to that. Some people will grasp onto the dream, white knuckling and clamping on for dear life despite all reason, and that's up to them, but I wish they'd maintain their parasocial attachments without having to lash out. You're entitled to your experience. But so are the rest of us. I implore you to keep your hinges on when engaging in online discourse about stupid rich people.

But I know a depressingly high number of people won't be able to do that.

It's as if we're so exhausted, so tired of bad news, that we can't bear to lose another hero. We need these uber-talented or uber-beautiful people to be better than us.

Unfortunately, the truth is they're as messed up as the rest of us.

His Greatest Role

A colleague beckons me into her office. I take a seat in front of her desk. I am working in the Los Angeles office full time, but I'm still technically a freelancer, and I am half in, half out. It's a lonely place to be.

I want to prep you for tonight, my colleague says. Tonight is the L.A. premiere of *Valkyrie,* and "prep" is when savvy staffers talk to red-carpet reporters about what to ask the stars at a given event. As it was explained to me when I first arrived in town and took a meeting in the L.A office, red-carpet reporting is not considered a simple task. You're expected to be ready if a surprise famous guest shows up and gives you an interview; you have to know what to ask them. Like when I studied up on Cheryl Hines and knew to ask her about the troubled starlet du jour, Lindsay Lohan. Cheryl spoke highly of the young actress, and I made an entire article out of her quotes.

There's something you need to know about Tom Cruise, my colleague says. *I'm telling you that he's been known to make reporters weak in the knees.* I must be making a face, because she half-smiles. *I know, I know.*

I've covered a ton of celebrities and will talk to a ton more, but she shakes her head. *You don't understand.* She is deadly serious. She is trying to help me.

Tom Cruise is not someone I've ever been particularly fascinated by or attracted to, for many reasons.

I've interviewed Val Kilmer for god's sake. He was an actual crush. I was professional and calm.

Just be prepared. He has a certain way about him.
I say, *Thank you.*
I think, *Whatever. Been there, done that.*

Tom Cruise is standing inches from my face on the most chaotic red carpet I've ever been on as of December 2008, bar the *Kingdom of Heaven* European premiere in Leicester Square. Tom's wearing that crooked aren't-I-charming grin.

He greets me by name before I can introduce myself. He employs his signature "you can't help but love me" tone. He wins. I *do* love him, and I daresay he had me at hello. "I'm Tom," he adds.

"Hi, Tom," I reply, going along with the farce and shaking his hand, probably with some palm-sweat.

He knows my name. *How does he know my name?*

His team would've had to make a list of all our names and match each one to the exact spot where each reporter is standing in order for him to greet me the way he did. The namecheck is a rare maneuver employed by somewhere in the realm of two celebrities, and I don't know who the other one is. But Tom is savvy; Tom *gets* it; perhaps Tom even enjoys seeing unglamorous journalists crumble beneath the weight of his charm.

"How are you?" he asks, as if he means it.

I am smart enough to answer briefly, because I know it's a trick. If he can get me talking, I'll have less time to pry information out of him, and then I'll have to cobble together a story out of movie posters and Tom Cruise grins instead of the zinging quotes I need.

"Great!" I almost yell. "And you?"

He opens his arms and raises them toward the heavens to let me know he's the happiest guy on planet Earth. I ask him the standard movie-related questions in rapid succession. I have become deft at four-minute journalism: *Your own stunts? Wow! The worst injury you've ever suffered for your craft? What's your favorite moment in this movie?* After he shares some mildly amusing on-set anecdotes, I hit him with the question the magazine really cares about: *What've you got up your sleeve for your daughter's sixteenth birthday?* Not controversial, but personal, and a half-decent answer will get us half a million clicks.

Instead of the generic *It's gonna be awesome, we're gonna yadda yadda,* or the icy *Not sure, next question* response we red-carpet types are used to, he comes out with something new: "Oh, that's a big one, isn't it? What was *your* sixteenth like?"

He wants to know—he *really* wants to know all about my best birthday. I tell him about how my parents were not always so organized and my sweet sixteen was unforgettable because they actually put on a party and bought a cake that had *my name* on it, evidence of advanced planning.

When the last word is out of my mouth and Tom's face comes back into focus, I realize I have fallen for his trick. It's not as if I wasn't warned.

Tom is a combo of cocky Maverick and peak Jerry Maguire, oozing charm and fixing those eyes on me. He's one of those people they invented the line "he makes you feel like you're the only person in the room" for.

I make one last attempt to save myself. "But, Tom," I ask again, "what're *you* doing for *your* daughter's sixteenth birthday?"

He answers with two good lines. It's also his wife Katie's birthday soon, and she doesn't know it, but Tom has put the *Valkyrie* cast up to something to surprise her, and he'll be doing little things just for her all week.

A publicist makes herself known. Tom finishes. "So…ha, ha, you know what I mean?" He says my name again as he departs. *Nice to meet you.*

And he is gone.

With exclusive stories about his two family birthdays, he gave me everything I need to write at least two articles, plus enough to feed a few good quotes to editors for bigger magazine stories including a potential cover. He made it fun. He treated me with dignity.

Someone near me mumbles, *How is it that he's never asked about Scientology?*

Oof. Back down to earth we go. This person is not wrong; Tom has gotten away with outlandish behavior that would've flattened a lesser mortal. He holds a powerful position, that of a near deity, in Scientology, which some countries call a cult and others recognize as a religion.

I certainly didn't ask him about it, even though his full immersion coupled with some perceived erratic behavior has been problematic for his image. Two of his most infamous missteps include the couch-jumping episode on Oprah's show, which viewers and the commentariat saw as "erratic" and "bizarre," and his disparaging psychiatry on the TODAY show, where he called Brooke Sheids "irresponsible" for using psychiatric medications to treat her post-partum depression.

He was also talking openly about Scientology in a way that must've given his public relations team hives. To *Rolling Stone* magazine, for example, he proclaimed, *Some people, well, if they don't like Scientology, well, then, fuck you. Really. Fuck you. Period.*

It was only two years before I meet him at the premiere, in 2006, when his star fell so far he wasn't even in the two-digit range anymore. He plummeted in popularity from number 11 on the most-liked celebrity list in the U.S. to a career-numbing number 197. His studio ditched him. Viacom's Sumner Redstone made a brutal statement: *His recent conduct has not been acceptable to Paramount.* (For more on that drama, I recommend reading the late sharp-tongued journalist Nikki Fink's *Deadline* piece *Who's Crazier: Viacom or Tom Cruise?* They don't write 'em like that anymore).

There are reports that Tom has benefited from low-paid or unpaid labor, such as when fellow Scientologists worked on his motorcycles. Tony Ortega, a journalist who's covered Scientology for years, claimed that members of Scientology's so-called "Sea Org" who worked on Cruise's property "were paid only about $50 a week by the church, even though their hours could reach 100 a week." Tom's net worth at the time was in the hundreds of millions.

Then there's the story of actress Nazanin Boniadi, a then-Scientologist who says she was recruited and groomed to be Tom's next girlfriend around 2005. She displeased the superstar right out of the gate. Her first transgression, as Scientology saw it, emerged the moment she first spoke to him and dared to say, *Very well done* after he was awarded Scientology's Freedom Medal of Valor. A scathing *Vanity Fair* article in 2012 explained, *Evidently that was not sufficiently doting; according to the source, her "Very well done" implied that Cruise was her junior. She spent two to three hours of her day, every day, purging herself of "negative thoughts about Tom."*

Still, things appeared to rebound quickly, according to the article. *Though the first month on the project was bliss, by the second month Boniadi was more and more often found wanting….[and], says the source, Cruise wanted Boniadi's incisor teeth filed down.*

The allegedly arranged romance didn't last long. When Tom soured on the actress, she told friends she was sad and upset about the breakup, and that's when things got really bad, according to *Vanity Fair*.

Boniadi's punishment was to scrub toilets with a toothbrush on her hands and knees, clean bathroom tiles with acid, and dig ditches in the middle of the night.

Scientology officials and Tom's reps deny she was put forward as a girlfriend for Tom or that she was punished. The organization has been accused of and/or sued for everything from child abuse to human trafficking to fraud; Scientology denies all of those allegations.

None of this stuck to Tom. He is Teflon. He is, in the year 2026, a bankable star of epic proportions. His *Mission Impossible* franchise has been a cash cow and breaks records. *Top Gun: Maverick* in 2022 was hailed as a career-best movie opening for him. In comment sections around the internet, you'll find people and bots falling over themselves to defend and minimize his deep roots within Scientology.

Why do we give Tom a pass? We know why, don't we? Watch footage of him at movie premieres, listen to him in modern interviews, and check out his recent box-office record. At the 2008 *Valkyrie* premiere, I got a sense of his charisma and the pull of that high-wattage smile and his star power. I watched him greet every single fan who came to see him, then turn back for more against the wishes of handlers trying to coax him onto the carpet, and when he said my name, I knew he was really interested in getting to know me as a human being (kidding).

He gets a pass because he might very well be one of the last great movie stars. We're not *supposed* to vet, judge, or prod these sublime beings. *Don't take away my fighter-pilot hero. Don't take away my star-packed Mission Impossible franchise, my gripping, heart-rending story, the stunts I get to watch while assuming Tom did them himself, like they're real.*

A Vox reporter examined how this happened, how the star mesmerizes us like a hypnotist.

So how did he do it? How did Tom Cruise go from America's 197th favorite celebrity to a bankable superstar once again? The answer seems to be deceptively simple: He kept working, and he stopped talking — about Scientology, and about almost everything else too.

We remember the exciting things, the positive things, because he wants us to. Tom Cruise will swoop in and save your ass from a burning car on the 405. Tom Cruise will be the only celebrity to make a point of knowing the name of a worker or a reporter or a server or assistant on the lowest rung—and then using that name through the entire interaction.

Hollywood is nothing if not a redemption arc, a never-ending story ripe for reinvention.

To me, Tom represents the extreme of the different faces celebrities put on—and the futility of trying to figure out who's behind the facade. It reminds me of life lessons from *Into the Woods: Nice is different than kind, right is different from good, and just because the wolf at the door is nice doesn't mean he's not still a wolf.*

Keep Your Finger Out of my Mouth

One of the grossest moments I'll ever experience with a celebrity happens at a 2009 Golden Globes afterparty. I'm cruising around with my tape recorder and a notebook in my handbag, talking to every relevant star I can see.

Jason Bateman has grown a beard, and it is a big deal. What's it for? Why is he suddenly hiding those dimples? *It's for a role*, he says.

He's super smiley and nice and cheeky like many of his characters. He acts like he's happy to talk to me, which is all I ask. If he wants to turn around after I'm gone and roll his eyes at his friends about how *People* magazine is interrupting him, that's his business. As long as I don't see it, it doesn't affect me. I've seen it before (not from Jason Bateman). I was at a party in London with some B and C-list British celebrities years before, and this very brash young tabloid reporter was telling a few colleagues about how *in* he is with the stars, and how friendly he is with all of them. You can see where I'm going with this. He walks up to one who's in a conversation with a circle of party guests while a couple of us sip our drinks from afar. The brash reporter chats with the celebrity like they're old pals. It's loud and features laughing and lot of *Daaahlings how aaaarrre yous*. He walks back toward us, winking smugly. Behind him, his best friend the celebrity is rolling her eyes, tilting her head subtly toward him, and shaking her head like she's telling her friends, *Ewww, sorry you had to experience that. Thank god he's gone.*

I hang out with Jason for a few minutes before I move on. Tea Leoni is laughing and super nice. Hot couple of the moment Zac Efron and Vanessa Hudgens walk through the party with a circle of protectors around them. I'm near them at the bar and before I can barely look their way, the circle makes a motion to push me back.

I know they're young, but they're also seasoned, though you wouldn't know it because their eyes are wide and they look depressingly uncomfortable.

After I've done a circle at another of the parties held at the Beverly Hilton tonight, I head outside to the breezy Los Angeles night. There, I notice a young sandy-haired guy I recognize from the hit medical drama *House*. I do a quick search to bring up his name. It's Jesse Spencer, Australian import.

I'm hanging out by the bar, and I say hi to him and his date.

Jesse smiles, ready to welcome me. Then his expression morphs into something resembling determination. He walks at me. He is in my face. I pull back slightly, but he reaches his hand out so quickly I can't stop it.

He unfurls his right index finger, and commands, "Go like this."

His mouth is open in a garish smile as he bares his teeth. His exquisite date, British singer Louise Griffiths, is giggling.

"Open ya mouth." Despite Jesse's solid Hollywood career, he retains a thick Aussie accent.

I do as ordered. I could get in trouble for disobeying a celebrity. Then, here it comes: His I-don't-know-where-it's-been fingernail scrapes against my front tooth. He pulls his finger back and shows me a disgusting fleck of green. "Ya got spinach in ya teeth. It's OK. Don't be embarrassed. Someone's gotta tell ya."

He smiles, but it is only partially for my benefit. This, I suspect, was more for his own entertainment than to save me from the humiliation of approaching Robert Downey Jr. with a slick of emerald slime on my incisor.

The interview itself, which I feel I have to conduct to save face, is unremarkable because I can't get over the sensation of his finger in my mouth. I find the ladies' room and rinse for a few minutes with vodka after, gargling and spitting into the sink.

Oscar the Grouch

My first Academy Awards red carpet is as chaotic as it appears on television.

It's a two-lane road covered in crimson, a traffic jam of beautiful people trying to pretend they're not jockeying for attention while those left holding the hats and purses of the beautiful people are repeatedly pushed or rudely told to *Get out of the way!*

Brad and Angelina are here, he nominated for *Benjamin Button* and she for *Changeling*, and they're talking about their kids being at home "throwing spaghetti" while they have a date night. I don't get near them. *People* has a certain L.A.-based team that covers the Academy Awards, and they dress up and watch from the pressroom or get a great spot on the red carpet. I'm shoved somewhere in the back, but I don't mind. It's exhausting up front.

After I watch Sarah Jessica Parker drag an uncomfortable-looking Matthew Broderick by the hand (literally) into the theatre, I find the shuttle to Elton John's watch party.

It starts well. I'm served a vanilla bean lemon martini by a friendly young fellow. He asks about me, and I tell him I'm from a big magazine. I shouldn't think of him as a bartender, he tells me. He's an actor and a part-time model, and he wants to be friends. We swap numbers.

Everything is purple and white and there's a celebrity at every turn. I approach my assigned table and see an imposing, dark-haired actor I recognize from TV and movies; I like him in *Law & Order: Criminal Intent*, and I've known him forever as *Sex and the City*'s Mr. Big, aka Big, aka Chris Noth.

I find I'm seated next to him, so I plop myself down. I situate my drink, my handbag, my phone; then I introduce myself. His face darkens when I mention the magazine. He utters some version of *Oh, GREAT*.

If I wasn't running out of fucks to give, I would've been hurt, but I need to know why about everything.

"What's the problem?" I ask, as if we're old friends. He is surprised at my bluntness. I don't have the patience for such bad manners. At least *fake* it when you meet your tablemate, man. Anyway, Mrs. Big leans across him and says hello. She's got a healthy glow, excellent manners, and is half his size.

"Your magazine misquoted me," Chris grumbles. "Got me in trouble." He's unapologetically grouchy, but doesn't want to give details. I'm dubious we "misquoted" him, partly because I don't remember the last time we wrote about him.

"That's not like them," I say. "We're usually a very nice magazine. Sorry about that. *I* don't misquote people, so don't worry."

He says something along the lines of, *Grumble mumble grumble*, and picks at his salad, then takes a drink of his something-or-other on the rocks. In the end, I warm him up and he becomes talkative and interesting, and his girlfriend, Tara, is the one with the manners and sparkling personality. At one point, Big even brings me a cocktail.

After dinner, the price of a chat with Sharon Stone is a dance. She's got short, spiky platinum-blonde hair, the deep smile lines she's had since before *Basic Instinct,* and a permanent smirk. I conduct an interview while bopping with her to the live band, at which point I learn she is not modest about her work with AIDS.

"I've been at it sooo long, my dear," she yells over the music. "I've been an AIDS worker since you were in diapers."

I hit her with a question from my Apropos of Nothing list. She's having nothing to do with it. "I have to ask how you stay looking so young," I say with long-practiced amazement. (It's important to try to look young, because looking your age is shameful, especially if you're over twenty-five).

"They've raised $3.8 million for AIDS tonight, baby. Just write that," she orders me, throwing her head back as she gyrates to the music. She's extremely hot in person, and she makes me chuckle. She's come to this party with a girlfriend's husband as her date, and all three of us unpack that. The wife is glad he's out of the house, is the gist. Unbothered that he's partying with Sharon Stone.

I bid them adieu and set off to look for an A-lister to interview. I pass a Godiva stand and pop a dusted cappuccino truffle in my mouth. I check my teeth and keep moving. I run into Angie Harmon, who's sweet and kind and funny. I love her in *Law & Order* and *Rizzoli & Isles,* just for starters.

Because it's the early 2000s, we talk about bodies and in particular, bodies after baby because she has a two-month-old at home. She's the only woman I can remember interviewing who makes me feel short. She says nice things to me, and we have a real talk about fitness. It's like speaking to an old friend.

I find Tia Carrere, who many people recognize from *Wayne's World* and *True Lies*, and have the same kind of frank, real, fun conversation, and I'm expected to ask her about her underwear from the Apropos of Nothing list, and she gamely goes with it. A sweet, funny, smart, nice woman.

I'm on a roll. Everyone's nice and normal and professional apart from Mr. Big, who I thawed enough with my bluntly questionable charms to end on good terms.

The awards ceremony over now, so the big names should start filtering in soon.

On my way to find actual stars, I see a potential warm-up act. Gordon Ramsay is sitting with his wife and some British guy I think I recognize from TV but can't place. No one at the magazine will print any quotes from him because he's not buzzy enough, but at least it'll show how hard I'm working tonight.

"Hey, Gordon," I grin at the British TV chef by way of a greeting, telling him who I am and who I write for. "What can we expect from your upcoming show? More swearing?"

"Cum, bollocks, shit, and piss," the guy sitting next to Gordon barks bizarrely in an English accent.

Tana, Gordon's long-suffering wife, glares at me. Gordon ignores me and says something to the weird guy, who I realize I *do* recognize as an aging bit-part actor. "You're Max Beesley," I blurt, though he's probably well aware of who he is.

I let it roll off and lean in. "Hi, Tana, I'd love to talk to you, too! For our Oscars issue. What can we expect on this season's show?"

"You've got a *ladder* in your tights," Gordon sneers out of nowhere as Tana says nothing. "Now, will you fuck off and fix it?"

The sweary actor with him snickers like a playground bully, a sort of laugh/snort, and Tana grins like the girlfriend of the head bully who thinks she's cool by association. I feel like I've been sucker-punched about this alleged "ladder," which in the U.S. is what we call a "run." I doubt very much my run-resistant tights have any sort of tear in them, but I can't be sure.

Talk about apropos of nothing. *Good gracious, what is happening?*

"I hate you," I reply in a deferential *ha ha, you got me* sort of tone, still trying to chalk this up to that famous British dark humor I loved so much when I lived in the UK. Truth is, I'm back on the school playground, powerless to do anything but laugh along at my own expense.

"It's not very nice to walk around with a ladder in your tights," Gordon keeps going, louder this time, pointing toward my upper thigh area. He means to humiliate and demean me, and it's working. I want to fight back or run, but I'm paralyzed.

"I have one? I do? Do I really?" My voice is nervously high-pitched. It's happening so fast there's no time to process how to handle it, or get out of it gracefully, so I revert to a sort of trauma response. Fight, flight, flee or fawn. I flip from fight to fawn, because the first one just made it worse.

"Yes!" Gordon yells. A thick swoop of hair stands up at the front of his head like the comb of a colossal blond rooster.

"Where?" I grab the front of my stretchy dress and pull down, trying to get it closer to my knees so he stops looking up my skirt.

"Up the back! You can't see it, it's right up inside your thigh. I'm being polite, and you tell me, 'I hate you.'" He's talking fast, in a cruel staccato. "Of course you can't see it, because it's right up the side of your bum."

Gordon takes a crooked finger and sends it in that general direction, though he stops short of touching my clothing or me. This hits me hard, I think, because it's sexual harassment, a heartbeat away from assault.

Don't piss off the celebrities. "I take it back," I say deferentially. "I don't hate you." *Ha, ha.*

Gordon decides it's time to tell me about the show, which he does in two monotone lines when all I want to do is retreat. At the end he barks, "Now—go sort your ladder out."

I walk away as fast as I can. This is not the worst thing that's ever happened to me. *Why am I so freaked out?* I head to the bathroom, sit on the toilet, and, shaking and breathing heavily, Google *Gordon Ramsay + misogyny*. An encyclopedia of dickheadedness pops up. He's allegedly cheated on his wife and publicly demeaned women.

I'm not the first woman he's deliberately humiliated on the job, and I surely won't be the last. The woman who revealed she was his "mistress" (her word) for years, Sarah Symonds, calls him a "bully, cheat, liar and serial philanderer." The *Daily Mail* in 2026 will give Symonds a platform to say she's *…traumatised by the alleged affair and the fallout that followed.*

Ramsay has repeatedly denied ever cheating on his wife with Symonds, who also says of a documentary that portrays him in glowing terms, *I am trying to heal, and then this appears everywhere. It makes me so angry.*

The thing is, I'm 99% sure my magazine has not written about this alleged affair, alluded to it, or amplified it, because Gordon is simply not that interesting to readers right now. I don't think they wrote about him being arrested and charged with driving under the influence of excess alcohol in London (the case went away due to evidentiary issues, according to reports) or his various court appearances for allegedly not paying taxes in two countries, or being arrested and cautioned for gross indecency in a public toilet at a London Tube station, which his reps called a "drunken jape."

The People, a British tabloid, exposed Gordon's 1993 arrest decades later, with the reporter writing, *When we asked loudmouth Ramsay about it, he was lost for words for once. "I'll call you back," he spluttered.*

Later, his PR people tried to gloss over the episode, as a "drunken jape" and "horsing around" in a statement they released after The People revealed it.

The reporter checked in with a legal expert, who said, *…gross indecency could involve acts such as oral sex or mutual masturbation.*

Meanwhile, I'm simply asking innocent, arguably dull questions, and Gordon goes apeshit.

I collect myself in the stall, freshen up, then make my way to the garden and outdoor bar for some air, hoping to catch up on my notes before the big stars arrive from the Kodak Theatre. The only butt-sized space left to sit is next to a smoking celebrity. I approach to see if he's up for a chat, though I fear this guy could be worse than the last.

"Hi, Simon," I greet him, tell him who I am.

He pats the space next to him. "Come. Sit."

I perch on the glorified ottoman, one butt cheek threatening to slide off.

"How's it going?" Simon Cowell asks me.

"Ah," I sigh. "Gordon Ramsay told me I have a ladder in my tights. I don't, though, do I?"

"No," he agrees. "You don't." He makes a face like maybe he knows what Gordon's like.

I turn on my recorder and fight an odd need to yawn. "What brings you to Elton's party tonight?"

"This is the only one I had an invitation to. That's why I'm here." He sucks in some nicotine.

Someone else stops by and we hang out for a bit. At one point I ask Simon about Terri Seymour, the British TV personality he was in a relationship with. "I'm sorry to hear about your breakup. How are things with you two?"

"We arrived together," he shrugs. "You know what? Always remain friends with your ex

girlfriends."

He seems happy to share, so I ask for more intel. "Are you dating again?"

"No."

"Really? Why not?"

He pauses, takes a drag.

"Are you coming on to me? Are you saying you'll have sex with me tonight?"

I blink. This is a new one. But I was born with a dry sense of humor, so I go with it.

I reply, "One-hundred-percent yes. Now what are you going to do?"

"Okay, you win. I'm now going to have to have sex with you."

The tone is light. It's risky and a bit weird, but it doesn't bother me. It's late, the cocktails are flowing, the party is raging, and Simon is trying to be funny. We part ways and later, after I send in my file, leaving out the embarrassing Ramsay attack, a colleague in London who's on the massive email chain replies to me.

SIMON COWELL!!!!

I head back toward the entrance to the party, not far from where the red carpet ends. I'm tired, and I'm still lacking A-list interviews.

Someone I recognize is coming through the grand entrance, the huge, gaping mouth of the party.

She is a sight for sore eyes. My face lights up and I spread my arms ready to welcome her to my country, my city. I think of all the things we already have to catch up on.

Hey! Here we are again. Victoria Beckham's here. Gordon Ramsay is an asshole. Which big names are you looking for?

"Hey!" I say, nice and loud so she can hear me.

It's my friend Mallory. But she looks past me like I'm not there, and I, still confused and clueless, say, "Hi! I'm so happy you're here."

She gives me a side-eye and a weird, terse, forced *hello* like you'd give an overzealous and stalkerish stranger on the street. She disappears into the party.

My face falls and I lower my arms as I watch her go. After the initial pang of hurt and shock, I find it incredibly bizarre and try to figure out what the hell just happened.

I get back to work, and as the night unfolds, it occurs to me—perhaps later than it should have—that she was probably flown to L.A. specifically to sneak into this party.

She can't be pegged as the tabloid gossip reporter she is, and she can't be seen with or associated with a reporter like me.

Still, there is never a catch-up after that, a nudge-nudge-wink-wink, a follow-up email. She ignores me throughout the party, pretends she doesn't know me, and we never interact again.

At least we'll have Lisbon. And Rome, and Windsor.

Nothing is real in this business. It's all smoke and mirrors, and an illusion.

End notes: Chris Noth, the Yale-educated actor I viewed as my grouchy yet ultimately amusing tablemate at Elton's party, turned out to be a card-carrying asshole. For starters, he admitted to cheating on his lovely wife, but then, in 2021, multiple women shared their stories of being allegedly sexually assaulted by him. One, in recounting her alleged rape to *The Hollywood Reporter*, said, *It was very painful and I yelled out, 'Stop!' And he didn't.*

Chris denied all the allegations, and in his one interview on the revelations in 2023, he said, *I strayed on my wife, and it's devastating to her and not a very pretty picture. What it isn't is a crime.*

I have trouble watching anything featuring his face now, including my favorite *Law & Order* franchise, *Criminal Intent*, and when an episode aired recently featuring a guest-star who came forward and described an uncomfortable experience with him on set, I had to turn it off.

Meanwhile, back at the actual awards ceremony, which I barely watched due to working the party, things were getting tense. This was the year in which the Academy

Awards decided to poke the beast and to make sure *no one* forgot Brangelina's messy origin story.

Rumors had been flying for weeks that Jennifer Aniston would be a presenter that night, and what do you know— she turned up. As she joked around with co-presenter Jack Black, cameras panned to Angelina and Brad. She was laughing. He was…smiling uncomfortably? In some people's opinion.

Panning to a top actor's ex-husband who's here with the significant other who may or may not have had a role in how and when a marriage ended, was a cheap move, many said later. It felt more like sensationalist reality television than an awards show meant to recognize extraordinary work.

As one reporter said later, *I have never, ever heard as big a gasp in the press room as when the TV telecast cut to a reaction shot of Angelina Jolie and Brad Pitt during Jennifer Aniston's presenting gig.*

Jen brought John Mayer as her date, and they were placed only a few seats away from Brad and Angie. Still, the four of them appeared happy and well adjusted. Then again, three of them are award-winning actors.

The Dehumanizing of Jennifer Aniston

S peaking of John and Jen, one night I see them together at the Sunset Tower Hotel's bar and restaurant, which is one of Jen's favorite hangouts.

I'm at a little table in the lounge section, near the hotel entrance, next to Vin Diesel and an older woman sipping tea. It's fascinating to hear his voice in the wild. It appears that in his private life, it is notably different. A bit higher, not so gravelly.

Sometime after nine p.m., a tiny figure in a casual black dress steps out of the restaurant and into the darkened lobby.

Jen knows everyone is watching her. Even though the place isn't packed, even though the patrons are Hollywood bigwigs or at least mediumwigs who aren't here to starwatch, she knows she's the main attraction everywhere she goes. As always, I'm struck by how little she is. When I describe celebrities as tiny, I don't mean skinny or short. I mean compact. I'm not alone in making this observation. Someone once described film and TV actors as Bonsai trees, and I understand the comparison.

Jen is half smiling and staring straight ahead, head held high, striding confidently toward the exit.

John Mayer is several feet behind her, be-bopping and uttering jazzy *doo doo dah* sounds as he snaps and looks around to see who notices him half-dancing his way through the lobby. He makes eye contact with me as I try oh-so-hard to appear like I couldn't care less that they're walking two feet away from me.

I never forgot that moment, because John came off like an unruly child, and she came off like his minder. Yep, I know it was only for a few moments, and I know it doesn't mean this was their dynamic as a couple, and I'm not saying I think John Mayer is or was immature.

This was my reaction to what I saw, period.

There is a line that shouldn't be crossed when reporting on celebrities. Behind that line are things like announcing pregnancies before the star reveals them—or any personal health information, for that matter.

With Jennifer Aniston, since the day she became a mega-celebrity in the nineties with the premiere of *Friends*, the line is crossed like Abbey Road in tourist season. She was one of the women regularly targeted by a certain blogger. I don't want to namecheck the scumbag who should be ignored into oblivion, but you know the guy who ran a blog in the early 2000s, the one who was known for his derogatory nicknames and humiliating "doodles" on paparazzi photos. Women were his target, and he took great joy in drawing penises, semen and other disgusting imagery across their mouths, faces and bodies. His rampant bullying, harassment, and misogyny was often aimed at stars like Lindsay Lohan, Paris Hilton, and Mischa Barton.

He'd often target Jen. One of his favorite nicknames for her was Chinnifer Maniston.

So, one day when she bumped into him, she calmly and kindly, in a way he did not deserve, held up a mirror to his behavior. As she tells it, *I ran into [gross misogynist] in a garage…I pulled up and we were sort of scoping each other out as I was pulling the car up. I just rolled down the window and I was like, "Hi." And he went, "Hi." We stood there like two deer in headlights. And I just said, "Come here. Just talk to me for a second." It was one of those great moments. It was a lovely meeting and I was just like, "Why are you so mean?"*

In a sort of meta-infinite-celebrity-cancellation circle, Jen reveals the details of this encounter on alleged bully Ellen DeGeneres's talk show in 2011, when Ellen is still riding high as daytime TV's Queen of Nice.

I was in the room for one example of one of the worst things Jennifer Aniston was ever subjected to in public as far as I ever saw or read (obviously only she knows what the actual worst is and where it happened). To this day I want to put the man in the hotseat and explain to him the reasons he sucks.

I'm at a presser in Conference Room A at a perfectly fine hotel in L.A. Jennifer Aniston and several other cast members take their places at a long table at the front of the room, ready to promote Christmas blockbuster *Marley & Me* (if you're sensitive like me, I'd check the website *Does the Dog Die?* before watching this one).

Jen appears confident and relaxed. She likes to toss her hair. I look around the room; interestingly, there are a lot of us misfits in this line of work, a lot of non-fashion-conscious, uncool, unglamorous people. Not for the first time, I wonder if the celebrities keep notes on *us*, and if so, what do they say?

We have been warned not to ask any personal questions. The press conference starts with queries about training the yellow Labradors who play Marley. A relatable exchange takes place, where the trainer replies, *We didn't train them. We did what I call anti training—we just encouraged very bad behavior.*

And my old pal Owen Wilson from Portugal chimes in, *I think you worked with my dog!*

People are raising their hands, and the microphone queen hands it to one of the professional junketeers (these are people who get travel and expenses paid for in exchange for writing about a movie). This man takes the mic and asks something along the lines of,

Jennifer, do you think you're really the right actress for the role of a mom considering you've never been a mother yourself?...This is a traditional wife and mother role. Some actors will say, 'I never could have played this role if I wasn't a mother.' Do you think you should have waited until you had your own kids?

He manages to twist the knife in two directions: Assuming a woman intends to have children, *must* bear children, and then ambushing her with a slap in the face telling her she isn't worthy of playing a role if she isn't a mother in real life.

I gasp audibly. Everyone is sitting quietly like good little junketeers. I'm disgusted, and I send the grey-haired man angry thoughts via an evil eye directed at the back of his head. For all we know, Jennifer is pregnant now, or was pregnant last week but lost the baby. And she has to face these humiliating, insulting questions from creepy men. For all we know, she's been trying to get pregnant for years.

Jen heroically stops herself from rolling her eyes and/or leaping off her chair and wrapping her delicate hands around his pencil neck.

I have been told by journalists who've interviewed her one-on-one more than once that she's known for her ability to skillfully respond to even the most invasive, surprising, and/or rude questions. (This also means that when she says the very rare sensational thing, like when she talked about Brad Pitt's missing sensitivity chip, she knows exactly what she's doing). She shows that skill today. She replies to the man *without* the derision he deserves:

"No! I wanted to be in the movie. I have been pregnant in so many movies it's ridiculous. Oh my god. The reason I wanted to be in the movie is it wasn't the girl trying to get the guy or the guy trying to get the girl…and then you get the movie where they ride off in the sunset. This is sort of the sequel to that."

I'm not on the panel, but I wish I was; there's no limit to the clapbacks I want to throw at this man. Let's start with this one: Owen Wilson plays the husband and father in this film. OWEN DOES NOT HAVE CHILDREN. Yet no one asked him, or even *hinted* that he shouldn't play a father. This year Robert Downey Jr. starred in the blockbuster *Iron Man*. Should he play the role of a brilliant scientist and superhero if he's never *been* a superhero? *The Dark Knight* was the number one movie of 2008. How dare Christian Bale play Batman when he doesn't own bat ears and can't bench press a thousand pounds or run as fast as an Olympian!

Within a few years, Jennifer would reveal publicly that, indeed, during this time in her life she was undergoing fertility treatments and enduring the agony and hellacious, life-interrupting, waiting game that goes along with it. And part of me still wishes I'd told that man to go fuck himself, but we all know that would never happen in a Beverly Hills hotel with celebrities and a bunch of journalists in the room.

My career would have been over. And I wasn't ready for that.

Not yet, anyway.

In 2016, Jen would reveal her feelings about all of this. She took the highly unusual step of writing a strongly worded op-ed in the *Huffington Post* lambasting this woman-shaming culture and slamming the celebrity/entertainment media for their (our) invasiveness and framing of women.

One passage read, *From years of experience, I've learned tabloid practices, however dangerous, will not change, at least not any time soon. What can change is our awareness and reaction to the toxic messages buried within these seemingly harmless stories served up as truth and shaping our ideas of who we are. We get to decide how much we buy into what's being served up, and maybe someday the tabloids will be forced to see the world through a different, more humanized lens because consumers have just stopped buying the bullshit.*

I recommend reading the whole thing. It was, in my opinion, a well thought-out feminist dissertation arguing that how we treat her in person and in print matters. How we portray her to tens of millions of people reading these magazines and blogs matters, because it affects all of us.

The problem was that many of her complaints are about things she participates in with her whole chest, like "racy" Smartwater ads where she's ultra-thin, lounging "suggestively" in bed, indicating she's on board with the notion that "sex sells," according to the New York *Post*. The paper flat-out called her a hypocrite and ran through everything she'd ever done that they perceived as asking for it:

As for what she decries as "the warped way we calculate a woman's worth," look no further than another Aniston business venture: her contract, rumored to be worth eight figures, with the skincare brand Aveeno, which has resulted in her wrinkle-free face staring out of billboards and magazines the world over.

And round we go, and nothing changes. Can we just…stop? I'm too old for this crap. No one knows how to talk about celebrities normally anymore.

Of course, back then, I got in on it too, and that fact annoys me to this day. I accepted an assignment to write a *Newsweek* op-ed about Jennifer's essay back when the publication was still a semi-respectable newsmagazine. In my piece, I criticized the actress for complaining about the way she, and by extension women and women in Hollywood, are treated and spoken about and demeaned.

My argument, as it was then and continues to be, is that every cog in this machine works together to maintain the status quo of sexism and misogyny via Hollywood and fame in general. I suggested Jen cannot have it both ways; she cannot put forward a carefully curated image of a perfect life and hair and skin and body, selling one beauty standard to a public who is then enticed and buys into it, and then complain that people scrutinize and criticize her for it.

But she and other celebrities and influencers don't do this alone. Everyone who churns out or consumes content like this is part of it, and we all have a role in keeping the wheels of this toxic machine turning and spewing out girls (people) with low confidence, body dysmorphia, depression and eating disorders.

At the time, I was too close to it to see that Jen's very personal op-ed, a first for her, was a response to something I wrote.

Jen published her heartfelt article on July 12, eleven days after my own letter calling out the industry went viral. At the time I thought, *Yep, she read my letter, and what an interesting coincidence.*

But…no. Not a coincidence. Her choice to speak out was clearly a direct result of my letter.

Looking back now, it's obvious. In my mini-memoir *Red Carpet Regret*, I wrote,

I've survived something like eight rounds of layoffs where talented colleagues were bitch-slapped into oblivion and, I hope, will never give their nights, weekends, relationships and sanity again to keep up **with an email chain about whether Jennifer Aniston is pregnant at 47 because of those tummy photos and what kind of mom will she be, when really she just had an extra burrito at lunch;** *but oh, wait, the rep says it's just a rumor so there's no story this week after all.*

In her essay, Jen wrote, *I have grown tired of being part of this narrative. Yes, I may become a mother someday, and since I'm laying it all out there, if I ever do, I will be the first to let you know. But I'm not in pursuit of motherhood because I feel incomplete in some way, as our celebrity news culture would lead us all to believe. I* **resent being made to feel "less than" because my body is changing and/or I had a burger for lunch and was photographed from a weird angle** *and therefore deemed one of two things: "pregnant" or "fat."*

It should have ended there. I regret taking the bait and writing a third piece for *Newsweek*. Not because I minimized some of Jen's well-made points, but because being part of the problem is not what *I'm* trying to do. Jennifer Aniston doesn't care what I write. But *I* do. Blame is useless. Keep your own side of the street clean. That's what I've been trying to do in the years since I wrote that letter, and since Jen wrote hers. We were both sides of the same coin.

To this day I wish I'd said nothing. *Newsweek* didn't even pay me for the work.

Side note on Ellen DeGeneres: I interviewed her and her wife, actress Portia de Rossi, one night, and Ellen did most of the talking. I was doubled over with laughter, tears falling down my cheeks as she told a story about how she was on the highway at night and saw a raggedy, skinny stray dog on the side of the road. She pulled over and beckoned, cooed, called out to the poor creature. She did everything she could to coax the animal into her car. People were honking and flashing their headlights as they sped by, but Ellen stubbornly refused to leave the dog at risk for being hit by a car or left to starve.

And then, Ellen said, it got closer, and I saw what everyone was trying to warn me about: it was a coyote. I'd been trying to get a COYOTE into my car.

She was one of the most fun stars I ever interviewed. As everyone knows now, the staff on her talk shows say she was horrible to work for. These reports have been as rampant in the blind items space as Harvey Weinstein's sexual assaults over the years. That whole time, the Queen of Nice was something else entirely.

Then again, Ellen apparently had a feud with Gordon Ramsay and banned him from her show, so that leaves me a little like…the enemy of my enemy is my friend?

Nah.

I continue to be Team They're All As Bad As Each Other.

A Low Julia

My one experience with Julia Roberts is extremely unsurprising. We're at a presser to promote beloved director Garry Marshall's *Valentine's Day*, a turgid cringefest of a movie where Jessica Biel plays a publicist who eats donuts while running on a treadmill and yelling at clients. In Conference Room B at the Beverly Wilshire hotel, I get to spend time observing Julia rule a room.

The organizers managed to contain the egos of three rows of celebrities in one place (they had high ceilings). Julia sits in the top back corner of the stadium-style seating, grinning like the Cheshire Cat. Her cackling movie laugh drives me bonkers. Below her are some of Hollywood's hottest men, including Bradley Cooper and Ashton Kutcher. On the lowest tier, Jessica Alba is flanked by a dimpled Jen Garner and the legendary Shirley MacLaine. We're still waiting for a couple of people as Julia banters with the cast.

Here comes Jessica Biel, who smiles shyly and takes her seat. I am not recording yet so I have to paraphrase what Julia says as Jessica settles in: *LOOK at those cheekbones. Oh, wow. What a beauty. Are you seeing this? Isn't she gorgeous?* Julia asks the room, forcing everyone in the bleachers and on the floor to agree with her. The other two American beauties, Jessica Alba and Jennifer Garner, sit quietly, looking mildly embarrassed and nodding with frozen smiles. I cringe, then watch Julia. She knows exactly what she's doing.

As the presser gets underway, Julia sits above us all like a one-woman Statler and Waldorf, quipping and making cracks. She gives the room what they want: relief from boredom. Shirley MacLaine looks over at Jennifer Garner and Jessica Biel sitting next to each other, and says, "What do all the women up here *eat*? I'd like to have a rundown—do you diet all the time? And is it worth it?"

Not one to let the spotlight veer off of her for long, Julia pipes up with a smirk and a glint in her eye, "You girls *are* slim…"

While Jessica Biel doesn't say much, Jennifer apologizes for being thin, saying breastfeeding keeps her fit and promising she'll "puff back up" soon enough.

The entire set-up is frankly an uncomfortable scene that doesn't allow for any depth (I know, I know) or complex discussion of the film or what Garry Marshall thinks of it. There's such a thing as too many big stars.

I've tried to avoid seeing Julia in anything since the T-shirt incident just a few years before this press conference.

Backstory: Julia met married cameraman Danny Moder while filming *The Mexican* in the year 2000 and, legend has it, she found him "yummy." They got together and went public with their romance.

Danny's wife of four years, Vera, was hounded by the media when this coupling was revealed, and after a while, she talked, telling a newspaper that *I'll never be able to forgive Julia. She's a husband stealer.* Vera reminded Julia through the press that how you get him is how you lose him.

I never found any quotes from Julia—who was in a relationship with *Law & Order* hunk Benjamin Bratt at the time—explicitly denying an affair with Danny while he was still married in name and in spirit, but she did give a vague explanation about how they each dealt with their responsibilities before getting together, whatever that means.

So far, so Hollywood.

What Julia Roberts did next is so beyond the pale, so petty, that I cannot be convinced that she is any kind of decent human being. She did this in 2002 when she was a grown-ass woman in her thirties, and it was a planned, deliberate act.

What happened?

Apparently, Danny's wife Vera wasn't giving up her husband fast enough for Julia. So the extremely famous actress, knowing she'd be followed and photographed by paparazzi, went out for coffee wearing a white T-shirt on which she'd hand-scrawled the words *A Low Vera*. She wore it with a gigantic smile and a smirk.

I shudder when I picture Julia making that shirt, bent over the white tee, cackling as she carefully drew out each letter, so proud of her clever play on words. *Get it? A Low Vera=Aloe Vera*. It's genius, Julia.

Worse, she later defended the infantile move on the then-biggest talk show in the country.

"It was private," she told Oprah of her motives, apparently lacking any modicum of the self-awareness required to understand she herself had made a point of doing this in *public*, and added, "I stand by my T-shirt."

I can't begin to fathom what kind of entitlement you must possess to think a fellow woman owes you access to her husband at the speed with which you demand it, and what kind of difficulty you must have regulating your emotions to serve up your drama to the public at the expense of the woman whose husband you're now living with.

Leaving Los Angeles

During my time in L.A., Michael Jackson dies. Certain people who were close to him, I'm told, are requesting and receiving briefcases full of cash in exchange for newspaper interviews.

Patrick Swayze dies. Farrah Fawcett dies. Ryan O'Neal, a handsome charmer who was possibly one of the worst human beings in Hollywood, is left behind. I found out things about their relationship I wish I never knew, specifically about the way he treated Farrah, for starters.

Brittany Murphy dies young, from a vague, suspicious, ominous thing involving prescription drugs and pneumonia. The husband she leaves behind is a grifter, a rapist (a former girlfriend will reveal this later), a liar, a thief, and one of the creepiest people I've ever covered. One day, in between calling around to figure out who this guy was—beyond a British man called Simon Monjack who was largely blamed in Hollywood circles for Brittany's decline in career and health—I get a call from a private number.

For reporters, blocked calls can be a source, a tip, a celebrity; it could also be someone I *really* don't want to talk to. This person had called me something like seven times in the past day but left no voicemail.

I answer this one, finally, out of curiosity.

"Hello," a man breathes heavily down the phone like his mouth is too close to the speaker. "I hear you're talking to people about me? I'm here. You can ask *me*."

He has an English accent. I know who it is even though we've never spoken, and my adrenaline whips up. It's

February 4, about six weeks after Brittany died. I'd been reporting on her death since day one, and almost immediately there were suspicions about her odd husband: *What did she see in him? Was he controlling her? He was in the house when she died. Could he….did he…what the hell happened to her?* I worked over Christmas. It remains one of the most bizarre stories I've ever worked on. To this day, the cause of death makes the gut tingle: Pneumonia, with anemia and prescription drugs as contributing factors—*that*'s what kills a thirty-two-year-old who presumably had access to the best medical care?

"Who is this?" I ask, knowing that will bother him. It does.

There is a pause and he grudgingly drawls, "It's Simon Monnnjaaaackk. Are you writing nasty things or nice things about me?" He speaks languidly, almost slurring.

I reply, "I'm a journalist, so I write about what people are saying; I'm just writing about what's news. How is Brittany's mom doing?"

"Not so good. Who are you talking to about me? Do any of these people even *know* me?"

Simon wants information from me that I'm not giving him; I ask him about Brittney's health and about his obviously fake "foundation" that's been collecting money in her name, and he, in turn, gives me very little back.

He will die a few months later from pneumonia and anemia.

I don't know what else to say about my time in L.A. that's particularly interesting. It's one star after another. Jack Black's sweet and self-deprecating and funny, and he says in all seriousness when I interview him at a weekend premiere, *This probably isn't where you want to be on a Sunday,* and I reply, *I get to talk to Jack Black. It's not all bad.*

Meeting Angelina Jolie is like getting an audience with royalty, and she's not cold but not warm either, kind of detached and above it.

I get to observe and meet Joan Rivers as a mother and a grandmother when I visit Melissa Rivers' Pacific Palisades home several times to talk to about her controversial turn on *Celebrity Apprentice* in 2009.

Joan bursts in like a hurricane, bustling around the kitchen in a fur coat, getting a drink from the fridge, talking about the grandson's tennis lessons in that *voice*, giving me a quick hello, not bothered I'm there, just living her life.

Charlize Theron is regal and serious, which I like. We talk about domestic violence. She lives with trauma that the public knows about; most of us don't show the world ours, but she does, and it's a lot to hold. Her mother killed her father in the family home in Johannesburg, South Africa in 1991. As Charlize's father was shooting through the bedroom door where she and her mother, Gerda, were hunkering down, Gerda shot back to save herself and her fifteen-year-old daughter. *In self-defense, she ended the threat,* Charlize would later say of her mother's fierce protective instinct.

Mark Wahlburg is tired and appears to have zero sense of humor about himself. I conduct a phone interview with him and ask how he liked the recent send-up on *Saturday Night Live,* in which Andy Samberg took on the soft, ethereal voice Wahlberg displays in various film roles. You know

I'm no Andy Samberg fan (bar some classic SNL Digital Shorts) but it was a pretty good imitation, pretty innocent.

Nah. I didn't think it was funny. Mark's tone says he hated it. I ask, What was it? Did it do you a disservice?

No, I'm not offended by it, he says. I just didn't think it was funny.

The tone says otherwise.

I was never fond of Marky Mark. People from Massachusetts never forgot his multiple racist attacks that left permanent physical and emotional scars on his victims. Per the Associated Press, *Court documents in the 1986 attack identify Wahlberg among a group of white boys who harassed a school group as they were leaving Savin Hill Beach in Dorchester, a mixed but segregated Boston neighborhood that had seen racial tensions during the years the city was under court-ordered school integration.*

The boys chased the Black children down the street, repeatedly shouting "n———-" and hurling rocks until an ambulance driver intervened. Wahlberg was 15 at the time.

Mark launched another brutal assault the following year. Reports the Associated Press,

In 1988, Wahlberg, then 16, attacked two Vietnamese men while trying to steal beer near his Dorchester home. According to the sentencing memorandum, he confronted Thanh Lam, a Vietnamese immigrant, as he was getting out of his car with two cases of beer. Wahlberg called Lam a "Vietnamese f——— s—-" and beat him over the head with a five-foot wooden stick until Lam lost consciousness and the rod broke in two.

In 2014, Mark, who allegedly hadn't made any approaches, apologies or amends to the Boston-area Vietnamese advocacy groups let alone his actual victims, filed an application with the Massachusetts Board of

Pardons to get his criminal record erased for his 1988 assault.

He did this because his burger restaurant chain needed a liquor license and he was afraid his conviction would harm his chances. The blowback was swift.

Why, one Asian-American advocacy organization asked, *should someone who has done nothing to support his victims or atone for his crimes get a pardon?*

One of Mark's victims, Kristyn Atwood, agreed: *I don't really care who he is. It doesn't make him any exception. If you're a racist, you're always going to be a racist. And for him to want to erase it I just think it's wrong.*

In 2016, Mark dropped the petition for a pardon and said on a Toronto Film Festival panel that going after that pardon in the first place wasn't really his idea, or his fault.

I didn't need that, I spent 28 years righting the wrong. I didn't need a piece of paper to acknowledge it. I was kind of pushed into doing it, I certainly didn't need to or want to relive that stuff over again.

Careful What You Wish For

I never settle properly or comfortably into the L.A. office. I'm relieved when, two years after stepping off the plane from Zurich, my husband is offered a job back in New England.

I'm ready to go. I'm ready to try *People*'s New York Bureau. I'm looking forward to covering more breaking news and human-interest (regular people) stories. I need a break from the Hollywood bullshit.

I move back to New England, a place I'd done everything I could to leave when I was eighteen, and I'm offered Monday shifts in the New York office. After eight years working for *People*, I'm finally ensconced in the home office, the legendary Time & Life building on Sixth Avenue, the one the *Wall Street Journal* called a "Mad-Men era Landmark," the one immortalized in Ben Stiller's *The Secret Life of Walter Mitty*. Here is where journalism legends were born, where Henry Luce's vision of a modern newsmagazine took off, where cocktail carts were wheeled through on closing nights. Where flagship publications like *Time* magazine, *Fortune*, *Life*, *Sports Illustrated* and, starting in the 1970s, *People* magazine, hooked millions of readers. I feel a buzz in its halls, like I'm inhaling the history of this career I've chosen.

The bad news is my commute is two-and-a-half hours door-to-door. To make the morning meeting, I rise at five a.m.

After a few months, I bow out of those shifts. Most evenings run late, and a five-hour round-trip commute isn't worth one day's pay.

I start working from home, making trips into New York City when needed. The celebrities aren't going to interview themselves.

We Meet Again

I'm excited to interview Val Kilmer once more, because whatever his reputation was back in the nineties, he's obviously not that guy. We're on a New York City sidewalk talking about his new movie *The Fourth Dimension*, in which he plays a motivational speaker called Val Kilmer.

Val greets me by name, and on the tape, his voice is sweet and upbeat, like he's happy to meet me. It's not hard, is it? At this point, if a celebrity doesn't touch me or yell at me, I'm a fan (and yes, I'm aware of how this sounds, that I'm in some sort of emotionally dysfunctional relationship with this job). Meanwhile, there is no world in which I will remind him we met in 2005, because that would be pointless.

Val is not young anymore, no longer Iceman, as he's done the most subversive thing a Hollywood actor can do: he's dared to age, just as I have since we last met.

I broach the fact he's entered his fifties, but he's not having it, and rightly so. He shifts to the subject of Samuel Clemens—whose pen name is Mark Twain—because Val has written a one-man show about the American author and will soon be playing Twain on tour.

"Mark Twain said, 'I wonder if there's ever a day you don't forget you're old?' You know, old people don't *feel* old inside, but their bodies tell them they are, and people treat them differently. But you feel like you've always felt—like yourself, as if you were still young. I've felt this way my whole life…I don't feel older."

He is trying to make me understand. "I don't feel my age," he says. "I'm in my fifties, but I feel the same way I've always felt."

In fact, he tells me, even *acting* old is a challenge. Preparing for Twain was "not different from any other role, but it's the oldest guy I've ever played so it's oddly challenging. It takes just as much energy to creep around as to run around. It's weird."

We fall into a discussion about Mary Baker Eddy, the founder of what would become Christian Science, which teaches the value of spiritual healing through prayer over mainstream medicine.

He's interesting and thoughtful, and just a sweetheart. He's not Iceman, because that was decades ago. But he's got life in him yet, and more to do.

A couple years after that meeting, Val would wake up in the night coughing up blood. In 2014-2015 he would be diagnosed with throat cancer, though he didn't tell us. We watched as he came out in public with scarves around his throat, having lost weight. He finally addressed the speculation in 2017, saying only that he had "a healing of cancer."

He was in and out of the hospital and used a feeding tube. In 2021 he reported he was cancer free, but weakened by the treatments that saved his life. In 2025, Val died of pneumonia at age sixty-five.

I was happy to have another chance with Val, but I could've done without a reunion with this next guy. I have no choice. I'm covering a screening of action flick *Escape Plan* in Times Square, where testosterone clogs the air as the film's headliners, Sylvester "Sly" Stallone and Arnold Schwarzenegger, wow the crowds.

Their rabid fans are nearly rioting behind ropes for their attention and their autographs. Arnold is not biting, for the most part. Sly throws his whole chest into it, signing everything they give him, making his fans lose their minds, and affably chatting with reporters. The guy might be problematic, depending on how you view him, but he sure is fun to interview (again, this is not an endorsement of him as a human being). It goes like this:

Me: "I'd love to chat with you!"

"Oh, really? Who's on the cover this week?"

"You, because I'm sure you'll give the best interview ever."

"If you want to sell any magazines, don't do that!"

"So, I hear you and Arnie are now BFFs. How in the world did that happen?"

"I don't know why we get along so well. We really disliked each other intensely for twenty years. I don't get it. It goes to show you: a good enemy is hard to find. And then eventually you start to appreciate something: maybe the reason we were so competitive is what made us get where we are. Seriously. I think it helps. It's what gets you out of bed in the morning and go 'oh, I can't wait to get at it again.'"

He's a delight. But now, here comes that guy from Paris, 50 Cents I think his name is. Still don't know his music, but his face I remember from the hotel lobby during Eva Longoria's wedding week.

I am sure he won't remember me.

He ignores reporters calling his name. I call out, too, because it's my job.

He beelines for me.

His long-limbed, glamorous publicist stays nearby.

Standing on a red carpet talking to him turns weird. After he moves on from me, I tell a reporter next to me, one I'd filled in about Paris earlier in the evening while killing time waiting for the stars to arrive, about how the interview just went. I don't remember what outlet she was working for, what she looked like, her name. But I was glad she was there.

Years later, in 2022, I launched a Substack newsletter called *The Landing* (as Sara Hammel), where I post about my investigations into sexual assault in the airline industry and expose predators who target flight attendants and women who dare to enter the flight deck (I don't call it a cockpit anymore).

On one occasion, I went off topic to write about 50 Cent's history with women, which includes an incident for which he was arrested and charged with domestic violence (he pled down to a lesser charge), civil lawsuits, and allegations of physical and sexual abuse of women. Multiple alleged victims were named in my open letter to Netflix, which ran in the *Daily Mail.*

In 2025, rapper Ja Rule Tweeted out my piece from *The Landing* and wrote, alongside a side-eye emoji, *@50Cents You got some explaining to do here Herman!!! An open letter to @netflix WOW…*

Unhinged

It's gala season in New York City. I'm at Cipriani to cover a benefit supporting and advocating for victims of sexual assault, domestic violence, and child abuse.

There are various television and film stars in the house tonight, but only one double Oscar winner. On this mild May evening, Hilary Swank is dressed in white, smiling, hitting the red carpet like a champ to lend her star power to a worthy cause.

I figure Hilary will be a decent interview. Top of her craft, not generally tabloid fodder, all-around inoffensive. When I volunteered in animal rescue in L.A., there was chatter that Hilary was so dedicated to the cause that she'd go out on the streets with organizations to save dogs and cats with her bare hands.

Even better, she's here supporting a cause that has affected too many of us. The broadest statistics from the National Sexual Violence Resource Center (NSVRC) show 81% of women and 43% of men have reported experiencing some form of sexual harassment and/or assault in their lifetime.

This is what's in the back of my mind when I meet Hilary Swank.

I ask the warm-up question, and she leaps on it. She knows the founder of this organization, and she's watched her friend build it into a force for change.

"To see this dream fully realized...look!" Hilary shows me the goosebumps dotting her arms. Her dress is sleeveless. "I get chills every year. I wouldn't miss a gala.

I've put it in my calendar so I wouldn't miss one wherever I was in the world!"

We talk a bit more. I ask her a few non-controversial, non-invasive questions, and in the end, we agree this is a great cause they're raising money for tonight. We can't look away anymore. This kind of violence has to stop.

"This is our shared journey, and we're not in it alone," Hilary says, her eyes flashing with what I read as empathy and passion.

We part ways and we both get on with the interviews we came here to do this evening.

I think maybe I'm a Hilary Swank fan now.

A half-hour later, it's time for dinner. I make my way through the event space with its majestic columns and vaulted ceilings, holdovers of its past as a 1920s disused bank. If you attend a function at Cipriani at any point between 2010 and 2016, you're likely to be offered burrata and layer cake. When I think of Cipriani, I think of zucchini chips, burrata balls, and Meringata alla Crema, an eight-layer crème and merengue cake that famously came between Denzel Washington and Food Network's Claire Robinson when they were both dining there one night, and Denzel ordered the last slice. Legend has it that he shared his piece with Claire, which is just as well, because that cake is RIDICULOUS.

I find my table, which is near the center, close to the front. There's going to be an auction, a presentation, speeches. But first, they wait for us to find our seats and greet our tablemates. I'm near an artist from Spain and next to an actor everyone loves and is beloved for his starring role in a cult-favorite TV show from years gone by (among many other roles). To my left is an empty seat with a phone on it. The actor, who I'll call Mr. Dashing, introduces himself to me, and to the artist on his right.

I keep an eye on the phone. It sits on the seat, alone and ripe, for long minutes.

I had a phone stolen at an event where Katie Couric, Matt Lauer, and Star Jones, and Barbara Walters were in attendance (that night I also interviewed rapper Flo Rida, who was a hoot and a great interview). I'm not accusing any of them of being the phone thief, but the point is, these devices are not safe when you abandon them in public.

The owner of the phone has returned. I greet Hilary Swank as she hovers over the chair and picks up the phone, then sits next to me. She's smiling widely at me.

I smile back. "Hilary Swank," I say, "careful with your phone…"

She makes a sheepish and thankful face, then giggles at me.

"Oh, you're right," she breathes. "I shouldn't do that. Thanks for looking out for it!"

She's so nice. So open. She must've enjoyed our interview. Mr. Dashing leans across me and introduces himself to Hilary. They chat briefly before she turns back to her left, where some of the charity's staff are sitting. We all get to talking, and the women from the charity share some statistics about sexual assault. We talk about the prevalence, the lack of progress. How everyone's here tonight to change that.

"Chances are," I say quietly, "if you look at the numbers, someone at this table has been a victim of sexual assault."

Hilary nods passionately. "Yes, *yes*. That's true!"

Someone else is talking now, but Hilary is still focused on me. She looks like a different person all of the sudden; her face is twisted into an angry mask.

"You're from *People!* I just realized it," she snarls. "I just got all sweaty under the armpits."

I am rendered speechless. I am resetting, trying to recognize this new Hilary. Hoping she doesn't tell me anything more about her armpits.

She makes demands. "*Please* don't write about anything I've said. I really didn't mean for this to be written about. *Really.*"

I'm shocked, but I'm also thinking, *Don't write what? That Hilary Swank appears engaged, empathetic, and totally against sexual abuse?*

"I'm here for the presentation," I assure her. "For the charity. There's nothing to worry about."

"You don't understand. The tabloids have been *terrible* to me, OK? *OK?!*"

She's *mad* at me for being here, though we had a nice interview maybe thirty minutes ago.

"But…but we just spoke on the red carpet…you don't remember me?"

She shakes her head. "I THOUGHT YOU WERE WITH THE CHARITY. I meet so many people. I didn't recognize you, OK? I've talked to a lot of people since then."

What hits me hardest, what gives me chills, is how deep and serious the discussion was at the table, how raw it must've been for some of us. It's hard to know who to trust on any given day. Until this moment, it felt like I was enveloped in a warm circle of trust. Surrounded by people who are here for the same reason, who take sexual violence seriously, who understand how delicate the framework around it is. Journalists are not the enemy.

Let me tell you, this girl can act. I can see why she won the Academy Awards for *Boys Don't Cry* in 2000 and *Million Dollar Baby* in 2005.

Anyway, I'm guessing it's occurred to her she's only making things worse by going off on me, because she turns away and stops speaking. A big guy with fluffy hair shows up late and drags a chair between me and Hilary. They start chattering away; he's a TV producer and sometime comic. Hilary whips out her phone and starts showing him pictures of her pets.

She shoots me looks, covers her phone with her hand, says loud enough for me to hear, "Don't let her see." (*Snotty look*). "Oh, just kidding!" She narrows her eyes. *Not kidding.*

I don't give a shit about our magazine's don't-upset-the-celebrity rule right now. I am done. I'm not going to be bullied by this woman, or by anyone who thinks they're above the rest of us. I level a calm gaze at her.

"You're mean," I say simply, effectively, and loud enough for her to hear.

She recoils as if slapped, then recovers quickly and goes back to showing off her photos.

"Are you enjoying the evening?" Mr. Dashing says, blissfully unaware of my Hilary drama. The first part of the presentation has concluded, and my tablemates start cutting into their chicken while I nibble on a roll. Hilary doesn't touch her food.

"I am," I smile. "It's a beautiful event. But I don't think everyone is as thrilled as you are to be seated next to a reporter."

"Oh?" Mr. Dashing keeps his face neutral. "Well. You can write anything you want about me. I'm happy to provide you with a scandal if you need one."

"I'll keep that in mind," I say, and finally start to relax.

He nods, then turns to listen to something the artist is saying. She's gorgeous and fascinating, so I join in in and manage to enjoy the rest of the dinner. I will forever love this actor, dashing and diplomatic 'til the end.

I think that night is the beginning of the end for me in this business. If it wasn't Gordon Ramsay yelling *Fuck* at me or Jesse Spencer putting his finger in my mouth or Andy Samberg talking about diarrhea and vomit, if it wasn't the fact I could never say anything or push back for fear of losing work, it's tonight.

I'm questioning my life choices. Because when I wrote about inequalities in women's sports and a legendary Division 1 basketball coach called me personally to yell at me and scare me off, I was braced. I knew he was furious about my investigation and was going to try to intimidate me, and I was ready for him.

This culture of precious celebrities who are untouchable and special for doing a job in entertainment, who can behave rudely or touch you or catcall you in a professional environment where you're expected not to challenge them, is not for me.

Comfort the afflicted and afflict the comfortable. That was my role when I began.

Not to sit and act like these people are special and I'm supposed to treat them differently than I would any other person.

But I stay, and I survive tonight's small stab of rebellion. I like this job, still.

Aspects of it, anyway. There's always the Meringata alla Crema.

I always have to know *why* about everything, such as, why did Hilary get so spooked?

Back home, I search *Hilary Swank + controversy*. Results burst onto the screen. British newspaper *The Independent*'s headline pulls no punches: *So, what first attracted Hilary Swank to Chechnya's brutal tyrant?* It tops an article that details how Hilary reportedly took hundreds of thousands of dollars to attend the thirty-fifth birthday party of despot Ramzan Kadyrov.

After Hilary's manager Jason Weinberg assured Human Rights Watch that his client had no plans to attend, the *Independent*'s reporter wrote, *Fast forward exactly nine days, and, well, I think you can guess what happened. Dressed to the nines, and watched by this newspaper's Moscow correspondent, Ms. Swank sauntered up Mr. Kadyrov's red carpet before delivering a charming speech about how much she had already enjoyed her stay in Grozny. "I could feel the spirit of the people, and I could see that everyone was so happy," she said. "Happy birthday, Mr. President!"*

It's not just Hilary, to be fair. There's Jennifer Lopez, plus Beyoncé, who sang for the Gaddafi family allegedly for upwards of a cool million (she later said she gave the proceeds to charity), and Mariah Carey and Kanye West who got paid to hang with some bad people.

This is some ugly history I did *not* know about Hilary. It's interesting that she seems to blame "the tabloids" for what she did. Here's an idea: If you don't want the media reporting your shitty behavior, don't do shitty things.

They say narcissists are drawn to Hollywood. If you ask me, masochists are drawn to celebrity journalism.

One Hell of a Morning Has Turned Into a Bitch of a Day

I meet Michael Douglas and Catherine Zeta-Jones at a Lincoln Center tribute to Barbra Streisand in April of 2013. Michael does most of the talking, though Catherine makes a point of chiming in to say how much she admires Barbra, who's the reason we're here. I mention how maybe this is a glamorous date night for the parents of two tweens. Michael plays along, while Catherine doesn't bite, staying quiet while he carries the interview.

I make a note that things seem slightly off with them. You can see it in images from that night; the smile doesn't reach her eyes. I don't speculate as to why this is or what could be wrong. There are a million reasons she could seem down, and why Michael could be covering for her when it's too exhausting to be sociable (introverts know what I mean).

I meet Liza Minelli, too, and I make a note in my file that she appears to be a bit wobbly, but it's a memorable life event to meet such a talent. Words bubble out of her, and she has a special, otherworldly quality. The daughter of Judy Garland, who I watched in *The Wizard of Oz* when I was growing up, is exactly as I imagined her.

And then Barbra herself, accompanied by husband James Brolin, is before me.

After some past ugly celebrity encounters, I always read up on my subjects before I meet them—and not just the fawning glossy magazine profiles. I check the blogs, the comment sections, the random newsletters. Barbra Streisand has been irrefutably difficult and rude to enough people over the years to earn a reputation for being someone you should be wary of approaching. One writer summed her up this way: *Not even the most worshipful of her biographers can disguise the fact that she's a pain in the ass.*

I throw myself at the mercy of the woman for whom The Streisand Effect was coined. This phenomenon came into the lexicon in 2003 when Barbra sued an aerial photographer for publishing pictures of the California coastline in which her Malibu home was identifiable, but her overreaction only succeeded in making the images go viral.

She's here now, and I'm ready. I'm thinking it could be fun. *Bring it, Babs.*

A couple of other reporters near me throw out some questions, and she answers them all. It's my turn. I know about her house, and I know she lives in Malibu, and I would've dreamed of living there, too—except for one huge drawback. I'm terrified of tsunamis. They're one of my biggest irrational fears.

"You live in Malibu, right?" I ask Barbra, who is a climate activist. "Do you worry about climate change affecting your home? I mean, they say the tsunami is coming…are you scared? When I lived in L.A.," I add, "I was terrified. It's matter of when, not if."

I have made Barbra Streisand laugh. She waves a hand like swatting away a gnat. *"Please."* She smiles like the iconic diva she is. "We live on a cliff. The water would have to come up ninety-five feet to get us. Don't worry about it," she advises me.

And there it is. I brought my fear of tsunamis to Barbra Streisand and asked her to give me therapy about it, and she did.

Days after that gala, Catherine Zeta-Jones, who is struggling with her mental health, checks herself into Silver Hill Hospital in Connecticut. Her reps tell us, "Catherine has proactively checked into a health care facility...[she is] committed to periodic care in order to manage her health in an optimum manner."

This is not the first time she has sought treatment at this hospital.

In 2010, Michael is diagnosed with stage four throat cancer. The ensuing months are rough on the family. Michael becomes a shadow of himself, appearing to lose significant weight while on a liquid diet during his treatment. Catherine struggles, too, and reaches a point where she feels she needs to seek mental health treatment. The actress does so, and takes an additional courageous step: She shares her diagnosis of bipolar II disorder in a *People* cover story to help further destigmatize mental illness.

"This is a disorder that affects millions of people, and I am one of them. If my revelation of having bipolar II has encouraged one person to seek help, then it is worth it. There is no need to suffer silently and there is no shame in seeking help."

By 2013, after Catherine completes the latest treatment she sought days after I met her at Lincoln Center, it seems Michael and Catherine are healthier, both physically and mentally. I'll interview both of them several times after this. They live in Bedford, not far from New York City.

As I get used to seeing them out and about, I get the sense that every New-York based reporter for a major news and/or entertainment media organization who's met Michael Douglas thinks they know him. He has that way about him. I've met him a few times, not including sitting across from him in that London courtroom, and his thing is being a regular guy.

He can also be open to a fault. Not that the media doesn't love it, but it gets him in hot water sometimes, though he's always able to laugh it off and move past it. One such misunderstanding happens in the wake of his illness.

Michael is promoting the well-received Liberace biopic *Behind the Candelabra*, and during a newspaper interview, he talks openly about his cancer. The reporter asked him a question I don't think I'd ever ask another human being, but that's just me: Did he regret his years of smoking and drinking which, the reporter wrote, is "usually thought to be the cause of the disease"?

Michael replied, *No. Because without wanting to get too specific, this particular cancer is caused by HPV [human papillomavirus], which actually comes about from cunnilingus…*I did worry if the stress caused by my son's [Cameron Douglas's] incarceration didn't help trigger it. But yeah, it's a sexually transmitted disease that causes cancer."

Hoooooooo boy. When I tell you the internet explodes when that comes out, I'm not exaggerating. People go wild speculating about Michael's past partners. It is…something. The magazine is careful in handling this story, even internally, because editors don't want to imply anything about anyone. It is delicate, to say the least.

His reps valiantly attempt to put the oral sex genie back in the bottle. "Michael Douglas did not say cunnilingus was the cause of his cancer," they say in a statement. "It was discussed that oral sex is a suspected cause of certain oral cancers as doctors in the article point out, but he did not say it was the specific cause of his personal cancer."

It's not particularly effective. And so, one night, word gets out that Michael is going to address the kerfuffle at an American Cancer Society event where he would be honored with the Marvin Hamlisch Memorial Award. I am dispatched to document his every word. He's relaxed and perfectly comfortable joking about it.

"I've become, I think, in the past twenty-four hours a sort of poster boy for oral cancer," he tells a room to applause, cheers and laughter.

"And just so we all understand, I think we would all love to know where our cancer comes from. I simply, to a reporter, tried to give a little PSA announcement about HPV, a virus that can cause oral cancer, and is one of the few areas of cancer that can be controlled and there are vaccinations that kids can get. So that was my attempt."

He ends with words of encouragement for those still undergoing treatment for their own cancer. He looks up at the audience in the balcony and roars, "All you guys up there, take care of yourselves. You go beat it!"

Later, I meet him at an intimate luncheon for the AARP where Michael and his *Fatal Attraction* co-star Glenn Close are having a rare reunion. I mingle with both Michael and

Catherine and, as always, they're approachable and easy to talk to.

On a different occasion, I get Catherine to myself for a few minutes, and to me, she is gorgeous (knowing that beauty is in the eye of the beholder. I'll never forget when a reporter at the magazine included his opinion about the looks of a mediocre reality star in a story, writing, *I'm in the presence of one of the best looking men in L.A.* I was like, that is not journalism; the reality star is gross. On the flip side, a staffer once returned from interviewing Cindy Crawford and told us flatly, still in a daze, *She's so stunning it's like staring at the sun.* Talk amongst yourselves. Leave the subjective observations out of the journalism).

Anyway, I can't stop looking at Catherine. She's upbeat and *so* excited to proclaim she's a dance mom. Her daughter Carys is a talented dancer who'll be performing tonight, and it throws me when I realize it was twelve years ago when I sat a few feet from Catherine in a London courtroom just a few days before she gave birth to Carys.

Later, after the performance, Catherine tells her daughter proudly, "You NAILED it!"

Another touching moment happens while I'm waiting to talk to Michael at the cocktail hour. He's approached by a man who appears to be in his eighties. Hands shaking, he pulls out what I think is a scrap book, but I can't tell because I'm hanging back so as not to intrude. The world swirls around Michael and he blocks it out like the *Matrix*. There is no one in the room but this man, who is probably Michael's father's age.

You might not remember me. I knew your father. I wanted to show you this.

Michael takes the open book the man holds out and studies the pages.

We were younger then, the man says with a smile in his voice.

Ahh…isn't that wonderful. Michael says it with deep appreciation. *Thank you. Thank you so much.*

It is a beautiful moment of human connection. It's clearly an important interaction for this man, who gives Michael the gift of paper, and Michael gives him the gift of his time.

When it's my turn to speak to him, Michael is as game as ever. He and Catherine have the same birthday, which passed just a few days ago.

"How were your birthdays?" I ask him.

Michael replies, "Quiet. Let 'em go by once in a while."

Let 'em go by once in a while sticks with me. You can use it for almost anything.

P.S. The chapter heading is a classic line from Michael Douglas's character in an eighties movie.

You Can't Spell Celebrity Without Taylor Swift

I f I can't find joy in watching Beyoncé hug Taylor Swift ten feet away from me, what am I even doing here?

I'm at Cipriani Wall Street for the Billboard Women in Music luncheon in December 2014. Taylor's album *1989* is ruling the music charts, and I'm surrounded by hitmakers and legends including Aretha Franklin, Idina Menzel, Ariana Grande, Jessie J, Iggy Azalea, and Charli XCX. They pose for red-carpet photos while we wait for Taylor, the Woman of the Year, to arrive.

Meanwhile, another megastar slips in: Queen Beyoncé herself. She poses for photographers but breezes past reporters and seemingly disappears—until Taylor enters the building. As starstruck little girls and big ones alike look on, Taylor heads toward the luncheon just as Beyoncé emerges from the shadows.

The room can barely contain the combustible collision of these two superstars. As they stand close (surrounded by security), they converse quietly, both smiling wide. A crowd builds around them as everyone tries to get photos and videos of the pair, but they're soon ushered out of view.

At one point I run into Taylor and throw a question at her, and I'll go my whole life saying she answered with a word. But I'm not sure if that's true. I have video of her looking at me while standing inches from my face, so that lends credence to the story I tell myself.

In a moment that exemplifies the state of entertainment media, absolute legend Aretha Franklin is wandering through arrivals alone, no entourage, no handlers. She's there for the picking, and I laser in. She's not dating a young hot reality star, isn't currently collab-ing with Calvin Harris (that I know of), nor is she regularly seen at Taylor Swift's Newport mansion, so the magazines and entertainment shows can take her or leave her. Which is gross to me, but here I am, a willing part of the culture.

I ask Aretha how she is, and we chat for a bit about the honor she is receiving today and how she can show a thing or two to these young upstarts.

"I'm well," she smiles. "I'm the lady next door. I'm thrilled to receive the icon award. It's fabulous, I hope that I have set a positive example for them."

Speaking of Taylor Swift, in the summer of 2012, at age twenty-two, she's dating seventeen-year-old high-school rising junior Conor Kennedy, son of Robert F. "Brain Worm" Kennedy. This romance takes over the entire internet.

The doyennes of Boston gossip, Laura Raposa and Gayle Fee, otherwise known as the Track Gals, are all over it.

Taylor goes all in quickly, buying a house across from the Kennedy Compound in Hyannis Port and launching herself as a potential Kennedy.

The Track Gals write in the *Boston Herald,*

They frolicked at the compound, where, according to Ethel Kennedy, Tay Tay, 22, was just like one of the family. In fact, Swift and the Kennedy dowager seemed to have a lot hotter romance than the singer and Ethel's 18-year-old grandson [his birthday was in July].

("I love her," Taylor said. "She's sensational inside and out," Ethel said.)

Unfortunately, Taylor makes a pretty big misstep early on, allegedly crashing a Kennedy family wedding that August, according to one member of the family.

The *Herald* reported it this way: *Ethel's daughter-in-law* **Vicki Kennedy** *told Taylor and Conor not to come to her daughter's wedding but they crashed anyway. And, Vicki told the Track, Swift was asked to leave twice—and wouldn't! "I personally went up to Ms. Swift, whose entrance distracted the entire event, politely introduced myself to her, and asked her as nicely as I could to leave. It was like talking to a ghost. She seemed to look right past me."*

That's the Kennedy side of the story. Taylor's spokeswoman quickly denies it ever happened.

There is no truth to that, she tells the *Herald*. *Taylor was invited to the wedding and the bride thanked her profusely for being there.*

When summer ends, I'm dispatched to the town of Deerfield, Massachusetts, where Conor will be starting his junior year. Word is Taylor will be visiting her boyfriend here at some point. I'm told to not set foot on the school campus, trespass, or engage in any other icky behavior, which is great because I never would. These are children.

Anyway, I'm strolling around the tiny "town," which is more like a street with a post office and a food truck. In the course of talking to people and making connections, I meet some students who know Conor. A girl stomps off to report me to the dean, though I am not on school property, or even close, but then I meet some boys who are excited to talk about what everyone's buzzing about in the halls of Deerfield High (or whatever it's called).

"The thing now is trying to get her to come...we have a Friday-night concert thing," says a pal of Conor, who turned eighteen in July. "One is in late fall, and people want her to come sing. It would be so funny for those two to sing together."

This surprises me. "Wait, what? Conor sings, too?"

"Oh, no." He shakes his head. "But Conor has the confidence to do it anyway."

I head back up that way once more after Taylor's been seen visiting Conor, and I end up at the tiny local airport, where I watch her private jet taxi away. I'm oddly surprised at how big it is. It's huge compared to the average PJ I've seen at the smaller airports, and the tail is decorated in pink and purple, I think.

Taylor has been getting some blowback for hanging around with high school kids, which I relate to, because I did it this season too and felt weird about it. There's the added suggestion she's "obsessed" with the Kennedys. In the October 2012 issue of *Rolling Stone*, she defends the coupling and calls Conor a "grown man:"

The way I look at love is you have to follow it, and fall hard, if you fall hard. You have to forget about what everyone else thinks.

I was hit over the head with their specific type of age gap when I was circling a high school campus to talk about the kid who's dating a world-famous singer with her own private jet; it was an uncomfortable assignment.

I'm not judging Taylor. Conor is of legal age, and age-gap relationships among celebrities are routinely normalized. I was around in the nineties when thirty-nine-year-old pervert Jerry Seinfeld was dating a seventeen-year-old girl, and all I remember about that time was it was largely accepted, no matter what people say now about how he was side-eyed and how it was a conversation point. I don't remember any of Jerry's colleagues publicly calling him out or doing anything other than welcoming the girl—emphasis on *girl*—and the romance into the *Seinfeld* fold. More recently, beloved actor Paul Walker was dating sixteen-year-old girls while in his thirties when he was alive. There are a ton of examples, and I don't have to drag up every one to make the point that we need to have a hard look at who we single out for criticism when everyone's of legal age.

By October, the same month Taylor's romantic portrayal of *falling hard* for Conor hits newsstands, the relationship is kaput, and by December, Taylor is dating Harry Styles of the boyband One Direction.

Monster

It's a clear March evening in New York City when I look into hulking Harvey Weinstein's dead eyes.

He's in his usual business suit.

I ask him if he has time for a chat.

"Sure," Harvey replies to me in a scratchy voice. "What's up?"

I'm on edge. I know how powerful this man is. I've heard what he's like, that he has a certain way of treating women. The blogs and comment sections and chat rooms have been simmering about this for years. Still, I figure, what's the worst thing an overly powerful Hollywood executive do to me in public? Walk away, snap at me, glower, ignore me. Been there, done that.

He tells me a bit about his current project, the new show opening this week. He professes his love and adoration for the Rockettes. He looks at me, looks away, then back at me, and then, weirdly, stares at my feet, as he talks. I ask him what he hopes will come of tonight's event to kick off the *New York Spring Spectacular*, a limited-time show featuring the Rockettes.

"People are loving the show, and it's selling like crazy. My kids like it!"

As for the Rockettes, who probably see him coming and squirm, he says, "They're pretty damn good!"

All in all, a benign experience, though he is mildly nauseating to be in close proximity to even if he's not molesting you. There he goes, comfortable among the beautiful people, not bothering Bella Thorne or Derek

Hough, who are friendly and red-carpet trained, saying all the right things in the chipper way they're meant to. (Bella is a sweetheart). Harvey, perfecting the bored I-own-all-of-this look, shuffles inside.

I know who he is when I meet him on this red carpet at Radio City Music Hall.

There is a woman inside the building right now who doesn't know. She will meet Harvey Weinstein for the first time tonight, and her life will change.

Depending how you look at it, due in part to her, so many other people's lives will, too.

When my fluffy story about the event runs, a colleague who'd interviewed him before almost didn't believe he was nice to me. *He's vile. He's rude. He's revolting.*

It happens lighting fast. Ambra Battilana Gutierrez is a twenty-two-year-old Miss Italy finalist who finds herself at a buzzy New York event surrounded by stars. I'm outside on the carpet; she's inside, where she's introduced to the legendary Harvey Weinstein.

He tells her again and again: *You look like Mila Kunis. You look like Mila Kunis.*

He swoops in to offer her a business meeting that he has fast-tracked—it'll happen the very next evening.

Ambra goes to his office. When he gets her alone, Harvey allegedly asks if her breasts are real. She says he does not wait for an answer; he lunges at her, "groping her breasts and attempting to put a hand up her skirt," as she asks him to stop, according to reports.

In what I view as an amazing show of courage and presence of mind—because when you take a shot at the king you better not miss—she immediately reports the assault to the NYPD. They take her seriously. Along with the Special Victims Division, they all form a plan for Ambra to meet with Weinstein a second time and record their interaction with the help of undercover officers.

The next day, she meets Harvey at the Tribeca Grand Hotel. He tries every which way to get her alone in his room. The recordings are harrowing, the transcripts chilling. You can hear the voice of the villain alternately coaxing and threatening, trying to seduce and then trying to scare.

He is heard asking Ambra to join her in his hotel room. She says "no" repeatedly but Weinstein persists, and when standing in the hallway outside his room, she confronts him about the groping incident the day prior and says she wants to leave.

AG: It's just that I don't feel comfortable.

HW: Honey, don't have a fight with me in the hallway.

AG: It's not nothing, it's —

HW: Please. I'm not gonna do anything. I swear on my children. Please come in. On everything. I'm a famous guy.

AG: I'm, I'm feeling very uncomfortable right now.

HW: Please come in. And one minute. And if you wanna leave when the guy comes with my jacket, you can go.

AG: Why yesterday you touch my breast?

HW: Oh, please. I'm sorry. Just come on in. I'm used to that.

AG: You're used to that?

HW: Yes, come in.

If she'd gone in, we can only imagine what would've happened. After minutes of excruciating back-and-forth, Harvey lets her leave.

When the disgraced mogul starts to make headlines for his disgusting behavior, I'm asked by editors for my reporting and observations from the night they met. What can I say? Medium affect, medium mood, basic quotes, not euphoric, not grouchy.

How can you tell if a man is searching for prey (that isn't you), and that he is twenty-four-hours away from allegedly assaulting his next victim? He doesn't show it in his eyes, or in public. He waits to get her alone. Always waiting for everyone else to be gone so they don't see his mask fall. It's his word against hers, and she's no one.

It was a previous event when I really felt I got a look at how he operates—and how those around him enabled his behavior. I was at an awards ceremony in New York City. Scarlett Johansson was there. Julianne Moore. Big, big names. Harvey was seated at a table at the front. Everyone wanted to get to him. Everyone wanted his attention.

A man was leaning in, close to Harvey's ear. I was around because I was looking for Scarlett. The man was pleading for attention. *Come on, man. She's right over there. Waiting. You gotta meet this one.*

He was tempting Harvey, tantalizing him, promising to bring him the prize like a cat bringing its master a trophy. *Look what I can do for you.*

She's a stunner. She wants to meet you!

I'll meet her. Hey: Don't worry. Gimme a minute. Harvey patted the man's shoulder like he's a good boy. *I want to meet her. Hey, I'll meet her, OK?*

You're gonna like her.

He turned to deal with the five other people wanting to talk to him. I left after that.

Despite Harvey's admission during an NYPD sting, District Attorney Cyrus Vance opted not to prosecute. I'm not going to get into the weeds with Cy Vance, but it's important to note that he came under scrutiny for accepting various donations connected to Harvey and to the Trump family, who Vance was investigating (he returned that donation and denied a connection in either case). The then-fledgling TimesUp organization wrote an open letter asking that he be investigated for refusing to prosecute Harvey in 2015. Vance still did nothing.

Harvey got caught anyway. By 2026, he will be a convicted rapist. In 2023 he was sentenced to sixteen years behind bars by Los Angeles Superior Court Judge Lisa Lench for his conviction of three felony sex crimes, including forcible rape, forcible oral copulation, and sexual penetration by a foreign object. Over time, something like one-hundred women came forward to publicly accuse him of sexual misconduct, rape, and/or harassment and assault, setting off an avalanche of civil and criminal legal proceedings that are still wending their way through the justice system in New York and California.

At this writing, Harve's sitting in Rikers Island, which by all accounts is a highly unpleasant place. He recently sat for an interview with *The Hollywood Reporter* and whined about how things weren't going well.

The writer lost me when he said in a promo video, …*did he feel bad for his crimes? The surprising thing was…he doesn't feel that he committed any crime, and he insists that he is innocent.*

If that surprises you, you're not paying attention.

Anyway, while I don't agree with platforming a rapist desperate for spin and recognition—his worst punishment is obscurity and impotence—it brings some solace knowing he's locked up at Rikers and has virtually isolated himself due to his immense unpopularity.

It was different when I was in state prison. I got up in the morning, I had breakfast, I saw friends, I spoke to people. We all watched TV together. I've been begging to go to state, but the DA's office says, "Because you have a trial upcoming, you stay at Rikers. We want to keep an eye on you." They kept an eye on me for 19 months now. I don't know where they think I'm going.

His notoriety, he says, means he doesn't go outside...*it forces me into isolation...I'm constantly threatened and derided. I wouldn't last long out there.*

Aw...that's a shame, isn't it?

Pacey and the Pantyhose Predicament

I never watched *Dawson's Creek*, but I know Pacey when I see him. I'm at a crowded film premiere where red-carpet arrivals will be followed by a screening and a party. A-listers are here, but so far they're not talking to me.

A star who's not on the list, a guy who appears to be someone's plus-one, skirts the carpet and moves stealthily, unnoticed, around the back of all the reporters and photographers.

I see him, though.

It's Joshua Jackson. I don't notice anyone else interesting coming down for an interview, so I ditch my spot and follow him.

I call out to him on the off chance. Katie Holmes is a big deal right now, and we always love Joshua of course, so I can ask him all about her.

"I'd love to ask you a few questions," I smile.

He stops, makes a *Why the hell not* face.

"Hey, sure," he replies, affable and cool and I have him all to myself.

And then…*oh, fuck.*

I'm in very big trouble.

It all started earlier in the evening when I dressed in a Spanx-like bodyshaper and then donned some semi-sheer black tights with a control top. The problem with control top is that when they start to slip, they roll down fast, because they're like a coiled spring.

And just before meeting Josh, I apparently did something—shifted excitedly or bent down to pick up a pen or who knows what—to cause the pantyhose to start rolling down.

I smile at him, make sure his eyes stay up *here*, and grab the elastic through my dress with one hand. The elastic is stuck halfway down my hip, so there is nothing to keep them in place. On the flip side of the carpet, where no one's looking, Josh stands in front of me and asks how I am. I am making deals with the universe. *Please, please, please let my pinching the elastic be enough.* The elastic shifts. I'm holding the left side up while the right is trying to roll all the way to my ankles, finding an easy, slippery path against the slick body shaper beneath. *PLEASE don't let my pantyhose roll down to my ankles with every photographer in New York standing by and Joshua Jackson in my face.*

The universe is not impressed. The pantyhose rolls down over my hips in one quick rush, and I reach down and grab the waistband again through my dress, pretending to simply be shifting dramatically on my feet. I'm holding the ultra-tight elastic bunched with my dress in my left hand while holding the recorder near Joshua's mouth in my right. They're stuck at the crevice at the top of my legs with only two fingers keeping them from dropping to my ankles. As I try to act normal, Joshua gives me an exclusive interview.

I ask him why he's skipping the red carpet; does he grow tired of people always wanting to be near him, always calling out to him? His answer is refreshingly honest.

"Have you ever met an actor who doesn't love the adulation?" he jokes. "No, but really, I love people. And all this comes with the territory." His voice, dark and strident, contains a Sting-worthy level of what the romance authors call "husky."

Josh insists that he happily basks in the attention that comes with his work, lately on Showtime's *The Affair*. He has deep-set eyes and a notch between his eyebrows. He's tall and solid.

I'm so happy when he leaves. I hobble to the bathroom, and by the time I get there, the tights are at my knees, and I make it to a stall without being seen or humiliated (that I know of).

I'll see him again, this time on a hot-summer's day at a polo match, when he's walking the carpet with his date, Diane Kruger. She talks to *Vogue* and some TV reporters but skips me and other entertainment outlets. Josh is relaxed and ready to talk to anyone. I catch him again.

We get to talking about travel and expat life, and I don't bother telling him I'm still dealing with reverse culture shock, because what did I say previously? *They do not care.* They're not here to get to know us.

Anyway, he tells me it was scary at first, but he'll never regret his time living in Paris with Diane Kruger. "Travel helps make you who you are. If you can, I highly recommend getting out of your comfort zone and seeing the world."

Since we're all here not just for polo but also for a champagne party, I ask him about his favorite story about bubbly.

"When we had on our first vacation together, we went to Tuscany and had, not prosecco, but proper champagne sitting on the battlements in Siena," he tells me of his first trip with Diane.

The pair of them are quite handsy afterward at the VIP party, and the file I send in that evening ends with, *They're nauseatingly adorable.*

Side note about Diane Kruger: Just a little sip of tea. And I know how this is going to sound. I really do. I'm not saying she deserves a medal. But women, picture it. You're at a big outdoor event. There is nowhere to "go" other than some "luxury" glorified port-a-potties in a trailer. You schlep across fields of grass in heels. You *really* have to go. You're turned away because apparently you don't have your pass on you. You are very famous.

Diane did not play the *Do you know who I am?* card. She could've. Remember, the bar for celebrity behavior and basic manners is way down low. In that situation I might've had to pull that card, if I was famous. I remember being impressed by her not causing a scene. She left and went to get her pass (or a staffer to escort her back. I didn't see the finale).

Anyway, when you run into Josh out in the world, it's like he is a regular person talking to a regular person which is, in fact, what is happening.

This is unlike Miles Teller, who showed up at one event and gingerly stepped onto the red carpet buffered by a circle of handlers who moved when he did, shuffled when he did, as if those of us behind the velvet rope might launch ourselves at him. Keep in mind there are mega-watt A-listers here who are not being carried like he is.

He avoids eye contact as he approaches my general area; his team corrals him, guides him, protects him from my invasive journalist tentacles. I actually don't care about getting quotes from Miles, so I'll live. But wait—it looks like he *is* going to talk to at least one member of the print press, but only to…*The Times? The Wall Street Journal?* No; he stops and does a quick exclusive in lowered tones with the New York *Post.* I roll my eyes, bite a hangnail, wonder if anyone can see what I'm thinking about all celebrities and reps right now: *You're not saving lives, you self-important twerps. You pretend to be someone else for a living. Get over yourselves!*

I never looked at Miles Teller the same again.

In a New York Minute

In one moment, in a literal flash, I do something to a celebrity that I regret. I'm at an *Avengers: Age of Ultron* screening in New York, and the red carpet is hopping. A couple of my favorites are coming toward me. Rob and Marisol Thomas (you know him from Matchbox Twenty) love to do red carpets together. They're fused at the hip and they'll chat as long as you need them to. I've met them before. The second time, I remind them about the first time.

"Just as when we talked here back in 2012, you guys remain ridiculously cute," I say.

Rob says, without missing a beat: "She's cute. I'm ridiculous."

Marisol replies to me, "Thank you! I wish I could stop time."

I ask, "What's your secret to continuing to be so happy together?"

Rob: "I don't know…"

Marisol: "Marry your best friend."

Rob: "Right. And then don't think about it too much."

So far, so drama-free.

I meet Geoffrey Arend, who's married to Christina Hendricks, and I see what the fuss is about. He has a way about him. A gentle, open, funny way. He talks to me about fellow castmates and new real-life couple Téa Leoni and Tim Daly (I've interviewed both, they're great), and I'll get a story out of it.

Time for the afterparty.

I'm walking in alongside Oscar-winning director Paul Haggis. I find Jeremy Renner, one of the first to arrive, dancing alone on the empty wooden floor, unbothered and unmolested as he performs moves I saw in a film once. The best way I can describe it is, if you slowed down the Carlton Dance to twenty-five percent, you'd have Jeremy Renner right now.

I look past him, see a friend, and we get to chatting.

That's when things take a turn.

Paul Bettany is moving through the party with Mark Ruffalo. As you know, I don't have celebrity crushes because I'm not fourteen, but there are a rare few for whom I have to remind myself of my professional role. Paul Bettany is one of those.

I'm so surprised to see him approaching that I blurt quietly to no one in particular, "It's Paul Bettany! I *love* him."

Paul Haggis hears this. "Why not go for it?" he says. "You might have a chance." He seems serious.

Paul Bettany's wife, actress Jennifer Connolly, is another one I love in every part she plays. She's with the guys, I see now. I say to Paul Haggis, "I don't think Jennifer would like that."

And then comes my obnoxious move.

I whip out my phone and take a quick snap of them. But it doesn't occur to me it's so dark in here the flash will kick in, partly because I almost never take pictures of the high-profile people I cover.

The flash blinds Paul Bettany and Mark Ruffalo, and they shield their eyes too late, and it's a big scene. I quickly duck and hide behind my friend, waiting for the three of them to pass. This might be my only regret throughout the celebrity part of my career. (Well, maybe I have a few other small regrets beyond taking this photo. If people dig them up, they can ask me about them, and I'll talk about the things I wish I'd never said or at least said better).

End notes on Paul Haggis and Paul Bettany: Haggis is now an adjudicated rapist. In November 2022, a New York jury ordered him to pay $10 million in damages for raping publicist Haleigh Breest in his Manhattan apartment nine years before. He was also arrested for a different alleged rape in Italy in 2022; a judge later dismissed those charges. But ya know, I met him twice, and he was so real and interesting to talk to. He doesn't *seem* like a rapist. (*Extreme sarcasm. They never do*).

As for Paul Bettany, in 2020, texts he sent to Johnny Depp in 2013 about torturing and murdering women came to light in a court case involving Depp's ex-wife Amber Heard. When I read those, my crush was cured instantly.

I'm not sure we should burn Amber, wrote Bettany. *She is delightful company and pleasing on the eye. We could of course do the English course of action and perform a drowning test. Thoughts? You have a swimming pool.*

Depp replied, *Let's drown her before we burn her!!! I will fuck her burnt corpse afterwards to make sure she's dead.*

To which Bettany wrote back, *My thoughts entirely. Let's be certain before we pronounce her a witch.*

If you are thinking about torturing and killing women, that is a red flag. If you are putting your fantasy in writing it and sending it to another man, there is something wrong with you.

I'm trying to remember all the brief but memorable celebrity encounters I had in New York.

At one event, I try to chat with Gillian Anderson, but she's not interested and ignores me. I watch her greet Stellan Skarsgård with a full smooch on the mouth.

He comes my way, and we get to talking. He's a cool character, and I can see why Paul Bettany and Jennifer Connolly named their kid after him.

"You've been in some controversial films," I observe after introductions. "You ever get any blowback for that?"

"Anything to do with sex is a bigger deal in the U.S.," Stellan says in that voice like sandpaper. He is laughing. "Growing up, my parents were naked around the house. I walk naked around the house. I was born naked—I don't know about you…"

"Yes, as far as I know," I confirm. "As was your son, I assume?" *Your gigantic, hunky son (s)?*

He doesn't bite. "You Americans are such prudes," he says in his thick Swedish accent. He's playful, but also serious.

He looks like he's having a better time than anyone, all the time. He's relaxed and confident, and so at odds with what Hollywood seems to be about; as the night progresses, I watch all the stars gravitate to him and I get the distinct feeling he's the mayor of Hollywood.

Let's talk about Bryan Cranston. This isn't tea, because you know this already, don't you? You know he's as salty and loose and as he seems in every interview or situation where he's playing himself. What you see is what you get.

My Apropos of Nothing list requires me to ask a slew of celebs what their television guilty pleasures are. Bryan says, "None. I'm not guilty about any of my pleasures."

His eyes are twinkling. *Breaking Bad* is ending soon, breaking the hearts of a million fans, and I ask him about it.

"I'm looking forward to seeing the reaction to the last eight episodes," Bryan says. "I think it's a very fitting ending for our show."

"But you won't tell me what it is, will you?"

He laughs. "I could say…well, you could slip me something [pretends to be stumbling as if drugged] and I might."

"Wait, you mean I could drug you and you'd tell me everything?"

"What?!" He's doubling over laughing. I think there was a cocktail hour before the red carpet. "Are you saying you're going to *roophie* me?"

"No, no," I half-laugh. "No way." I'm trying to move away from this line of discussion as I don't want either of us to get into trouble or be misunderstood.

I don't file about the roophies that night. I don't want either of us being scrutinized for a wacky misunderstanding. Rape drugs, or Rohypnol, are not funny, and we were not minimizing how horrific they are when used for nefarious reasons. We were laughing at how we got here, how an innocent chat spiraled. We both pulled back and had a good interview, though he never told me how *Breaking Bad* was going to end.

There was that time Katie Couric slapped me. I'm at an NBC-sponsored event, and Katie is dating a new man, so I ask her about it.

"I know you might want to smack me for asking this (ha, ha), but we'd love an update on your love life considering what's been in the news lately," I inquire charmingly.

Any celebrity journalist worth her salt knows Katie can get prickly when asked about her personal life. In response to my intrusive question, she maintains that famous watermelon-wedge smile as her hand slides smoothly across my cheek in a faux-slap.

I move on to the next question, and then to the next celebrity. She doesn't like me, either. Hoda Kotb has spoken publicly about her man, how in love they are, and there are rumors they might get engaged. I ask her about that.

"How rude!" She snaps.

I don't remember what happened with Hoda after that. I don't like offending people. I don't know if she's like that as a person or if I hit a nerve, but I moved on quickly.

The nicest person I talk to that night is Matt Lauer. Earnest, gives me time, answers all my questions. Of course, he'll later be revealed to be a fucking prick and alleged sex offender. He's accused of sexual assault by multiple women, with one alleged victim writing in a *New York Magazine* piece that Matt, who was fired in 2017 after the allegations came out, forced her to have anal sex while they were in Russia covering the Olympics. He says there was consensual sex only and denies he assaulted her. He's never faced any criminal charges.

Never forget that nice is different than good.

Michael Stipe is so sweet and serious and earnest. Same with Salman Rushdie, who tells me he re-reads James Joyce's

Ulysses every ten years. Alan Cumming is humorless and irritable. He simply doesn't like me. He would reveal later that this time in his life was incredibly difficult and he was going through some things.

Elsa Pataky, actress and wife of Thor, is routinely called "thirsty" on celebrity blogs. They say the petite Spanish beauty clawed at fame's door begging to be let in, and now that she's inside it's still not enough for her. From where I'm standing on this charity gala's red carpet, Elsa is something else: Cooperative, fun and helpful. Not to mention stunning and happy.

In contrast, her six-foot-three Australian husband Chris Hemsworth looks like he's about to cry. He's utterly bereft because reporters are not asking him the right questions. He's careful not to come off angry; instead, he tries to connect with us, bring us in on it: *Guys, come on. We're here for a good cause. We're here to talk about making the world a better place!*

We're here for a gala to save the oceans, but we all want to ask about Chris's brother Liam, who's engaged to Miley Cyrus. When he's asked about Miley, Elsa takes over. "We love her. She's wonderful, and as long as Liam is happy, we're happy." She radiates joy.

Chris is the first and only celebrity I've met who I believe *might* genuinely wish fame and worship didn't accompany the money and the job of acting. In part because he's said as much, and also because he's the first A-lister I've met who's balanced respect and empathy toward reporters with his annoyance and disappointment in us.

Anyway, Chris ends up giving me some of what I came for. I ask him what's most important in this life. "This cause matters so much to me," he tells me. "The environment, too. Our children deserve a clean planet. They need a *live* planet."

"And fatherhood," I say, "that's important, too?"

"It's amazing," he tells me. "It's everything." And *boom*—I've got a story.

When the smoking-hot couple leaves the carpet, I zoom over and privately ask Elsa how she's doing. "Great," she says, either excited to meet me or faking it very well.

"What's it like being in the spotlight? It seems to me that for every compliment there's a bunch of abuse that follows…"

"I don't know," she replies, thinking about it for a moment. "I am just myself. I am very, very happy, and maybe that bothers some people."

Chris takes her hand, and she crinkles up her eyes, smiles at me, waves…and I think, *There is no photo or movie screen that does them justice.*

It's great fun to make Ricky Gervais laugh. Ricky is the one entertainment professional I can say anything to and he'll crack up. He's problematic, a disappointment to the LGBTQ community for his transphobic remarks and "jokes," and is rightly criticized for punching down in various arenas—I'm not a fan of his portrayal of people with disabilities, for another example—and he knows it, and he doesn't care.

When I'm covering a premiere at a museum, Ricky is laughing again at something I've asked him. I turn to his longtime love, bestselling novelist Jane Fallon, and jab my thumb toward her man. "You must laugh all the time living with this guy."

"I do," she deadpans. "I laugh until I'm *sick*." She puts a heavy emphasis on *sick* as if she's literally going to blow chunks.

Ricky doubles over.

One of his co-stars in the movie, Dan Stevens, walks up to us in the quiet room away from the melee of the afterparty. Ricky, who starred with him in *Night at the Museum*, introduces us.

"Meet Dan. He's newly famous. The girls like him. You can see why, can't you?"

"Absolutely."

Finding himself in the spotlight, Dan reveals an aw-shucks shyness. Soon enough, I figure, he'll be jaded and suspicious of people like me. "Didn't you play Sir Lancelot in those movies?" I ask. "I mean, you went full knight—talk about a chick magnet, right?"

"My wife, in particular, loves the knight thing," Dan replies, smiling shyly.

I nod to indicate yes, I understand he is married.

"What are your fans like? Do the ladies ever get a bit pushy around you?"

"My wife keeps me in check," he says.

It's kind of sweet the way he keeps mentioning her. Either he thinks I'm lusting after him or he wants fans to have no misconceptions about his marital status. Or maybe he's just a nervous blurter, which I can entirely relate to.

And, finally, shoutout to Matt Bomer, who's starring in the stripper film *Magic Mike* around the time I meet him. We've found a tiny pocket of space in a small, *very* over-packed restaurant where a fancy private dinner will soon begin.

He's giving me his full attention and telling me funny stories about fatherhood and about manscaping for his role as a stripper in the movie. We've got a good rapport and I'm going to get a few articles out of this one interview.

I am in hell.

It's the time of year in New York when it's not that hot yet, but the humidity is at five hundred percent. I emerge from the subway late, and I'm panicking because I don't want to miss my interviews. I fast-walk, then jog, toward the restaurant. It's about a half mile away.

I feel a light breeze, so I keep my pace up. I don't feel like I'm exerting myself. After sitting on public transportation for over two hours, this is refreshing.

I make it to the restaurant to find it packed to the rafters. This is not a roomy Outback Steakhouse; it's your standard trendy, downtown New York "cozy" place, and it has far too many hot human bodies inside it. About two minutes after I enter, Niagara Falls unleashes from my pores. I am sweating visibly, profusely. Water is dripping down my face and down the back of my neck, wetting the under-layer of my blonde hair so it's dark, like I've been swimming.

This has never happened to me. It's the perfect storm: The body heat inside has created a steam-room effect, resulting in extra humidity and a significant spike in temperature compared to outside. After that jog, it's like every drop of humidity in this room is condensing on my face; I must've worked harder than I realized. I think, *Am I (early) premenopausal? What is happening?*

Before I do any interviews, I find the bathroom. *I can clean up. Some paper towels and deep, still breaths should do it.*

Wrong.

The restroom is one stall with the door leading directly to the restaurant. It is marginally bigger than an airplane bathroom, and I've jumped from the frying pan to the fire. There is exactly no air in here and the sweat keeps coming no matter how many paper towels I use. I try a ponytail to get the hair off my neck and pull it back from my face. Surely that will cool me down.

Nope. My hair looks wet in the front and the back. The outer layer of still-dry hair is all I have to keep me looking somewhat presentable. I take down the pony. I have to get out of this heat box, because it's making things worse.

Most other people in the restaurant seem fairly composed, and I imagine if you were one of the first to arrive and your car dropped you at the door you'd have been fresh and would've acclimated to the atmosphere as the place filled up. Because I was last in, it was already a steam room and I'd run a half mile with a handbag and a laptop, and I was cooked.

If you want to see actual footage of me, look up the "Ted Striker sweating" GIF from the movie *Airplane!* The obvious solution is to go outside and cool down for a few moments. But the dinner starts soon, and the reps tell me if I want the celebrities I'm being paid to interview this evening, time is of the essence.

So here I am with TV and movie star Matt Bomer, who's talking to me like nothing is wrong. He's keeping his game face on like my mascara isn't running and my face isn't pomegranate red.

I have never been so grateful for a person's handling of an awkward encounter. He could've done almost anything other than what he did. He could've asked me if I was OK, or if I needed a tissue, or made any sort of gesture that would call attention to my condition and make me feel more awkward, upset, and humiliated than I already did.

He talked to me with a straight face as I tried to look like I wasn't melting.

Yes, the bar is way down low. But don't we all know people in our regular lives who wouldn't have had that much grace? Good job, Matt.

Thanks For Everything, Kevin

A celebrity poetry reading followed by a full bar equals great chats with New York-based actors. I bump into Parker Posey as we get our drinks at the bar and I introduce myself. She nods agreeably, conspiratorially, like we're both in on a secret.

"I'll give you quotes," she says. "I'm not going to mess around. I know you're *working*. I mean, sometimes I do evade and avoid, but I know it's a job and I'll give you good quotes."

Obviously, I love her immediately. I ask what she's been up to lately.

"I love reading great writers," she says. "Standing on stage and doing readings. I could do that 'til the cows come home. This is what I do since my movie and TV career are gone."

"*Whoa*. What? No," I say, shaking my head violently. "You were just in a movie with Nicole Kidman!"

She shrugs, waves me away. "I was supposed to do a reading in New York Wednesday night, but I wasn't feeling well. I fainted on Tuesday."

"*Wait*. You fainted? Are you OK?" *Is this a story?*

"It's not a huge deal." She shrugs. "It's just vasovagal syncope."

"Poor you," I say. We finish our drinks and I thank her and set off again to find more interview subjects and look up "vasovagal syncope."

I see Kevin Kline and think, why the hell not. He's been in the news lately for allegedly slamming Las Vegas as a vacation destination, and Vegas is pissed. He's standing with a man who has *fan* written all over him. Kevin is nodding and agreeing with whatever the guy is saying, but glancing around at the same time. I catch his eye and hold up my notebook to prove my officialness.

I introduce myself and ask if he has time for an interview.

"Of course," he booms as if he's on stage doing Shakespeare.

The fan thanks him and bids him adieu as I muscle in. We exchange pleasantries, and I eventually ask him if he really doesn't like Vegas.

He's happy to clear up the scandal of the decade.

"That's not true! But I heard that. They couldn't have been nicer when we filmed there. I said it's not a great place to *unwind* and find serenity and tranquility. As one would want to say, duh! That's not what Vegas is for."

He has a hyper, hilarious delivery. It's not often you get to talk to someone who starred in both *Sophie's Choice* and *Dave*. He's married to Phoebe Cates, an eighties icon I loved in everything, most of all the coming-of-age movie *Shag*, and of course the horrific Christmas movie *Gremlins*.

I have been told by editors to check the Apropos of Nothing List and ask people about their favorite beaches tonight, and I figure Kevin will be game. I ask what he does to relax. He stares off into the distance, presumably considering my question.

"Beaches can be tranquil," I prod after a few moments of silence.

"What?" He pretends to be confused.

"What I'm getting at is, do you have a favorite beach?"

"You're writing a story about beaches?" He leans in to peek at my notebook. "What've you got so far?"

"Orient Bay nude beach in St Martin," I say. "Just kidding. You're the first I've asked."

Crap, I've done it again. These people are not your friends; avoid risky asides.

"There's a nude beach in St. Martin?"

"Yes, but the nude people there are not the ones you necessarily want to see naked."

We're standing close because the party is packed. I try not to invade his space.

"They never are," he nods in agreement.

There is a pause, during which he appears to be thinking very hard.

"My favorite beach…"

Pause.

"You know, I've been to so many."

Twenty-second pause.

"You don't have to be anywhere, do you?" His grey-blue eyes meet mine.

I can't help it. I burst out laughing until I tear up. I wipe me eye. Normally I'd own up to the fact that I'd asked a dud of a question and move on. But in his own way, Kevin's not letting me.

"OK," I say, "You don't have to answer if you don't want to. But—*but*. Who doesn't love beaches?"

"People who have fair skin and have to slather on inches of high-powered SPF sunscreen," he informs me, "and for whom it takes an hour to find the shade under which to hide or put sunscreen on and you're all greased down. 'Isn't this wonderful?' I *do* love the ocean, though."

"What's your favorite ocean?"

"I'm glad you asked." He's not.

He pauses to sign an autograph, then turns back to me and makes a great show of pretending to think about my question.

"Come on. What's your favorite ocean?" I'm trying not to laugh.

"That would be, hands down…" He rubs his temple. "Name a few oceans."

"Who doesn't like the Pacific?"

Long pause.

"The Caribbean's beautiful."

Pause.

"Or is that a sea?" I ask.

"I believe so," he agrees. "I like the ocean Freud talked about. I like oceanic feelings. You'll have to do an Internet search for that one."

"It sounds made up," I say.

"Oh, no no *no*," Kevin chastises me. "Freud wrote at length about an oceanic feeling. I like all the oceans, actually. I like the idea of oceans, I think we need more of them. I'm all for oceans."

I nod along with him, make a show of taking notes. "You're clearly pro-ocean."

"They're an unstoppable trend…they're here to stay," he says. "When they overflow because of the ice caps, all the science-doubters can put on their little water wings and float about saying, 'Isn't the ocean wonderful? Right here in my backyard.'"

There are tears rolling down my cheeks. Unfortunately, some official-looking people, probably heads of the charity, interrupt us. "I'd better let you get back to your fans," I say, smiling and wiping my eyes. "Thank you—really."

His eyes are wide. "Stay." He keeps eye contact. "Come on."

He's an actor and a gentleman, but I have to leave because that little voice is reminding me again of what can happen if you offend or annoy a celebrity whether you realize it or not.

Did I tell you about that magazine reporter in a certain city who was known to be young and cool, and was covering a party one night, and chit-chatted with some Hollywood types and had a drink with them, and the next day their publicists called magazine editors to complain the reporter was bothering them?

A cautionary tale if there ever was one. That's not going to be me.

"Thanks for everything, Kevin," I say, and I wave goodbye.

The End Was Very Sudden

The entire time I was working for *People*, I was also writing novels. When I was in the Paris Hyatt Vendôme lobby killing time and trying to blend in with other hotel guests during Eva Longoria's wedding week, I was writing *The Promise*, book-club fiction with a mystery at its core. When I was on the train heading to interview Roger Federer in Basel, I was writing *The Lake Toplitz Code*, a thriller set in Switzerland, which got me a wonderful agent but no book deal back then (it'll be released on May 19, 2026).

It was my fifth effort, *The Underdogs*, that got me a book deal. Farrar, Straus & Giroux was going to publish my mystery for young readers, one with a wild twist, in May of 2016. This was huge. This was my dream.

After I inked the deal, I let my agent and my editor know we had a head start in the publicity game: My book would be featured in one of the most-read magazines in the world, because *People* has given space to contributors' books since before I started working there in 2002. I'd built up enough goodwill that they'd definitely treat me the same as everyone else who had a book coming out, from freelancers to top editors.

As the first half of 2016 flew by, my workload for the magazine was on the lighter side, which was fine, because I was working on my promotion plan for *The Underdogs*, which included emailing magazine editors to figure out timing for a reveal.

It wouldn't matter that my book was a novel and had nothing to do with celebrities. They'd featured all sorts of books over the years, including chick lit by one of their American freelancers. Since landing in New York, I'd personally been assigned to write about books that had nothing to do with celebrities or entertainment, and as I did my research, I thought, *Who is this a favor for? People* editors were making exceptions left right and center.

But for some reason, they drew the line at me.

I emailed everyone I could think of who I'd worked hard for. After nearly fourteen years covering everything from school shootings to Oscars to missing children to *Space Chimps*, working Sundays and Christmases and getting stuck in dark alleys when murderers were on the loose, one editor after another said no or ignored me.

In April, I covered a dinner in New York City. Katie Holmes was there, as was Scott Eastwood, and my last "interview" of the evening—a few words thrown back at me by an unenthused actor—was with Robert De Niro.

I kept trying to get editors to acknowledge my upcoming book from a major publisher.

I wrote an article around the *The Underdogs*, which was set in a fictional town in Massachusetts that happens to be the hometown of a certain big star, and sent it to editors I'd worked closely with for years. The TL:DR reply: *No thanks.*

I thought, that's all she wrote.

I'm done.

It was the double standard that got me. The drawing of the line at *me.*

So, in June of 2016, I did what I do, and I wrote. I described what had happened and how I felt about it, told them I quit, and screamed from the rooftops about *The Underdogs*, a book set in the New England tennis world I still love more than any other I've written. I sent the resignation letter to all staff.

I watched it go, and I thought about how this fourteen-year journey was ending, and how my first assignment so long ago was with a Spice Girl and my last was with Robert De Niro.

I didn't think anyone would read the letter or the mini-memoir I'd dashed off and published as an eBook on Amazon. Especially after I sent the resignation letter to a few editors I knew at other publications—after all, this was about *The Underdogs*, and I was putting everything I could into promoting it—and no one picked it up. I went on a short book tour and started writing my next novel. I moved on with my life.

And then, just before midnight on June 30, I received a DM on LinkedIn from a guy I didn't know, a financier from New York: *Your letter…wow. Congratulations, and just…wow.*

I had *no* idea what he was talking about.

I frantically searched my name and found that the legendary media reporter Keith Kelly had excerpted the letter in the New York *Post*.

I was going viral.

The DMs poured in from strangers, all of them supportive. My favorite remains one I received from an air traffic controller: *Your resignation letter is AMAZING!!! CONGRATS! You have most of the Air Traffic Controllers in [BIG CITY] wanting to do the same! But I told them all "you don't have the balls that she does so shut up and go back to work!"*

I was ill-prepared for this kind of attention, to say the least. I had almost no social media presence, with maybe five-hundred followers on Twitter and a new, half-hearted Instagram account. My Twitter following swelled to 900 (lol) before long. I didn't capitalize on it, I didn't post much. A few editors from various publications called me, and I took assignments as they came in. I went to Europe.

I was so used to being behind the scenes that I had no idea how to be the center of attention. Like many authors and journalists, I despise being in the spotlight. I just wanted to write another book.

As for my *People* colleagues, I lost a couple of acquaintances and gained some new friends. I received nice notes from senior staffers I'd worked with peripherally but had never spoken to, who said they had clearance to post on People.com directly: *I wish you'd asked me. I would've posted about your book and asked forgiveness later.*

People like that are part of the reason I stayed so long. I worked with some amazing and talented journalists I still call friends. I was honored to receive personal notes from others I didn't know who shared their own experiences of being treated poorly by a magazine they'd loved working for. I received a couple of apologies from staff who had nothing to apologize for, and crickets from the people who the letter was directed to.

It was heartening, and a relief, to know so many of my fellow journalists understood the difference between exposing bad behavior—however indiscreetly and controversially—and betraying a confidence and a source. The stories they told me were worse than mine. The messages have long since been deleted and there is no world in which I'd ever reveal any of what they shared with me, or who they are. I remain honored they trusted me.

A bunch of staffers who were there when I left, some of them mentioned in my mini-memoir, have since been laid off or moved on after continued rounds of layoffs. This was expected but still depressing. I wouldn't wish that on anyone.

After quitting the magazine, I went all in on books. I'm particularly proud of my military biography/memoir *The Strong Ones: How a Band of Civilian Women Made Their Mark on the Army,* a No. 1 bestseller on Amazon and an uplifting story about the power of women and of fighting for what's right. I wrote the screenplay, too, and was a quarterfinalist in the prestigious Academy Nicholl screenwriting competition. A dozen production companies, including Robert De Niro's, read the script, but no one has optioned it so far.

In 2021, I tried something new. I started two publishing imprints: One Moment Books for short biographies/nonfiction and One Moment Books DARK for mysteries and thrillers. My first book was a royal biography focusing on Prince Harry and Meghan. This kind of work, to me, was more about history and less about celebrity. I was keeping it low-profile and decided to launch the first book under a pen name to see what would happen. As I was getting ready to publish, I asked my husband, *What should my pen name be?*

We had a private joke in the family that there was a sixth (non-existent) sibling called Courtney, and he said, *Why not Courtney?* Great idea, I thought. I didn't think for a second that this book, which I was not putting any money into promoting, would take off. If I'd known I'd be stuck with the name Courtney Hargrove for the rest of my life, I would've chosen more carefully and had some fun with it (not that there's anything wrong with the name, but we came up with it in under a minute).

Courtney/Sara has published nineteen books, with fifteen currently for sale, including three No. 1 Amazon bestsellers. Courtney outsells Sara by about five hundred to one.

Would I do it again? Should you do it?

My take is that you get one shot. I waited until I knew I was done with mainstream media and celebrities. For when I could take the consequences. I had a robust body of work behind me. The stakes for me were not as high as they would be for many other people.

I never regretted it, but one thing I wish was different was the overall tone of the letter. I haven't read it in years and don't think I ever will again, but at the time, I thought it was funnier than it was. The anger, which we all know is covering for the hurt, came through more than I realized, more than I wanted.

I didn't miss the celebrity side of my job. I didn't miss being on call to scramble on a Sunday morning only to go two weeks with no work.

I missed what wasn't there anymore. I missed journalism, budgets for real reporting, collaboration, paper, and being on the scene. The future was already underway, leading to an industry being forced to embrace AI slop and jump on trends. Scraping other people's social media posts or regurgitating old news was not something I was interested in.

I can tell you this, too: With the way the world changed in ten years, the way just being alive seems fifty times harder and high anxiety is the new baseline, I would never handle a resignation now the way I did back then. Not in a million years. That letter was of a time, and that time has passed.

I hope you found some lighthearted enjoyment in this journey, and if you have questions or would like to interact with me, find me on my Substack, *Everything Is a Mystery.*

xo Courtney Hargrove, aka Sara Hammel

P.S. The title of this chapter, as many people know, is a nod to the movie Fletch, starring the king of problematic celebrities, Chevy Chase.

About the Author

Royal biographer and thriller writer **Courtney Hargrove** is the pen name of an award-winning journalist and #1 bestselling author with decades of international experience writing for magazines and newspapers including *People, Newsweek, U.S. News & World Report, The Sunday Times Magazine (UK), Glamour, Shape,* and more.

Sara Hammel's first novel *The Underdogs* (Farrar, Straus & Giroux BYR, 2016) was an Amazon editor's pick and #1 new release. Her memoir/military history book *The Strong Ones: How a Band of Civilian Women Made Their Mark on the Army* was an overnight #1 bestseller on Amazon in 2021.

She was the first-ever recipient of the Jane Cunningham Croly Award for Excellence in Journalism Covering Issues of Concern to Women from the General Federation of Women's Clubs. Later winners include luminaries such as Marianne Pearl, and judges were legends in journalism like Judy Woodruff. Hammel contributed to the feminist anthology *Letters of Intent* (Free Press/Simon & Schuster, 1999) along with icons Gloria Steinem, Ntozake Shange, and Judy Blume.

She runs the Substack *The Landing,* where she exposes predators in the airline industry and gives a voice to victims and survivors of pilots who continue to get away with sexually assaulting women in the workplace.

**With a twist you won't see coming, this atmospheric thriller from #1
bestselling author Courtney Hargrove is set in the stunningly treacherous
Alpine landscape of Switzerland and Austria.**

Dead mountains, dead lake…

*What lies beneath Austria's deep, dark Lake Toplitz? This legendary
location nestled in the Dead Mountains is believed to be one of the hiding
places for billions of dollars in Nazi gold. It holds secrets and treasures no
one has been able to bring up despite doomed searches that have killed
unlucky fortune hunters for decades.*

Until now.

Other Titles by Courtney Hargrove

Mysteries & Suspense

The Duchess Scarlett Mysteries

The Expatriate Mysteries

History of the British Royals

The Harry & Meghan Biography Series, Volumes 1–4

www.ingramcontent.com/pod-product-compliance
Lightning Source LLC
Chambersburg PA
CBHW071452140726
47997CB00005B/1695